IS THERE A FUTURE FOR MARXISM?

By the same author

ALTHUSSER'S MARXISM
SOUTHERN AFRICA AFTER SOWETO (*with John Rogers*)

IS THERE A FUTURE FOR MARXISM?

Alex Callinicos

HUMANITIES PRESS
Atlantic Highlands, New Jersey

First published in 1982 in the United States of America by
Humanities Press Inc., 171 First Ave., Atlantic Highlands,
NJ 07716

ISBN 0-391-02360-8

Printed in Hong Kong

Contents

Preface and Acknowledgements

Without the help of a number of people this book would not have appeared. I would like to thank the following especially: Tony Cliff, Tony Dodd, Duncan Hallas, Chris Harman, Alan Montefiore, Mike Rosen, Joanna Seddon, Colin Sparks. David Edgar first stirred me from my dogmatic slumber and made me realise that there was a case to answer. I am also grateful to the Master and Fellows of St Peter's College, Oxford, and to John Winckler and Anne-Lucie Norton at Macmillan's. The usual disclaimer that no one but myself is responsible for the outcome is more than usually appropriate in this case. I am painfully aware of the provisional and sketchy nature of the arguments in Chapters 5, 6 and 7. However, I offer this book in the hope that it may make some contribution to clarifying the issues raised by current debate on marxist theory.

Definitions

The following terms have much currency in contemporary marxist writing. Since I have found it necessary to use them, and since they have a technical meaning, these definitions may be helpful.

Mode of production designates more than simply the economy. It is best understood as a set of relations of production, the forces of production corresponding to them, and the social relations which can be deduced from these relations. So the concept of the capitalist mode of production includes not simply all the economic determinations elaborated by Marx in *Capital*; it also includes, at the minimum, some basic definition of the capitalist state.

Social formation is, by contrast, a more concrete concept. No mode of production in the pure form ever exists. What does exist are definite social formations in which different relations of production co-exist with, however, one set of relations prevailing over the others. Thus Marx in *Capital* analyses the (economic level of the) capitalist mode of production, Lenin in *The Development of Capitalism in Russia* (some aspects of) the Russian social formation. Nicos Poulantzas, populariser of this jargon, writes that 'social formations are not . . . the concretisation and spatialisation of modes of production existing already in a state of abstract purity, but rather the particular form in which modes of production exist or are reproduced'.[1]

Discourse is a generic term for both the activities of speaking and writing and their result, bodies of utterances and inscriptions.

Introduction

Is there a future for marxism? The question will annoy those opponents of marxism for whom it is a demon to be exorcised, a paroxysm unamenable to rational discussion, an error long ago refuted, stemming from the darker side of the human soul. It will also irritate those marxists who believe that to ask such a question is to admit the possibility that the answer might be 'No'.

At one level the relevance of marxism has never been greater. Capitalism is, by common acknowledgement, undergoing its most severe crisis since the 1930s. The world economy is in the grip of a lethal combination of inflation and overproduction, while in the years since 1968 massive social struggles have shaken western state monopoly capitalism, eastern bureaucratic state capitalism and the dependent capitalisms of the south. These same years have seen the revolutionary left – marxists more radical than the Communist Parties – win, in the main western-European countries at least, a toehold in the industrial working class.

And yet there has been no decisive breakthrough by the working class anywhere in the world. In western Europe, while the Communist Parties have continued their rightward evolution, the far left have been unable to win the durable support of even a large minority within the workers' movement. The result has been a severe crisis which has gripped the bulk of the European revolutionary left. The Communist Parties have not, since the ebbing of the eurocommunist tide, been immune from this crisis. There has followed a systematic questioning by many on the left of, not simply isolated propositions, but the entire body of concepts constituting historical materialism.

It is this 'crisis of marxism' to which this book is addressed. Chapter 1 will outline the lineaments of the crisis. It remains briefly to indicate the co-ordinates governing my arguments.

1

In the first place, this book is devoted to the clarification of concepts rather than their utilisation. As such, it is a work in marxist philosophy, an attempt to isolate and examine some of the presuppositions of marxist theoretical discourse. It is, therefore, a contribution to the already vast literature in which contemporary marxism has feverishly examined its entrails, taking the epistemological auguries. This may be regrettable, but, in present circumstances, it is a necessity. What is in question is marxism's adequacy both as a scientific discipline and as a guide to political practice. It is not possible to meet this challenge without a return to fundamentals.

The focus of my discussion of the 'crisis of marxism' is provided by the work of Louis Althusser. My reasons for concentrating on Althusser and his followers are in part personal and parochial. Their writings were of great importance in my own intellectual and political formation. Moreover, Althusser has been the chief influence in the revival of British marxism (in the universities and polytechnics, at least) over the last decade. However, there are more general reasons for selecting this focus. Althusser's impact has been felt by socialist intellectuals across Europe, from Sweden to Spain. His is undoubtedly the most important single attempt to redefine the essentials of historical materialism in the 'return to Marx' of the last fifteen years.

Moreover, there are certain important structural features which France, from where Althusser and his school originate, shares with those other European countries where revolutionary impulses have been most strongly felt since 1968. France, Italy, Spain, and Portugal all have in common mass Communist Parties, a sizeable far left, a significant increase in working-class militancy over the last fifteen years, long-entrenched right-wing regimes. Althusser's influence has been felt in all these countries. Britain, too, although it fits this pattern far less well, has experienced in the last decade a sharpening of the economic class struggle. It is significant that the major European country which has proved largely immune from the althusserian bacillus is west Germany, where there is neither a mass Communist Party nor a militant trade-union movement.

Althusser's work, therefore, has been felt to be of general relevance. Furthermore, as we shall see, his intervention represents an extremely ambitious attempt to restate marxism in terms of a set of categories largely derived from post-war French philosophy. In itself, there is nothing new in this phenomenon: the influence of the neo-kantians and Weber on the austro-marxists and Lukacs, of Croce and Bergson on Gramsci is well-known. But this particular attempt at a synthesis of marxism and 'bourgeois idealism' is of interest, first, because of the intrinsic importance of contemporary French philosophy and its subversion of traditional notions of consciousness, language, knowledge, and secondly, because the failure of this attempt has contributed to the rise of a new school of radical intellectuals which, starting from the same philosophical themes, has sought to provide an alternative to marxism. I am referring to Michel Foucault, Gilles Deleuze and their followers. Foucault in particular, having acquired by the mid-1970s the same status in Parisian intellectual circles which Althusser had enjoyed a decade earlier, is now beginning to have a major impact elsewhere in western Europe. His examination of existing society (and, tacitly, his critique of marxism) in terms of 'power-knowledge' are seen by many disillusioned with marxism to provide a radical alternative to the traditional left.

The reference-point for this book is, therefore, not simply the rise and fall of althusserianism, but also the 'nietzschean' challenge offered to marxism by Foucault and Deleuze. Chapters 2, 3 and 4 are devoted to these matters. In the rest of the book I examine certain major conceptual difficulties of marxist theory – the dialectic, determination by the economy and the status of theoretical discourses – before discussing the implications of these issues, in the final chapter, both for our understanding of contemporary capitalism and for revolutionary strategy and tactics.

Finally, I suppose I should lay my cards on the table. This book is a reasoned defence of marxism. But *which* marxism? Lenin's? Stalin's? Mao's? Trotsky's? Isaac Deutscher identified two main marxist traditions: 'classical marxism', stemming from Marx and embracing Lenin, Luxemburg and Trotsky in particular, and 'vulgar marxism', the crippling distortion of marxism already at work in the Second International but codified under Stalin. Perry Anderson (following Merleau-Ponty) introduced an additional nuance by opposing to both these traditions (but especially the first) a third – 'western marxism', the tradition, located in the universities rather than the working-class movement, concerned with philosophy rather than economics or politics, idealist rather than materialist, which evolved in western Europe following the defeats of the 1920s and 1930s. My basic reference-point is provided by the classical tradition. The future of marxism lies with Marx and Engels, Lenin and Trotsky, Luxemburg and Gramsci, rather than with Kautsky, Stalin or Mao. However, we cannot simply 'return' to the classics. We shall in the course of this book discover some of the contradictions and silences present even in *Capital*. Classical marxism is not a monolith, a seamless robe. Its gaps, aporias, too-hasty answers created the space in which vulgar marxism emerged. Western marxism's concern with epistemological questions is not simply, as Anderson suggests, a flight into idealism, but a response, however inadequate, to real problems. Classical marxism requires conceptual development as well as application in concrete analyses and embodiment in revolutionary organis-ation. This book is a small contribution to that task.

1 The 'Crisis of Marxism'

THE GHOST OF STALIN

If there is any one point at which the 'crisis of marxism' can be said to have gone public, it was on 13 November 1977. There had of course been many symptoms of the crisis before that moment – most notably, perhaps, the sudden prominence of a group of young Parisian intellectuals who in 1976–7 produced a series of books and articles in which they proclaimed marxism a machine for the construction of concentration camps. The *nouveaux philosophes*, as one of their number dubbed them, achieved rapid prominence in the French media (after all, France was then in the lead-up to the legislative elections of March 1978, which the Communist–Socialist Union of the Left was then expected to win). They even made the cover of *Time*, which solemnly announced that Marx was dead (when had it ever thought otherwise?). But despite all the fuss and the fact that the *nouveaux philosophes* had mostly been active members of maoist *groupescules* in the immediate aftermath of 1968, their message carried little authority with those who preferred to remain on the left rather than succumb to the eager embraces of President Giscard d'Estaing.

Far more significant then was Louis Althusser's contribution to the conference held in Venice on 11–13 November 1977 devoted to the theme 'Power and Opposition in Post-revolutionary Societies'. Organised by the Italian far-left group *Il Manifesto* to counter the Venice Biennale, that year devoted to dissidents in the eastern bloc of a largely reactionary persuasion, the conference sought to examine both the nature of 'really existing socialism' and its implications for the western-European left. In her opening address Rossana Rossanda declared that the experience of stalinism had placed in question 'the very idea of socialism, not as a generic

5

aspiration, but as a *theory of society*, a *different* mode of
organisation'. The result was 'a crisis of marxism, of which the
nouveaux philosophes are the caricature, but which is experienced by vast masses as an unacknowledged reality'.[1]

Althusser, speaking during the conference's final session,
developed Rossanda's reflections further:

> What is this crisis of marxism? A phenomenon which must
> be grasped at the historical world level and which concerns
> the difficulties, contradictions and dilemmas in which the
> revolutionary organisations of struggle based on the marx-
> ist tradition are now involved. Not only is the unity of the
> international communist movement affected, and its old
> forms of organisation destroyed, but its own history is put in
> question, together with its traditional strategies and prac-
> tices. Paradoxically, at the moment of the most serious crisis
> which imperialism has ever known, at a moment when the
> struggles of the working class and of the people have
> reached unprecedented levels, the different Communist
> Parties are all going their own separate ways. The fact that
> the contradiction between different strategies and practices
> is having its own effects on marxist theory itself is only a
> secondary aspect of this profound crisis.[2]

Thus for Althusser the 'crisis of marxism' is principally the
political crisis of 'official' marxism, of the 'international
Communist movement', manifested first in the split between
China and the USSR and then in emergence of eurocommunism as a current largely independent of Moscow. The
crisis of marxist *theory* is a 'secondary aspect' of these political
changes.

Althusser, however, goes on to say the following about the
crisis of marxist theory:

> We cannot consider our historical, political and even
> theoretical tradition as a *pure* heritage, which was distorted
> by an individual called Stalin, or by the historical period
> which he dominated. There is not original 'purity' of
> marxism that only has to be rediscovered. During the whole
> testing period of the 1960s when we, in our different ways,
> went 'back to the classics', when we read and re-read Marx,

Lenin and Gramsci, trying to find in them a living marxism, something which was being snuffed out by Stalin-type formulae and practices, we were all forced, each in our own way, even within our differences, to admit the obvious – namely, that our theoretical tradition was not 'pure'; that, contrary to Lenin's over-hasty phrase, marxism is not a 'block of steel', but contains difficulties, contradictions and gaps, which have also played, at their own level, their role in the crisis, as they already did at the time of the Second International, and even at the beginning of the Third (Communist) International, while Lenin was still alive.[3]

This is a passage of great significance. For who more than any other in the 1960s went 'back to the classics' but Althusser? The very titles of his two most famous works, *For Marx* and *Reading Capital*, imply that their purpose was to extract the essential principles of historical materialism through a reading of the classics, and above all *Capital*. Now this 'pope of theory', as Elmar Altvater and Otto Kallscheuer described him, announces the failure of his project, declares it to have been a search for a non-existent object.[4]

The issue more than any other around which the 'crisis of marxism' has been seen to concentrate is that of the Soviet Union. The decay of the Western Communist Parties' loyalty to the motherland of socialism, gradual in the years following Krushchev's denunciation of Stalin in 1956, given a push by the Russian invasion of Czechoslovakia in 1968, accelerating rapidly in the mid-1970s when the Communist Parties seemed on the verge of office and were eager to brush up their image, has meant that stalinism is no longer a taboo subject in their ranks.

The motor of this process has been the transformation of the European Communist Parties into classical reformist parties. Stalin's triumph in the USSR meant that the Communist International ceased to be the world party of socialist revolution its founders had intended some time in the mid-1920s. However, the Communist Parties remained part of an international movement, subordinated to Moscow. There was always implicit in this situation a tension between the Communist Parties' role as instruments of Soviet foreign policy and their roots in the workers' movements of their own countries.⁵ The adoption of the strategy of a popular front against fascism following Hitler's conquest of power in 1933 was in part a response to initiatives by various European Communist Parties as well as a result of Stalin's interest in an alliance with 'democratic' imperialist powers such as France and Britain. The popular front period and its sequel in the period between the German invasion of the USSR in 1941 and the outbreak of the cold war in 1947 enabled the Communist Parties to present themselves increasingly as national parties based on the native popular traditions of their own countries and pursuing their own roads to socialism. Even the expulsion of the Communists from the French, Italian and Belgian governments in 1947 led to a new inflection rather than to the abandonment of the nationalist and class-collaborationist rhetoric of the popular front – an appeal for an alliance of democratic and popular forces against, not fascism this time, but the alien threat of American imperialism which threatened to transform western Europe into an economic and military dependency of Washington and Wall Street. The subsequent development of the theory of state monopoly capitalism by the European Communist Parties involved a further shift within the same basic framework: the enemy was now identified as being the small band of monopolists in control of an increasingly socialised economy; the solution an alliance of all anti-monopoly elements (including 'progressive' sections of the bourgeoisie).⁶

The characteristic themes of eurocommunism – of the need to construct a broad democratic alliance with the objective of establishing an advanced democracy in the country concerned – therefore overlay, and were a continuation of, a strategy dating in all essentials from the Seventh Congress of the Comintern in 1935. The difference lay chiefly in the willingness of the European Communist Parties to criticise forthrightly both the record and the present-day reality of the soviet bloc. This was largely a matter of political necessity. As in the mid-1970s the possibility of Communist Parties participating in governments in France, Italy and even Spain seemed a real one, the right-wing parties and press naturally concentrated much of their propaganda around one simple issue: the election of a government including Communists would lead ineluctably, so they argued, to the horrors of stalinism. The ineffectual attempts of the last major brezhnevite Communist Party in western Europe to ride to power on the backs of the Armed Forces Movement in Portugal of course added force to these arguments. The Communist Parties needed to establish their democratic credentials. Particularly important was the need to stress that a government of the left would not involve any dangerous rupture with the existing economic system nor the replacement of the existing state machine with organs of popular power. So, for example, to avoid the danger of a Chilean-type 'destabilisation' of a Communist-governed Italy the Italian Communist Party opted for a historic compromise with the ruling Christian Democracy, while the French Communist Party abandoned the formula of 'the dictatorship of the proletariat'. The political strategy of the western Communist Parties, as outlined by Santiago Carrillo in his book *Eurocommunism and the State*, revived the classical themes of social democracy as outlined by Bernstein and Kautsky, above all in their stress on the continuity of the political institutions of parliamentary democracy in the transition from capitalism to socialism.[7]

This shift, less in strategy than in rhetoric, and the accompanying willingness of the Communist Parties to distance themselves from stalinism and the Soviet Union, depended on the effective independence of these parties from Moscow, a product of their success in rooting themselves in their native working-class movements and the Soviet State's emergence as a super-power capable of dealing with the US on equal terms and therefore much less reliant on the international Communist movement as a tool of diplomacy. A space was thus created within which Communist Party militants could, for the first time, openly discuss the nature and history of the USSR, at the same time as the Communist Parties sought to define their political strategy as a distinctive line evolved independently of the Kremlin. Reflection upon the nature of the Soviet Union became closely linked to discussion of the nature of socialist democracy and the problems of strategy and tactics facing the western-European workers' movement.

Other factors served to give these debates an added force. The development of opposition to bureaucratic rule within the Soviet bloc had repercussions in the west. The publication of Solzhenitsyn's grim masterpiece *The Gulag Archipelago* in the mid-1970s roughly coincided with the opening of the debate on eurocommunism. The book was to have a very powerful impact on French intellectuals of the left as much as of the right. The PCF, slow to break the mould of unquestioning loyalty to Moscow set by Maurice Thorez during his long reign as secretary-general, was therefore hit much harder by the sudden exposure to the light of day of what Althusser called the 'unfinished history' of stalinism than its subtler and traditionally more independent Italian counterpart.

There thus emerged, as Althusser put it, 'the simple but serious problem: . . . *what social relations today constitute the Soviet social formation?*'[8] Without for the time being examining any of the answers offered to this question, let us first note the terms in which it is posed. Althusser referred to

> the extreme difficulty (everyone working seriously on the problem knows this very well) and perhaps even, in the present stage of our theoretical knowledge, almost the impossibility of providing a really satisfactory marxist explanation of a history which was, after all, made in the name of marxism![9]

'*Almost the impossibility of providing a really satisfactory marxist explanation . . .*' What an admission. Althusser's former pupil Regis Debray, theoretician of guerilla warfare in Latin America and later an adviser to the French Socialist leader Francois Mitterrand, went even further, writing in reply to the *nouveaux philosophes*' claim that marxism displays a totalitarian logic leading inevitably to the Gulag:

> Owing to Marx and his descendants, something is known about the exploitation of man by man. Very little is known about the domination of man over man, regarding which marxism falls short. . . . Only once we know how to integrate patiently the achievements of modern science: biology, thermodynamics, information theory, history of religions, ethnology, psychoanalysis, etc., will we one day be able to comprehend and not condemn phenomena as decisive as the cult of personalities, (yesterday, today, and tomorrow),

the permanence of the institution, the constant reinforce-
ment throughout the planet of national particularities
and their attendant technical and political centralis-
ations, the fragmentation of universalities postulated for
the benefit of lived identifications, the sacralisation of
power, etc.[10]

Debray's argument virtually concedes the point at issue. For
what else did Marx claim to do than to explain 'the domination
of man over man' in terms of the 'exploitation of man by man'?
In a passage to which we will have occasion to return, Marx
writes:

> It is always the direct relationship of the owners of the
> conditions of production to the direct producers . . . which
> reveals the innermost secret, the hidden basis of the entire
> social structure, and with it the political form of the relation
> of sovereignty and dependence, in short, the correspond-
> ing specific form of the state.[11]

Yet Debray is in effect arguing that marxism cannot explain
the 'specific form of the state' either east or west (or south for
that matter). The door is thus opened to those, such as both
the *nouveaux philosophes* and, as we shall see, Michel Foucault
and Gilles Deleuze, who argue that society must be understood in terms of relations of power rather than relations of
production.

Some who do not necessarily share Debray's elegant pessi-
mism concerning the prospects for socialism in the west[12] are
tormented by the same doubts concerning marxism's ability to
account for 'really existing socialism'. Paul Sweezy writes of a
'deep crisis in marxian theory' arising from the failure of the
' "socialist" societies (to) behave as Marx – and I think most
marxists until quite recently – thought they would'.[13] This is a
highly significant admission from one of China's chief defen-
ders in the west. For other marxists the crisis centres more
directly on the problems of socialist strategy in the west. Lucio
Colletti declared in a celebrated interview:

> Not only has the falling rate of profit not been empirically
> verified, but the central test of *Capital* itself has not yet come

to pass: a socialist revolution in the advanced west. The result is that marxism is in crisis today, and it can only surmount this crisis by acknowledging it.[14]

THE CRISIS OF THE EUROPEAN REVOLUTIONARY LEFT

Naturally enough, the non-occurrence of revolution in the west was most serious for those socialists who believed that the Communist Parties, by taking a parliamentary and pacific road to power, had betrayed the heritage of Marx and Lenin. The year 1968, and those immediately following, had transformed the situation of the revolutionary left. The student movement of the late 1960s provided them with a mass audience. The events of May and June 1968 in France – the greatest general strike in the history of the European proletariat – were the curtain-riser to a wave of working-class struggles which shook western Europe from end to end: the 'May in slow motion' in Italy 1968–9; the working-class resistance to the Heath government of 1970–4; the Portuguese revolution of 1974–5; and the 1975–6 strike wave which sounded the death-knell of the Franco regime in Spain. David Widgery accurately described the mood of revolutionaries in those heady days:

> It was as if an international political pageant was being acted out – the ideas we had treasured in pamphlets and argued about in tiny pub rooms were now roaming alive, three dimensional. Marxism had come out of the cold.[15]

The late 1960s and early 1970s saw a very rapid expansion of the far-left organisations: by the middle of the latter decade, all the major European countries had revolutionary groups each with several thousand members and with peripheries numbering sometimes in tens of thousands. In Italy the three main organisations had, in 1976, 30,000 members and half a dozen members between them, while each produced a daily paper. In Portugal in 1975 the far left was able to lead very large street demonstrations of workers and soldiers and to exert an influence even in governmental circles thanks to its sympathisers in the Armed Forces Movement.

However, this dramatic improvement in the situation of the revolutionary left gave way, with parallel rapidity, to a severe crisis. The collapse was greatest in those countries where the most ground had been gained previously. In Portugal the far left virtually disappeared following the right wing's successful exploitation of a botched attempt at a coup d'etat by military elements sympathetic to the Communist Party on 25 November 1975. In Italy the parliamentary elections of June 1976, when the parties of the left failed to win a majority, led to the dissolution of one group, Lotta Continua, and splits in the other two main organisations, PDUP-*Il Manifesto* and Avanguardia Operaia. There followed a drastic decline in the influence of the Italian far left. When in 1977 a student movement developed in protest against the Italian Communist Party's support for the Christian Democratic government it was as hostile to the organised revolutionary left as it was to the reformist parties; support grew for groups committed to something closer to anarchism than a leninist strategy – the movement generically known as the *autonomisti*. In the rest of western Europe the main far-left organisations experienced crises, perhaps less acute than those in Portugal and Italy, but nonetheless serious.

There is no need to examine the crisis of the European revolutionary left in detail – this has already been done in a masterly fashion by Chris Harman in a recent article in *International Socialism*[16] – but its main elements should be outlined. The very rapidity of the revolutionary groups' growth after 1968 created the conditions for the crisis. The sharp increase in the class struggle bred a mood of 'revolutionary impatience' – the belief that revolutionary situations could be expected to develop quite quickly out of existing social conflicts. Moreover, in the years immediately following 1968, the bulk of the membership of the far-left organisations were students or ex-students and the political traditions of many of these organisations, notably the maoists (predominant in Italy, Spain and west Germany), denied the industrial working class the central role in the revolutionary process. The result was a tendency to by-pass the traditional political and trade-union organisations of the working class – to believe, as the Fourth International did following 1968, that the universities could be the fulcrum of the revolution, or to concentrate, like Avanguardia Operaia, on building rank-and-file committees outside the unions. Finally, the almost universal resolve of the far left after 1968 to build leninist parties tended to involve the adoption in practice of a model of organisation in fact derived largely from the zinovievite Comintern of the mid-1920s or, worse, from the stalinist parties before their decline into 'revisionism' after 1956 (the latter being especially true, of course, of the maoists). The internal regimes of many of the revolutionary groups therefore made discussion difficult and encouraged little reflection on the concrete problem of how to develop support for their ideas in the conditions of western Europe today.[17]

However, the development of revolutionary consciousness among workers did not unfold in the linear manner expected by the far left. The radicalisation caused by the struggles of the late 1960s and early 1970s found political expression largely in the growth in support for the traditional reformist parties. Not only did the Communist Parties in Italy, France, Spain and Portugal enjoy a marked increase in membership and influence, but the Socialist Parties in these countries enjoyed an extra-ordinary revival. There was little, perhaps, that the far left could have done to prevent this – despite their expansion after 1968 they remained too small to offer a credible political alternative – but very often their response to the change in the situation was to leap from one extreme to the other. Where once they had believed that the traditional reformist parties could be ignored and by-passed, now they began to hang their hopes on the electoral successes of these parties. As Chris Harman put it:

> All too often the former 'ultra-lefts' reacted [to the reformist revival – AC] by substituting a new form of impatience for the old. In the past they had believed that an activist revolutionary minority could by its own radical action transform society *for* the working class; now they believed that manoeuvres with reformist parties could transform society *for* the working class. In neither case did the class itself have to develop a revolutionary party and a revolutionary consciousness.[18]

So in France the Ligue Communiste Revolutionnaire (French section of the Fourth International) and in Italy the three main groups centred their expectations upon the election of a government of the left, implying that a Socialist–Communist coalition could inaugurate a rupture with capitalism.[19] The ebb of the eurocommunist tide – which in Italy began with the disappointing election results in June 1976 and was underlined by the set-back suffered by the Italian Communist Party in the 1979 general elections, while in France it was marked by the break-up of the Union of the Left in September 1977 and the right-wing victory in the legislative elections of March 1978 – could only cause a severe crisis in the revolutionary left.

It should be clear, however, that the different forms taken by the 'crisis of marxism' among Communist Party members like Althusser and in the far-left organisations are part of the same set of inter-connected phenomena. The revival of the traditional workers' parties in the 1970s provided a common focus for revolutionaries and reformists alike. Even if the far left had been less naive in pinning such great hopes on the prospects for electoral victories by the left, it was impossible not to be affected by a mood in which an end to decades of right-wing rule was confidently expected. Moreover, many of the younger activists especially in the Communist Parties had been radicalised by the experience of 1968 and after. The revival of marxist theory provided a common reference point for Communist Party intellectuals and revolutionaries alike: Althusser, Poulantzas, Bettelheim, Mandel were read by and influenced both. The left's electoral set-backs gave rise to a ferment of debate, notably in the French Communist Party. Althusser and his collaborator, Etienne Balibar, had already opposed the Party's abandonment of the formula of 'the dictatorship of the proletariat' in 1976; in the aftermath of March 1978 they launched into a frontal assault on the Communist Party leadership and internal regime.[20]

Other factors contributed to the crisis, and especially encouraged the questioning of the leninist model of political organisation. One was the so-called 'crisis of militancy' – the strains imposed on activists especially in the far-left organisations by a decade or more in which they had devoted their lives whole-heartedly to a revolution which was not as close as it had once seemed.[21] Of greater and more universal significance was the emergence after 1968 of movements whose social composition, objectives and forms of organisation appeared to fit traditional marxist models badly if at all – the so-called 'new social movements' or 'autonomous movements' of women, homosexuals and immigrant workers. The development of the women's liberation movement in particular posed problems for orthodox marxists, since many feminists argued that the struggle against sexual oppression transcended class divisions and could not be conducted within the framework of a socialist party. Their arguments were given added force by the crass and male-chauvinist attitude initially displayed towards the women's movement, not only by the Communist and Socialist Parties, but by the far left. In Italy in particular the rebellion of women within the revolutionary groups contributed materially to their crisis, playing, for example, an important role in the break-up of Lotta Continua. In the wake of this crisis many argued that the development of revolutionary consciousness would depend less on a centralised party winning the support of the majority of workers than on the evolution of a cluster of loosely-structured movements each combatting a particular form of oppression.[22]

MARXISM IN BRITAIN

So far we have concentrated upon the 'crisis of marxism' as it has manifested itself on the continent. It remains to say a little about the situation in Britain. The most obvious difference lies in the non-existence of a mass Communist Party. The loyalties of the organised working class have been monopolised by the Labour Party since before the First World War. This is not to dismiss British communism as negligible or irrelevant: in the years following the October revolution the Communist International grafted itself upon a native British marxist tradition with both strengths – solid proletarian roots, and weaknesses – a tendency towards syndicalism and sectarianism.[23] However, from the 1920s onwards the Communist Party of Great Britain, although the driving force of the trade-union left, was never able to break out of a minority position within the labour movement, nor to contribute to the development of marxist theory. The Communist Party leadership's subservience to Moscow was to exact a severe cost – the gains made in the popular-front period of the 1930s and between 1941–5 when the Russo–British alliance was at its zenith were undermined by developments such as the Hitler–Stalin pact and the Soviet invasion of Hungary. The events of 1956 in particular led workers and intellectuals alike to pour out of the party.

However, 1956 helped to create a small space within which marxists could exist outside the Communist Party. The development of the Campaign for Nuclear Disarmament provided them with an audience. The main focuses were (and are) provided by *New Left Review* and various trotskyist groups. *New Left Review*, founded by dissident Communist Party intellectuals such as Edward Thompson, sought initially to develop a form of non-stalinist marxism rooted in the native radical traditions of the British left. In 1962 an abrupt change took place with the installation as editor of Perry Anderson, who announced the intention of remedying the defects of marxism in Britain by the wholesale importation of 'western marxism' – firstly mainly Sartre and Gramsci, but then Althusser and Colletti. This shifting intellectual focus was accompanied by a rather nomadic approach to politics: in the mid-1960s hopes were placed mainly in the apparent successes of various reformist parties – notably, the inclusion of the Italian Socialist Party in government coalitions (the so-called 'opening to the left' by Christian Democracy) and the election of the Wilson government in Britain; later in the decade attention shifted to guerilla struggles in the third world, while after 1968 a strategy of building 'red bases' in the universities was advocated; in the early and mid-1970s, however, a partial rapprochement was reached between *New Left Review* and the orthodox trotskyism of the Fourth International, announced by Anderson in his essay (and tacit self-criticism) *Considerations on Western Marxism*.

Further to the left, the various groups which emerged from the splits in the Fourth International could claim a continuity, through Trotsky, with the traditions of the October revolution and the early Comintern. In most cases, however, they displayed a sectarian preoccupation with their own differences sometimes verging on the pathological, as in the case of the Workers Revolutionary Party (formerly the Socialist Labour League). However, it was a group stemming from the trotskyist tradition, the Socialist Workers Party (formerly the International Socialists), which was the chief beneficiary of the student movement in Britain. By the mid-1970s the Socialist Workers Party was an organisation of three to four thousand members, with some support in the working class, a group comparable with the main far-left organisations on the continent.

The crisis of the revolutionary left was not to leave Britain immune. The Socialist Workers Party had anticipated that the struggles which had brought the Heath government down would continue, after a short interruption, under Labour, leading to the radicalisation of significant numbers of workers and a consequent growth in support for the revolutionary left. In fact, the class struggle did not follow this linear course: after 1975 the continued ideological and political grip of labourism on the organised working class led to a drastic fall in strikes; even after the revival of economic militancy in 1977 and then in the winter of 1978–9 strikes tended to assume a defensive character in the face of an offensive by an increasingly aggressive and cohesive employing class, while shop-floor organisation in such traditionally strong sectors as engineering and shipbuilding was clearly in decline.[24] The result was a period of confusion, disorientation and division within the Socialist Workers Party, with many of the issues involved in the crisis of the far left in countries like Italy – notably, the relation of movements against racial and sexual oppression to the class struggle and the internal regime – being debated. If the crisis was less severe than on the continent, this reflected the fact that in the period after 1968 the Socialist Workers Party had not, on the whole, shared the more extreme illusions of the European revolutionary left, whether 'ultra-left' or 'opportunist'.

The crisis was felt more severely inside the Communist Party of Great Britain. Throughout the period since 1968 the Communist Party has been in decline as an organisation. At the heart of this decline has been the increasing integration of the party's trade-union activists into the official machine. This development has made it more and more difficult for the Communist Party to serve as the focus for rank-and-file militancy in the unions – its traditional role, whatever the political acrobatics imposed by Moscow, since the 1920s. The party was forced to present itself less as an autonomous political force than as an adjunct to the left wing of the Labour Party. It was this change in the role of the Communist Party as much as the desire to climb on the eurocommunist band-wagon which led the party congress in 1977 to adopt a new version of its programme, *The British Road to Socialism*, which explicitly endorsed a gradualist strategy centred around the election of a 'Labour government of a new type'.

There were those, however, within the Communist Party who wished to go much further. The Communist Party, even while its working-class base contracted, managed to recruit quite a lot of students and youngish white-collar workers, some of whom had been through one or other far-left group. Moreover, it benefitted considerably from a phenomenon we shall discuss a little more below, the growth of a politically inactive marxist intelligentsia in British higher education. Since the Communist Party, unlike the far-left groups, did not expect intellectuals to become involved in routine political work, it provided a comfortable home for many of these academic marxists. The annual Communist University of London provided a venue where they could discuss their ideas, attracting at its zenith in 1978 over 1000 students. Increasingly the young recruits to the Communist Party after 1968 began to develop their own distinctive position to the right of the party leadership. Opposed to the traditional Communist Party focus on trade-union activity, they dismissed the wages struggle as 'economism' and advocated a shift in attention towards struggles located outside the workplace, notably those around community issues, womens' rights and (peaceful) opposition to racism and fascism, and an explicit political orientation on Tony Benn and the Labour left. The 1977 congress was followed by two years of wearing debate and continued organisational decline culminating in the 1979 congress where the party traditionalists were victorious over the right, reasserting the party's orientation on the industrial working class, even though the Communist Party's decay at the roots made it doubtful that this decision would be implemented.[25] Themes similar to those raised by the new right in the Communist Party were developed with more clarity elsewhere on the left. Most significant, perhaps, was the evolution of althusserianism in Britain. For a brief period in 1971–3 a journal entitled *Theoretical Practice (TP)* had sought to develop a distinctively althusserian strategy for Britain. It soon succumbed to the dissensions of the editors. Individually, however, those involved in *TP* continued to exert an influence, notably through their involvement in journals such as *Economy and Society* and *Screen*.

Then there appeared in 1977–8 a two-volume work, *Marx's 'Capital' and Capitalism Today*, by four ex-editors of *TP*, Anthony Cutler, Barry Hindess, Paul Hirst and Athar Hussain, which represented a sharp break with orthodox marxism. *'Capital'*, the authors declared,

> does not provide us with the basis for the kind of work we need to undertake. In key areas of theory it is either inadequate in what it does say or it enforces silence through the intervention of the questions and concepts which it brings to the fore.

The

> conception of value and the law of value which is present in the discourse of *Capital* . . . and the concepts and problems dependent upon it should be rejected. It is necessary to displace mode of production as a primary object of theorisation in marxist discourse. The concept of class struggle cannot be retained in its classical form and . . . there can be no justification for a "reading" of politics and ideology for the class interests they are alleged to represent. It follows that the working class is not automatically or essentially socialist, that working-class politics are not automatically progressive.[26]

These propositions, presented with great intelligence and force, provided a coherent rationale for those in the Communist Party who wished to redirect socialist politics away from the industrial working class. For some, *Marx's 'Capital' and Capitalism Today* and the other writings of Hindess and Hirst provided a bridge out of marxism entirely towards an exploration of the problems posed by Michel Foucault and his collaborators. Such an evolution was especially marked in the case of the journal *Ideology and Consciousness*.

Support for a shift away from the traditional preoccupations of marxism came from other quarters on the left of a very different theoretical provenance from the former followers of Althusser. A collection of essays entitled *Beyond the Fragments* by Sheila Rowbotham, Lynne Segal and Hilary Wainwright argued forcefully for forms of socialist organisation deriving from the experience of the women's movement and focussing less on the struggle for political power than on the prefiguration of the future society. In 1978 E. P. Thompson published a lengthy essay entitled *The Poverty of Theory*. Designed as a counterblast to the influence of Althusser and his followers, the essay provided, as we shall see, as powerful an argument for abandonment of the central concepts of classical marxism as did the work of Hindess, Hirst and their co-thinkers.

Underlying these debates, and to some extent the changing character of the Communist Party of Great Britain, was a social phenomenon of some significance. There now exists in Britain a socialist intelligentsia explicitly pledged to marxism of some size and significance. Several factors came together to make this development possible: the expansion of higher education, especially in subjects such as sociology; the student movement of the late 1960s and early 1970s; the general atmosphere of crisis which has become ever more pervasive in the last fifteen years. The phenomenon is not confined to Britain; it is to be found in the main western European countries and to some degree in north America.

What distinguishes this group from earlier generations of marxist intellectuals is its confinement to academic institutions. Perry Anderson wrote of western marxism, as it emerged in the writings of Adorno, Althusser, Della Volpe, Colletti, Marcuse, Sartre, Lukács and others in the last fifty years that 'the first and most fundamental of its characteristics has been the structural divorce of this marxism from political practice'.[27] In the 1970s what had been true of a few individuals has become a description of a mass phenomenon. These words of Frank Parkin are, sadly, wholly accurate:

Contemporary western marxism, unlike its classical predecessor, is wholly the creation of academic social theorists – more specifically, the creation of the new professoriate that rose up on the wave of university expansion in the 1960s. The natural constituency of this marxism is not, of course, the working class, but the massed ranks of undergraduate and postgraduate students in the social sciences; its content and design mark it out exclusively for use in the lecture theatre, the seminar room and the doctoral dissertation.[28]

This development has been, perhaps, more marked in Britain, partly because of the relative poverty of marxist culture in this country before the 1960s, partly because of the absence of any mass party paying even lip-service to marxism. The hold of labourism on most workers has provided the new academic marxists with an alibi for pursuing their natural inclinations and remaining in the comfort of their studies. A semi-autonomous culture has been created within which the work of academic marxists is produced and consumed; journals such as *Screen, Capital and Class, Radical Philosophy, Economy and Society, Ideology and Consciousness, History Workshop* are part of this culture, as are the frequent specialist conferences organised under the auspices of these publications. In some subjects – most notably, history – marxists and *marxistants* enjoy a considerable influence. Some have celebrated this rise of 'Anglo-Marxism'[29]; others, above all Edward Thompson, denounced 'those barrels of enclosed marxisms which stand, row upon row, in the corridors of polytechnics and universities'.[30] It is, at any rate, a new and puzzling phenomenon – a free-floating socialist intelligentsia unburdened by practical political commitment.

Therefore, if acted out on a smaller stage and with a less dramatic script than on the continent, the 'crisis of marxism' in Britain was no less real for all that. Riven with doubts about 'really existing socialism', about strategy in western Europe, about the very status of their discourse, the marxist left found themselves in disarray. This situation was all the more serious in the light of the resurgance of the right, both politically, as evidenced by the election of a Tory government in Britain, and intellectually, with the growth of interest in economic liberalism *a la* Milton Friedman.

If the political confusion was perhaps greatest in Italy, the intellectual retreat of marxism was most dramatic in France. Sartre, when he declared in *The Problem of Method* (1957) that marxism was the definitive philosophy of the time, had spoken for a generation of French intellectuals. Today, little more than twenty years later, all that has changed. In an important survey of recent French philosophy which appeared in 1979 Vincent Descombes wrote of 'the complete effacement of marxism from the French scene'.[31] Two examples may help to bring the point home. The works of Claude Levi-Strauss have had an enormous impact on the post-war French intellectual scene. Books such as *The Savage Mind* were explicitly described by Levi-Strauss as inspired by marxism. Yet in 1979 he told an interviewer, the *nouveau philosophe* Jean-Marie Benoist, 'I think the marxist, communist and totalitarian ideology is only a ruse of history to promote the accelerated westernisation of peoples who have remained outside until recent times'.[32] For those who may doubt that Levi-Strauss' marxism ever ran very deep there is another, more tragic example – the suicide of Nicos Poulantzas.

Poulantzas, a member of the Greek Communist Party of the Interior resident in Paris, was the most influential marxist political theorist of the last decade. Among the reasons given for his death was depression caused by the defeat of the Union of the Left in France and the wars between 'socialist' states in Indochina. His last book, *State, Power, Socialism*, had ended on a pessimistic note. Accepting the risks involved in the gradualist strategy advocated therein – 'we could be heading for camps and massacres as appointed victims' – he concluded: 'if we weigh up the risks, that is in any case preferable to massacring other people only to end up ourselves beneath the blade of a Committee of Public Safety or some Dictator of the proletariat'.[33]

Even more shattering was the death on 16 November 1980 of Helene Rytman, wife of Louis Althusser. An autopsy revealed that she had been strangled, to the horror of Althusser's friends and colleagues, who had refused to believe his claims that he had killed her. The examining magistrate who visited Althusser in Sainte-Anne hospital was unable to charge him with murder because, in the words of *Le Monde*, 'the philosopher seemed unable to understand the meaning of this judicial act'. Three psychiatrists were given the task of establishing whether Althusser was insane at the time of his wife's death. This tragic episode was a terrible reminder of the fact that even marxist philosophers do not occupy the geometric space of pure reason but are combatants in what Althusser himself called in his essay 'Freud and Lacan' 'the only war without memoirs or memorials, the war humanity pretends it has never declared, the war it always thinks it has won in advance, simply because being human is nothing but surviving this war'. Althusser had long suffered from severe and recurrent bouts of depression and was in the depths of melancholy at the time of this tragedy, but its causes may have been political, stemming from the 'crisis of marxism', as well as personal. This at least is what Jean Elleinstein, who had fought the PCF leadership from the right flank of eurocommunism as Althusser had from the left, thought: 'The state of the world, the state of contemporary France could only have contributed to aggravating [Althusser's] illness'.

The remainder of this book is concerned with the 'crisis of marxism' in the form it has taken at the theoretical level, particularly in France. Both the most influential version of marxism to have come out of that country – that contained in the writings of Louis Althusser – and the theories elaborated in opposition to it have been produced within an intellectual framework decisively influenced by a new conception of language. Any consideration of the 'crisis of marxism' must, therefore, begin with the remarkable philosophy of language which so came to dominate the French intellectual scene in the 1960s.

2 In the Beginning Was the Word

THE REVOLUTION OF LANGUAGE

> The real metaphysical problem is the word. The epoch
> when the writer photographed the life about him with the
> mechanics of words redolent of the daguerrotype, is
> happily drawing to a close. The new artist of the word has
> recognised the autonomy of language and, aware of the
> twentieth-century current towards universality, attempts to
> hammer out a verbal vision that destroys time and space.[1]

These words were written by Eugene Jolas in 1929 in an article
entitled 'The revolution of language and James Joyce'. They
are applicable to one of the most striking phenomena of
western intellectual culture in this century – the manner in
which language has somehow folded back onto itself, its
nature defined, not by the relation between words and things,
discourse and a reality that exists independently of and prior
to it, but by its own inner structure. Language, in much of
western philosophy and literature, has broken loose from
reality and become an autonomous, self-referential process
extending to infinity in all directions.

   In a sense the starting point of contemporary French
philosophy, as it has developed since the 1950s, can be said to
be the denial of the traditional doctrine of language, according to which, as Michel Foucault put it, 'discourse . . . is but a
slight addition which adds an almost impalpable fringe to
things and to the mind; a surplus which *goes without saying*,
since it does nothing else except to say what is said'.[2] The
traditional conception of language, as it is developed, for
example, in such seventeenth century discussions as the Port
Royal *Logic* or Locke's *Essay Concerning Human Understanding*,

involves two elements. First, the meaning of a word is held to consist in the entity outside language to which it refers – to adopt modern terminology, the sense of a word is its reference. Further, since such doctrines of language are usually connected with theories of knowledge which hold that the ideas or sense-impressions present in consciousness mediate between human beings and the external world, what we have is a structure of *representation*: ideas are the signs of things and words the signs of ideas.[3] Language is conceived of as a collection of signs whose nature depends on their relation to entities outside language. Secondly, the problem naturally arises of the security of this relationship. To put the question somewhat anachronistically: what criteria exist to ensure the correct use of a given word to refer to a particular set of ideas/things? The guarantee is provided by the *subject*. In secure possession of his consciousness and its contents, which can be distinguished, arranged and generally put to work at least in principle prior to the existence of language, the subject assigns meanings to words and ensures their correct usage. This doctrine of language, therefore, depends upon a certain ordering of philosophical categories – one which, in the course of the seventeenth century, in the writings of Descartes and Locke and the traditions deriving therefrom, accords primacy to the subject as the self-defining point from which the orders of thought and of the world are constructed. Language, in this epistemology, becomes a simple receptacle for the contents of consciousness – essential from the point of view of convenience as a store of information and a means of communication, but subordinate to and dependent upon the intuitive relation between the subject and his ideas and impressions.

It would take us too far from our subject to discuss the nuances of what I shall call the classical doctrine of language and of the epistemology on which it depended, or to trace their gradual subversion, first by such heretical and apparently marginal figures as Spinoza and Vico, then in the full light of day by German idealism and its heirs. Let us turn to consider the work whose alternative conception of language has had such a decisive influence on contemporary French thought – Ferdinand de Saussure's *Course in General Linguistics*. Only some of the themes of this revolutionary work (first published posthumously in 1915) need be emphasised here.

Saussure begins his discussion of the general principles of linguistics by criticising those who 'regard language, when reduced to its elements, as a naming process only – a list of words, each corresponding to the thing it names': this conception 'lets us assume that the linking of a name and a thing is a very simple operation – an assumption that is anything but true'. He insists that 'the linguistic sign unites, not a thing and a name, but a concept and its sound-image'. In order to emphasise the point he introduces a new terminology: the sign comprises two elements – the *signifié* or signified (the concept) and the *signifiant* or signifier (the sound-image). Thus the sound 'tree' is linked to the concept of a tree rather than the entities which in the real world fall under this concept:

> Language can ... be compared with a sheet of paper: thought is the front and sound the back; one cannot cut the front without cutting the back at the same time; likewise in language, one can neither divide sound from thought nor thought from sound.

The process of signification involved in language consists in the movement from sound-image to concept and back, the movement backwards and forwards from signifier to signified.[4]

This concept of the sign and of signification in itself involves no radical breach with traditional notions. Roman Jakobson has pointed out that Saussure's conception of the sign is the same as its mediaeval definition as *aliquid stat pro aliquo* – something which stands for something else.[5]

Saussure's innovation lay in the way in which he conceived the conditions of possibility of signification – of something standing for something else. Having asserted the arbitrary nature of the linguistic sign – in other words, the proposition that the relation between signifier and signified is a purely conventional one, involving no element of, say, resemblance or association between a sound-image and the concept for which it stands – he insisted that signification depends upon the relations holding between the units making up a language. These relations he designated by means of the concept of linguistic *value*. The analogy with exchange-value is explicit:

> To determine what a five-franc piece is worth one must therefore know: (1) that it can be exchanged for a fixed quantity of a different thing, e.g. bread; and (2) that it can be compared with a similar value of the same system, e.g. a one-franc piece, or with coins of another system (a dollar, etc.). In the same way a word can be exchanged for something dissimilar, an idea; besides, it can be compared with something of the same nature, another word. Its value is therefore not fixed so long as one simply states that it can be 'exchanged' for a given concept, i.e. that it has this or that signification: one must also compare it with similar values, with other words that stand in opposition to it. Its content is really fixed by the concurrence of everything that exists outside it. Being part of a system, it is endowed not only with a signification but also and especially with a value, and this is something quite different.[6]

Saussure is not, however, merely delineating two distinct aspects of language – signification and value. He is asserting that *signification depends upon value*, that the relation between sound-images and concepts depends upon the relations within the two series of the signifier and the signified. Thus: 'It is quite clear that initially the concept is nothing, that it is only a value determined by its relations with other similar values, and that without them the signification would not exist'. Further:

> The conceptual side of value is made up solely of relations and differences with respect to the other terms of language, and the same can be said of its material side [i.e. the signifiers – AC]. The important thing in the word is not the sound alone but the phonic differences that make it possible to distinguish this word from all others, for differences carry signification.[7]

Let us note that value consists not simply in the relations between words or concepts, but in their *differential* relation – the differences between them. Thus the French word *'mouton'* cannot in all contexts be substituted for the English word 'sheep' because *'mouton'* corresponds to the two English words 'sheep' and 'mutton'. Again, 'synonyms like French *redouter*, "dread", *craindre* "fear", and *avoir peur* "be afraid" have value through their opposition', while, 'the terms *a* and *b* as such are radically incapable of reaching the level of consciousness – one is always conscious only of the *a/b* difference'. Considerations of this sort lead Saussure to conclude:

> In language there are only differences. Even more important: a difference generally implies positive terms between which the difference is set up; but in language there are only differences *without positive terms*. Whether we take the signified or the signifier, language has neither ideas or sounds that existed before the linguistic system, but only conceptual and phonic differences that have issue from the system. The idea or phonic substance that a sign contains is less important than the other signs that surround it.[8]

Language, therefore, for Saussure, consists in two parallel and interdependent series, the signifiers and the signified. Each series is constituted by the relations between its elements, sounds and concepts respectively. These relations and the elements themselves are produced by difference. One can see here the starting point for some of Saussure's most well-known themes – notably his insistence on the priority of *langue*, 'the whole set of linguistic habits which allow an individual to understand and to be understood', over *parole*, its usage in speech, and of synchrony, the relations constituting *langue* at any one time, over diachrony, the evolution of language.[9] It is this sense that Saussure is called the father of 'structuralism' – he regards the system of difference constituting *langue* as the privileged level of linguistic analysis.

More important from our point of view are the philosophical implications of this conception of language. In the first place, language has been lifted off reality. The sense of a word or sentence is no longer its reference to an entity outside language. As Frederic Jameson writes of Saussure:

> The lines of flight in his system are lateral, from one sign to another, rather than frontal, from word to thing, a movement already absorbed and interiorised in the sign itself as

the movement from signifier to signified. Thus, implicitly, the terminology of the sign tends to affirm the internal coherence and comprehensibility, the autonomy of the system of signs itself, rather than the constant movement outside the symbol-system towards the things symbolised.[10]

Language, in other words, has become autonomous, a self-contained system.

Secondly, meaning no longer inheres in individual words or sentences. It depends upon the relations constituting language. As Gilles Deleuze put it, *'sense always results from the combination of elements which are not in themselves significant'*.[11] Thirdly, and closely following on the previous two points, the 'combination of elements' is constituted by difference. The concept of *difference* has a number of connotations. One, obviously, is that of the hegelian dialectic, which conceives reality as a self-contained whole developing according to the contradictions internal to it. Again, there is Heidegger, whose critique of western metaphysics involved centrally the claim that the latter had failed to think difference – the difference between Being as such and entities.[12] As we shall see, the concept of difference plays a role of crucial importance in the writings of Althusser, Foucault, Deleuze and Derrida.

Finally, the conception of language developed by Saussure involves, implicitly at least, the dislodging of the subject from the position it had occupied in philosophy since Descartes. The subject was no longer the source of meaning, the guarantor of the relation between word and object. This displacement of the subject was, as the implications of the new conception of language unfolded, to give rise to its *decentring*: from being the secure foundation of thought and the world (and, therefore, by implication, of language) the subject became a result of certain relationships which both were prior to and exceeded it.

This decentring of the subject, and the adoption of a conception of language deriving from Saussure were part of a wider shift in philosophical preoccupations in post-war France. Vincent Descombes characterises this shift as follows:

We can see in the recent evolution of philosophy in France the passage of the generation of the 'three H's', as one said

after 1945, to the generation of the three 'masters of
suspicion', as one will say in 1960. The three H's are Hegel,
Husserl, Heidegger, and the three masters of suspicion are
Marx, Nietzsche and Freud.[13]

The earlier period, that following the Second World War, saw
the subject left intact in its position of primacy: Descombes
shows how the cartesian *cogito* continues to structure the work
of Sartre, for example.[14] The Hegel of these years was the
Hegel of *The Phenomenology of Mind*, his dialectic one of
consciousness, the subject of history no longer Absolute Spirit
but Man. Of decisive importance was what Descombes rightly
calls the '*anthropological version* of hegelian philosophy' offered
by Alexandre Kojeve.[15] His lectures on Hegel at the Ecole
Pratique des Hautes Etudes between 1933 and 1939 (later
published as *Introduction to the Reading of Hegel*) were attended
by, among others, Raymond Aron, Maurice Merleau-Ponty,
Georges Bataille, Jacques Lacan and (possibly) Sartre. Even
Jean Hyppolite, who expressed strong reservations about the
attempt to transform Hegel's philosophy into the drama of
man's passage through the world,[16] as Mark Poster puts it,
'directed his students to the *Phenomenology*, not only in his
translation and commentary, but even in his work on Hegel's
logic'.[17] Among these students were Althusser, Deleuze,
Foucault and Derrida.

Ironically, therefore, the return to Hegel in post-war France
was rather a return to the humanist philosophy of Feuerbach
and the other young hegelians of the 1840s. Like David
Strauss, those who followed Kojeve's reading of Hegel saw the
Phenomenology as 'the alpha and omega of Hegel's works'.[18]
The fact that the *Phenomenology* was, for Hegel, the preliminary to *The Science of Logic*, where the unfolding structure of
conceptual thought is shown to govern the very movement of
reality in an extraordinary bringing down to earth of the
Christian *Logos*, was largely ignored.[19] The dialectic in post-
war Paris was conceived of as the history of the successive
forms of human consciousness. It is in this light that the
considerable interest in Georg Lukács' *History and Class
Consciousness* (1923) must be understood. In this work Lukács
sought to rescue marxism from the evolutionist and fatalist
interpretation given it by the Second International. He read

Capital as the analysis of the way in which the reification of the worker, his transformation into a commodity, is reflected in all the different aspects of social life, and argued that the nature of reification implied the general rationalisation and bureaucratisation of western society, a process already emphasised by his friend Max Weber. Lukács differed with Weber in arguing that a change in working-class consciousness, the adoption of a revolutionary orientation, would dissolve the structures of reification. The proletariat assumes the attributes of Absolute Spirit; as with Hegel the turning point comes with the realisation by the subject that the apparently objective structures of reality are the estranged expressions of its own essence. It is only the nature of the subject that has changed – no longer the *Logos*, but the proletariat. The primacy accorded to the subject and the interpretation of history as the successive forms of human consciousness remained unaltered albeit grafted onto historical materialism.[20] To dislodge the subject from his sovereign position necessitated, therefore, a critique of the dialectic.

It also, apparently, involved a new approach to language. In a paper given in 1964, Foucault referred to the 'suspicion of language' characteristic of western civilisation – 'suspicion that language doesn't say exactly what it says', that it conceals hidden meanings, that 'it in some way outflanks its properly verbal form, and that there are plenty of other things in the world which speak, and which are not language'. This suspicion gives rise to different techniques of interpretation, of putting language to the question, of which the nineteenth century, with Marx, Nietzsche and Freud, produced a new variant.[21]

This new technique of interpretation involved a rejection of the idea that language secretes within itself layers of hidden meaning. Nietzsche had effected 'the reversal of depth, the discovery that depth was only a game, and a fold of the surface'. Words no longer formed an hierarchy leading down into the depths whose exploration was the task of interpretation. They spread across the surface of things into infinity: 'Beginning with the nineteenth century, signs are linked together in an inexhaustible network, itself also infinite, ... because there is an irreducible gap and opening.' The openness of language reflects the fact that it does not depend upon a meaning external to it. Even 'interpretation can never be completed' since 'there is nothing to interpret, for fundamentally, all is already interpretation, each sign is in itself not the thing which offers itself to interpretation, but interpretation of other signs'. Thus 'interpretation finds itself before the obligation of interpreting itself to infinity', a situation which carries with it the danger of 'the disappearance of the interpreter himself'.[22]

These propositions (which owe much to Nietzsche, something to Freud, very little to Marx) are obscure and difficult, and, as the discussion which followed Foucault's delivery of this paper shows they puzzled some of his audience very much. A good deal of this chapter, as well as of Chapter 4, could be said to be devoted to clarifying them. Arguably, they can only be understood if we start from an inflection introduced into saussurian linguistics by Claude Levi-Strauss and Jacques Lacan.

THE SUBVERSION OF THE SIGNIFIED

As we have seen, Saussure conceived of language as forming two parallel series each constituted by the differential relations internal to it – signifiers and signified. There is no order of priority between the two: sound-images and concepts, sensible and intelligible, are indissolubly linked, form, as Saussure puts it, two sides of a piece of paper. The change introduced by Lacan and Levi-Strauss, in their different ways, was to insist on the primacy of the signifier over the signified, a process which has led, in the philosophies of Deleuze and Derrida, to the denial that the process of production of meaning can find any secure resting point in a signified external to language.

One way to understand the assertion of the primacy of the signifier is as follows. Let us reverse the relationship and assert the primacy of the signified over the signifier – of concepts over sound-images. Such a move leaves the subject secure in his place: it is he who assigns words to the role of standing for his thoughts. There are semiotic systems which seem to fit this picture – the Highway Code or Semaphore, where a limited number of signs are conventionally defined to stand for certain concepts. One difficulty with language conceived along these lines is that these codes can transmit only a limited number of messages. Yet one of the characteristics of language agreed on by all sides is its ability to transmit an infinite number of messages. How can a theory of language which asserts the primacy of signified over signifier account for the production of *new* meanings? Is an act of intuition binding together a concept and a sound-image necessary in each case? The dependence of this conception of language upon the creativity of the subject reaches its most extreme here.

Levi-Strauss can be taken to argue that the production of new meanings can be explained if we assert the primacy of the signifier over the signified in the sense that there is 'a superabundance of signifiers, relative to signified', 'a surplus of signification'. This dislocation between the two series constituting language arises from the following situation:

> Whatever the moment and the circumstances of its appearance in the scale of animal life, language could only be born all at once. Things could only be made to signify all at once.... But, this apparently banal remark is important, because this radical change is without counterpart in the domain of knowledge which develops slowly and progressively. In other words, at the moment when the entire Universe, at one blow, has become *significant*, it has not become thereby any better *known*.... What results from this? That the two categories of signifier and of signified were constituted together and simultaneously, as two complementary blocs; but that knowledge ... only got under way very slowly.[23]

It follows that

> Man from his origin disposes of an integral system of signifiers which he must allocate to a signified, given as such without thereby being known. There is always a discrepancy between the two, which could be resolved only by the divine understanding, and which results in the existence of a superabundance of the signifier, relative to the signified on which it can pose itself.

This discrepancy explains the existence of notions such as *mana* in certain 'primitive' societies, as 'oomph' (Levi-Strauss was writing in 1950) in western popular culture:

> Always and everywhere, these types of notions intervene, a little like algebraic symbols, to represent an undetermined value of signification, in itself devoid of sense and therefore susceptible to receive any sense, whose unique function is to overcome a gap between signifier and signified.

To these notions Levi-Strauss gave the name of 'floating signifier', 'the servitude of all finite thought (but also the gage of all art, all poetry, all mythical and aesthetic invention)': The possibility of producing new meanings arises from the 'superabundance of the signifier'.[24] Clearly Levi-Strauss' introduction of this concept, and, underlying it, of the proposition that there is a discrepancy between signifier and signified such that the former series has priority over the latter (the signifier 'poses itself on' the signified) reflects his own preoccupations: in particular, his conceptualisation of society as a symbolic order governed by the laws of language:

> Like language, the social *is* an autonomous reality (moreover, it is the same reality); the symbols are more real than that which they symbolise, the signifier precedes and determines the signified.[25]

Similarly, Lacan has sought to employ the concepts of structural linguistics in his reinterpretation of psychoanalysis. One of the interesting features of this reinterpretation was that it took the form of a 'return to Freud'. This is the theme, for example, of the famous Rome report delivered by Lacan in 1953. But, as is indicated by the title of that text, 'The function and field of speech and language in psychoanalysis', this return is of a peculiar sort. Shortly afterwards Lacan succinctly summed up its main themes:

> What the psychoanalytic experience discovers in the unconscious is the whole structure of language. Thus from the outset I have alerted informed minds to the extent to which

the notion that the unconscious is merely the seat of the instincts will have to be rethought.[26]

Lacan, therefore, is particularly concerned to challenge the interpretation of Freud according to which psychoanalysis discovers in the unconscious, repressed, biological instincts. Profoundly influenced by Hegel and Heidegger,[27] he argues that lack and separation are constitutive of human experience. The human child is born incomplete – expelled from security of the womb, in its early years of life completely dependent for its survival on others. The unconscious is the record of its transformation into a human subject, a process the decisive stage of which is the Oedipus complex – if successfully resolved the latter leaves the child, by its acceptance of the lack at the very heart of its being, a lack symbolised by the phallus either which it does not possess (if female) or of which it can be deprived (if male) by the father, lodged in the symbolic order which Lacan, following Levi-Strauss, conceives of as being the order both of language and of society. It follows that 'Freud's discovery was that of the field of the effects in the nature of man of his relations to the symbolic order and the tracing of their meaning to the most radical agencies of symbolisation in being'.[28]

Clearly this theory necessitates a confrontation with Freud's theory of the instincts and of sexuality – if the latter is not about a biological substratum lurking beneath conscious experience, what is it about? Lacan insists on the centrality of desire to psychoanalysis: *'Desidoro* (I desire) is the Freudian *cogito'*. But the drives (it is thus, rather than by the traditional 'instinct', that Lacan and his followers translate the freudian concept of *Trieb*) do not represent the completeness of biological needs repressed by civilisation. They are themselves fragmented and partial: 'Sexuality is realised only through the operation of the drives insofar as they are partial drives, partial with regard to the biological finality of sexuality'. They are partial because sexuality itself is caught up in the fundamental lack at the heart of human existence:

> If all is confusion in the discussion of the sexual drives it is because one does not see that the drive represents no doubt, but *merely* represents, and partially at that, the curve of

fulfilment of sexuality in the living being. Is it surprising that its final term should be death, when the presence of sex in the living being is bound up with death.[29]

The hegelian overtones of this passage are very strong. Hegel conceived of sexual reproduction as the moment at which the living individual both realised itself and discovered its finitude – its entanglement in a process in which the species continued while the individuals perish having reproduced themselves: 'in the process of generation the immediacy of the living individual perishes'.[30] It also recalls Heidegger's analysis in *Being and Time* of human existence as constituted by its relation to death.

Lack, therefore, is constitutive even of sexuality and the drives. As Anike Lemaire puts it, for Lacan

> the eroticised partial instinct refers back to the organic need which founds it, but it also refers back beyond this to a lived experience of radical lack resulting from separation from the maternal body.
>
> For Lacan, lack is the void, the zero, that which lies before the instinct. It refers to the absence of an anatomical complement and induces organic need.... Lack is what precedes the instinct 'expressed' by the erotogenetic zone and the letter. It also precedes the desire expressed by a signifier. Lack implies the idea of the lived drama of an irreversible incompleteness rather than that of some erotic appeal.[31]

Desire is to be distinguished, Lacan argues, both from biological *need* and from *demand*. The latter 'bears on something other than the satisfactions it calls for. It is demand of a presence or of an absence – which is manifested in the primordial relation to the mother'. Demand, therefore, arises from the incompleteness inherent in man. It is in principle unsatiable because it seeks, not the satisfaction offered by the meeting of some physical need, but the restoration of the original unity with the mother from which the subject was progressively exiled from birth. 'Desire is neither the appetite for satisfaction, nor the demand for love, but the difference that results from the subtraction of the first from the second,

the phenomenon of their splitting (*Spaltung*)'. Desire is the
process through which the subject, on the basis of the partial
sexual drives fragmented by his fundamental incompleteness
and finitude, seeks to win the recognition of the Other. 'Man's
desire is the desire of the Other.'[32]

This analysis recalls those pages of the *Phenomenology* in
which Hegel outlines the dialectic of master and slave, pages
which fascinated Kojeve by depicting a life-and-death struggle whose stake was not power or physical satisfaction but
recognition by the other. Reversing the cartesian *cogito*, Hegel
insists that self-consciousness, far from being primary and
self-subsistent, depends upon the existence of other subjects:
'Self-consciousness exists in itself and for itself, in that, and by
the fact that it exists for another self-consciousness; that is to
say, it *is* only by being acknowledged or "recognised"'.[33]

Lacan's innovation was to identify the intersubjective relations on which self-consciousness depended with the symbolic
order of language and society. It is at this point that the
reinterpretation of the theory of the instincts meets saussurian linguistics: 'desire is an effect in the subject of the
condition that is imposed in him by the existence of the discourse, to make his need pass through the defile of the
signifier'.[34] Fragmented from birth, the subject in its passage
through the world struggles for recognition by 'another
self-consciousness', above all, the mother. This struggle can
only take place within language, the framework within which
self-consciousnesses exist and relate to each other. Its
effects – and in particular the effect of the subject's full entry
into the symbolic order at the Oedipal stage – are to be found
in the unconscious. It is in this sense that we must understand
two characteristic lacanian theses – that 'the unconscious is
structured like a language' and that 'the unconscious is the
discourse of the Other'.

But the repressions necessitated by the process through
which the subject is formed as a self-conscious member of
society deny him access to the record secreted within himself
of that process. Inverting Descartes, Lacan asserts: 'I think
where I am not, therefore I am where I do not think'. I am, not
within the circle of self-consciousness, but somewhere else, in
the unconscious. The subject has become decentred: its
meaning no longer lies in the self-certainty of the *cogito*, but in

'the other scene, *ein andere Schauplatz*, of which Freud speaks in *The Interpretation of Dreams*', where '*it* speaks (*ça parle*)'. Its presence is to be detected in the gaps, the slips of the tongue, of everyday talk and the fragmented discourse of the dream. It is to be understood by means of the tools provided by linguistics:

> Interpretation is based on no assumption of divine archetypes [a la Jung – AC], but on the fact that the unconscious is structured in the most radical way as a language, that a material operates in it according to certain laws, which are the same laws as those discovered in the study of actual languages.[35]

However, Lacan does not simply take over Saussure's concepts, but transforms them. The signifier becomes constitutive of *langue*, as is clear from the following passage:

> The first network, that of the signifier, is the synchronic structure of the language material insofar as in that structure each element assumes its precise function by being different from the others; this is the principle of distribution that alone governs the function of the elements of the language (*langue*) at its different levels. . . .
> The second network, that of the signified, is the diachronic set of the concretely pronounced discourses, which reacts historically to the first, just as the structure of the first governs the pathway of the second.[36]

Signifier and signified are no longer two parallel series whose relation to each other (as essential, remember, as that between two sides of a piece of paper) is determined in each case by the differential relations between its elements. Instead, the signifier has been mapped onto the saussurian concepts of *langue* and synchrony, and the signified onto those of *parole* and diachrony. The signified no longer represents the concept towards which the signifier points, but instead the concrete uses to which the differential relations constitutive of language (=*langue*=the signifier) are put.

The nature of the change involved can be better understood when we take note of another of Lacan's moves.

Following Saussure and Jakobson, he asserts that language has two dimensions. The first is that of the paradigmatic or associative, which enables the *substitution* of one word for another. The second is the syntagmatic, which renders possible the *combination* of words to form a sentence or chain of sentences. Jakobson had already gone a stage further by identifying the two dimensions with two traditional figures of poetry and rhetoric: *metaphor*, in which a word or sentence is substituted for a similar word or sentence, and *metonymy*, in which a part is allowed to stand in for the whole (he gives an example of the latter from Tolstoy's *War and Peace*, where 'bare shoulders' is used to designate women at a ball).[37] Lacan now identifies the two poles of language with the two mechanisms through which the freudian dream-work operates to transform the latent content of the dream (repressed thoughts) into a quite different manifest content. Condensation, the process through which different meanings are fused in order to occult a censored thought, is assimilated to the pole of paradigm/association/substitution/metaphor; displacement, the transposition of one term for another with syntagm/combination/metonymy.[38]

The effect is to transform language into an endless play of substitutions and combinations of signifiers in which safe anchorage in a signifier outside this play is never reached: 'No signification can be sustained other than by reference to another signification'. Signification consists not in crossing the bar separating signifier and signified (Lacan employs what he insists on calling the 'algorithm' S/s to represent 'the signifier over the signified'), but in the reference of one signifier to another: 'We can say that it is in the chain of the signifier that the meaning "insists" but that none of its elements "consists" in the signification of which it is at the moment capable'. Meaning is produced not through the signifier pointing to the signified, but in the production of meanings other than its own through the signifier's metaphorical and metonymic relations with other signifiers: 'What this structure of the signifying chain discloses is the possibility I have . . . to use it to signify *something quite other* than what it says'. This 'notion of the incessant sliding of the signified under the signifier' recalls Levi-Strauss's concept of the 'floating signifier', of a 'surplus of signification' which renders possible re-orderings of the relations between signifiers and the production of new meanings. It enables Lacan to conceptualise the process through which the dream-work occults, distorts, transforms meanings through a multi-levelled cluster of associations. Furthermore, desire is assimilated to metonymy. Entry into the symbolic order of language means that recovery of the lost unity with the other is endlessly deferred. By passing through the defile of the signifier need becomes desire, the endless process of displacements characteristic of metonymy. The openness of language corresponds to man's incompleteness.[39]

The disjoining of language and reality involved in Lacan's assertion of the primacy of signifier over signified had also a practical purpose. It served to challenge prevailing psychoanalytic orthodoxy, especially in the United States (Anglo-Saxon analyists were frequent victims of Lacan's considerable resources of sarcasm and vituperation) which held that the aim of the therapeutic technique was the adaptation of the patient to reality. By asserting the primacy of signifier over signified Lacan sought to return to Freud's original conception of the 'talking cure', of analysis as a potentially interminable process in which new layers of meaning could be endlessly unravelled from within the unconscious. But Lacan's reinterpretation of Freud had wider philosophical implications. First, it involved a much more radical assertion of the autonomous and self-referential character of language than Saussure had been prepared to make. Signifiers in their different metaphoric and metonymic dimensions spread across the surface of things to infinity in exactly the fashion described by Foucault in his paper on the 'masters of suspicion'.

Secondly, Lacan dislodged the subject from the pivotal position it had been accorded by Descartes. The existence of the subject as autonomous and self-certain pertains, according to Lacan, to the imaginary order, the register conceptually and chronologically prior to the individual's entry into the symbolic order in which thought takes the form of images rather than words. To this order corresponds the mirror-stage, the early months of life in which the child, totally dependent on others, comes to view his body, initially as a collection of fragments, then as a totality corresponding to the bodies he observes – his mother, other children, his own image in the mirror. The child imagines himself to be a whole and the world to be an extension of his needs and demands; he is incapable of engaging in genuine inter-subjective relationships. The autonomy of the subject is a phantasy produced within the imaginary. Only when the child enters the symbolic order can he relate to other self-consciousnesses, and here he is caught up in a new form of alienation – subordination to the signifying chain.

The subject is outside himself, in the 'other scene' of the unconscious, where the process through which he came to submit to his alienation is recorded. The 'self's radical excentricity to itself' which Lacan, following Freud, claimed to have established represented a fundamental challenge to any philosophy which rested upon the notion of the subject.[40]

Lacan's *Ecrits*, published in 1966, consolidated the growing reputation he had already acquired through his seminars and articles. Fortuitously, that same year saw the appearance of Foucault's *The Order of Things*. Devoted to 'an archaeology of the human sciences', the book's conclusion secured for it a *succès de scandale*. Foucault wrote:

'Among all the mutations that have affected the knowledge of things and their order . . . only one, that which began a century and a half ago and is now perhaps drawing to a close, has made it possible for the figure of man to appear. . . . Man is an invention of recent date. And one perhaps nearing its end'.

If 'the fundamental arrangements of knowledge' were 'to crumble, as the ground of classical thought did, at the end of the eighteenth century, then one can certainly wager that man would be erased, like a face drawn in sand at the edge of the sea'.[41]

The year before *For Marx* and *Reading Capital* had appeared; the year after no less than three major books by Jacques Derrida were published. This bunching together of a number of books all sharing a common 'anti-humanism' in the sense of denying the epistemological priority of the subject and of man, all to some degree influenced by Saussure, seemed to represent the emergence of a new 'structuralist' school. In reality, it was a matter of convergence rather than of shared doctrine.

Derrida in particular developed the philosophical implications of the new doctrine of language.[42] At the source of both the classical theory of language and the cartesian concept of the subject lies, he claims, a notion of *presence* constitutive of western metaphysics. Here he follows Heidegger, who detected at the beginnings of western thought, in the Greek philosophers, 'the treatment of the meaning of Being as *parousia* or *ousia*, which signifies, in ontologico-temporal terms, "presence". Entities are grasped in their Being as "presence"; this means that they are understood with regard to a definite mode of time – the "Present"'.[43] Metaphysics, according to Derrida, places language and history in relation to a present in which the subject has direct and immediate access to reality, a situation identified with or modelled upon theological conceptions of God's revelation of himself to his creatures. Our thought is dominated, Derrida claims, by this present in which the curtain slips aside and the essence of reality spreads out before us, directly accessible to our gaze. There thus arise myths of the Fall – the loss of presence – and Redemption – its recovery; history is merely a secularisation of these myths – 'history has always been conceived of as the movement of a resumption of history, as a detour between two presences'.[44]

Derrida is particularly concerned with the form taken by the metaphysics of presence at the interface between thought and language. Here we find the subordination of writing to speech, of the written to the spoken word – a doctrine which Derrida calls phonologism, whose history, he argues, is closely linked to that of the cartesian cogito, where 'the motif of presence was decisively articulated'. For Descartes the subject is 'a self-present substance, conscious and certain of itself at the moment of its relationship to itself'. The contents of its consciousness are directly accessible to it. Words involve the passing of presence outside itself in communication with others.

The priority of speech over writing reflects its greater proximity to self-consciousness – the fact that speech can be experienced as 'auto-affection', as hearing oneself speak. Language as such is the deferral of presence, its interruption by a web of signs: speech, however, is the point at which this deferral nears zero, at which the production of signs remains closest to the circle of self-consciousness. 'This experience lives and proclaims itself as the exclusion of writing, that is to say of the working of an "exterior", "sensible", "spatial" signifier interrupting self-presence'.[45] Derrida detects this phonologism at work in the writings of Rousseau, Husserl and even Saussure (remember that for the latter the sign is the unity of concept and *sound-image*).

Derrida's aim is to 'deconstruct' the metaphysics of presence by, in the first instance, reversing the order between speech and writing. This reversal should not be taken too literally. What interests him in writing is its capacity to interrupt presence, the fact that it necessarily involves the spatial organisation of material inscriptions – marks on a page. One way to conceptualise writing is through the notion of the *hinge* (*la brisure*) which designates both the break between written signs – they are different from and external to each other, spread across the surface of the page – and their articulation together to form units of meaning, words, sentences, etc. The exteriority of inscriptions to each other means that they can never be recaptured by presence and reduced to its inner unity; hence the hostility of metaphysics to writing. 'The hinge marks the impossibility that a sign, the unifier of a signifier and a signified, be produced within the plenitude of a present and an absolute presence'.[46]

Reversing the relationship between writing and speech enables Derrida to develop fully the consequences of 'the thesis of *difference* as the source of linguistic value' advanced by Saussure.[47] For difference necessarily involves the soldering together of presence and absence. Reference to absent terms is intrinsic to the signifying chain whether they are to be found 'vertically' in the paradigmatic dimension of language – the substitution of terms involved in metaphor – or 'horizontally' in the syntagmatic dimension – the combination of terms characteristic of metonymy. The concept of the trace serves to underline the play of presence and absence inherent in difference. Vincent Descombes explains the function of this paradoxical concept:

The present is present only on condition that it is related to the absent in order to distinguish itself (to an absent which is the past or the future). Metaphysics, according to Derrida, would be the act of effacing this distinctive mark, this trace of the absent thanks to which the present is the present. One then observes this: *trace* ordinarily means the present sign of an absent thing, a sign which this absent has left, after its passage, on the places where it has been present; but if every present bears the trace of an absent which delimits it (and in this sense constitutes it, produces it, enables it to be what it is), then it is necessary to think paradoxically an 'originary trace', that is a *present trace* of a past *which has never taken place*, a 'past absolute'.[48]

Meaning, therefore, does not rest on the deferred fullness of presence; it is produced across the play of difference, a play which depends upon the necessary absence of certain terms.

Play is the disruption of presence. The presence of an element is always a signifying and substitutive reference inscribed in a system of differences and the movement of a chain. Play is always the play of absence and presence, but if it is to be thought radically, play must be conceived of before the alternative of presence and absence. Being must be conceived as presence and absence on the basis of the possibility of play and not the otherway around.[49]

These concepts – writing, hinge, difference, trace, play – (and there are others, necessarily, since deconstruction itself involves the constant substitution and displacement of meanings) enable Derrida to think through much more rigorously than Lacan or Levi-Strauss the primacy of the signifier. The distinction between signifier and signified, he argues

leaves open in principle the possibility of thinking a *concept which is meaningful in itself* (un *concept signifié en lui-même*), in its simple presence to thought, in its independence of language, that is of a system of signifiers. ... Beginning from the moment, on the contrary, when one puts in question the possibility of such a transcendental signified and when one recognises that every signified is also in the position of the signifier, the distinction between signified

and signifier – the sign – becomes fundamentally problematic.[50]

Language becomes an absolutely autonomous self-referential
process in which each signified in its turn is a signifier and so
on to infinity:

> *There is nothing outside the text.* . . . There have never been
> anything but supplements, substitutive significations, which
> could only come forth in a chain of differential references,
> the 'real' supervening and being added only while taking on
> meaning from a trace and from an invocation of the
> supplement, etc. And thus to infinity.

Derrida recognises that this deconstruction of the sign involves
the subversion of the traditional concepts of science and truth,
resting as they do on the notion of a real world independent of
discourse.[51]

Derrida does not believe that it is ever possible to escape the
boundaries of the metaphysics of presence. This is reflected in
his 'concept' of *differance*. This neologism is what Lewis Carroll
would call a 'portmanteau word'. It combines the meanings of
the two verbs 'to differ' and 'to defer'. It affirms, first, the
priority of play and difference over presence and absence,
and secondly, the necessity within difference of a relation to
presence, a presence always deferred (into the future or past)
but nevertheless constantly invoked. Presence is as intrinsic to
difference as absence. The result is that difference conceals
itself within the play of presence and absence:

> The trace must be thought before the entity. But the
> movement of the trace is necessarily occulted, it produces
> itself as self-occultation. When the other [presence – AC]
> announces itself as such, it [the trace, i.e. the present trace of
> absence – AC] presents itself in the dissimulation of itself.

Differance, then, is 'the obliterated origin of absence and
presence'.[52] The concept of the sign can serve as an example.
As we have seen, Derrida regards this concept as necessarily
involving the possibility of a 'transcendental signified' outside
the play of difference. Language, therefore, is ineradicably

metaphysical.[53] We cannot escape metaphysics except by a flight into silence. For Derrida the deconstruction of metaphysics involves, therefore, challenging metaphysics on its own terrain: 'The passage beyond philosophy does not consist in turning the page of philosophy (which usually amounts to philosophising badly), but in continuing to read philosophers *in a certain way*'.[54] And read them he does. As David Wood puts it,

> To say that his work is heavily parasitical on other writing is not just to utter a truth about all writing, but to say something special about his. . . . In a whole series of texts, of which *Marges* and *Glas* are the prime examples, he doesn't just feed off his prey, he hatches his eggs inside their flesh. Sartre once talked about the worm in the heart of being. The possibility of a derridean in-worming lies at the heart of every text.[55]

Deconstruction amounts to a sort of textual politics, the subversion of literary and philosophical texts from within. Not surprisingly Derrida's example has been of greatest inspiration to literary critics – to Julia Kristeva and the other members of the *Tel Quel* group during what Frederic Jameson wittily calls their 'left heideggerian'[56] phase in the late 1960s and early 1970s, and in the Anglo-Saxon world to those contributing to journals such as *Yale French Studies* and the *Oxford Literary Review*.

Others were prepared to go further than Derrida – most notably, as we shall see, Gilles Deleuze. But undoubtedly the former's work has demonstrated with great rigour (I cannot say clarity, since Derrida's writings tend in their construction to reflect his theses concerning the ambiguous, self-referential, pluri-dimensional character of language) that the new conception of language stemming from Saussure carries within it a formidable challenge to orthodox philosophical conceptions.

We could sum up the nature of this challenge as follows. In a well-known article Bertrand Russell distinguishes between 'knowledge by acquaintance' and 'knowledge by description'. 'I say that I am *acquainted* with an object when I have a direct cognitive relation to that object, i.e. when I am directly aware

of the object itself'. I know an object by description only
indirectly, by means of a description (i.e. a unit of discourse)
which picks out a segment of the realm of objects. Russell
argues that 'all propositions intelligible to us, whether or not
they primarily concern things only known to us by description, are composed wholly of constituents with which we are
acquainted'.[57] In other words, knowledge by description is
derivative from and subsidiary to knowledge by acquaintance.
This is a version of a theme characteristic of an old philosophical tradition. Like Descartes and Locke, Russell believes that
the subject has direct access to the contents of his
consciousness – he is, in Derrida's terms, 'self-present' – and
that it is from this primordial knowledge by acquaintance that
our knowledge of the world is constructed. Knowledge is in
the last instance *immediate* knowledge: there can ultimately be
no intermediary between the intuitive contact of subject and
object.

For Derrida this argument would be an example – perhaps
the most important example – of the metaphysics of presence.
He wishes to reverse the order and assert that all knowledge is
knowledge by description. Our relation to the world is
necessarily a discursive one; we have no access even to the
contents of our consciousness prior to discourse. But since
Derrida also denies the possibility of a transcendental
signified – of any meaning prior to the interrelations of
signifiers – and thereby disjoins discourse and reality, does
not the rejection of knowledge by acquaintance place in
question the possibility of *knowledge* itself? For does not the
concept of knowledge presuppose that of truth, which in turn
involves the possibility of a relation of correspondence between discourse and a reality independent of discourse?
Derrida seems to set us adrift in the play of presence and
absence, in the endless proliferation of signifiers. It is in this
state of far more radical doubt concerning the possibility of
knowledge than any entertained by Descartes that the revolution of language seems to leave us. Not only *meaning*, but *truth*
itself has been subverted.

The 'revolution of language' clearly represents a radical
challenge to marxism. First and most obviously because its
epistemological implications, briefly indicated here, seem to
compromise materialism, at least in the sense given it by Marx

and Lenin; the latter wrote that 'it is this sole unconditional recognition of nature's *existence* outside the mind and perception of man that distinguishes dialectical materialism from relativist agnosticism and idealism'.[58] For Derrida the belief in any 'transcendental signified' existing outside, if not 'the mind and perception of man', then discourse is merely a relapse into the metaphysics of presence.

Furthermore, the 'revolution of language' seems to undermine the marxist conception of the social whole. There are, in fact, two main ways in which the relation between the economy and the social whole has been conceptualised by marxists. The first is that of cause and effect: the economic base acts upon the politico-ideological superstructure, which reacts back on the former, but only within certain limits. The second is that of essence and phenomenon. An example is provided by Lukacs in *History and Class Consciousness*. The different aspects of the social whole are conceived as expressions of its hidden essence – the transformation of the worker into a thing. This approach involves the subject: it is the proletariat's *failure* to perceive itself, not as a commodity, but as the productive basis of society, the subject of history, which renders possible the reified structure of capitalism. Both approaches are compromised by the approach we find in Derrida, for example. Causality in the traditional sense of the word implies a linear relationship between two stable objects or events, A, B, such that A acts upon, or gives rise to, B. Yet the stability possessed by the two series of signifiers is only temporary and relative; it exists only so long as their opposition is not displaced by a new one arising from the transformation of signified into signifier, or vice versa. Furthermore, as we have seen, the subject is reduced by the 'revolution of language' to the status of a subordinate agency of impersonal structures. It is in this respect more than any other that the very diverse work of Lacan, Levi-Strauss, Althusser, Foucault, Barthes, Kristeva, etc. has come to receive the appellation of 'structuralism' (much against the wishes of many of them) – whatever their differences, they all assent to the 'decentring' of the subject. This demotion of the subject is as applicable to collectives as to individuals – to the lukácian proletariat as to the cartesian self.

At this point some readers will ask why this strange

concoction of Parisian intellectuals should be of any interest or relevance to marxism. Are we not dealing with two discourses which meet at no point, whose basic assumptions are quite different, which are, in short, incompatible? And indeed many marxists have responded in exactly these terms – 'structuralism', they have argued, is merely the latest version of idealism, a form of bourgeois ideology alien and hostile to marxism. This response, in my view, is untenable. There are two main reasons I would give for taking the 'revolution of language' seriously, apart from the obvious one that attaching a label to something one dislikes or fears does not count as refutation.

First, the philosophical case made out by Derrida and others is a formidable one. This is to accept neither the detail of their arguments, nor the conclusions drawn from them, and certainly not to endorse the attempts by various British and American academics to parrot the usually inimitable rhetoric of one or other Parisian *maître à penser*. It is simply to assert that there is no knowledge other than by description. Discourse is no mere intermediary between thought and reality; thought takes place within discourse, through the combination of phonemes into words, words into sentences, sentences into larger discursive units. As Wittgenstein showed, even the description of one's private mental life is dependent upon the existence of a public language based on a set of rules shared by a community of speakers. Consider the alternative, which is to assert that knowledge by acquaintance – the direct, intuitive contact of subject and object – is possible. This implies the existence of a form of experience which is indubitable, where the experience itself is the sole and indisputible criterion of validity of knowledge given in that experience. Spinoza wrote that 'he who has a true idea, knows at that same time that he has a true idea, nor can he doubt concerning the truth of that thing'. He sought to clarify this claim by comparing truth to light: 'just as light shows itself and darkness also, so truth is a standard of itself and falsity'.[59] The metaphor of truth as light is deeply rooted in western thought. It assimilates knowledge to vision. At its core in the theological concept of *parousia*, the revelation of God's presence in his creation, his self-disclosure to man, the form of experience whose object directly guarantees its validity as knowledge. This concept is still at work in empiricist theories of knowledge, where the information conveyed in sense-experience is treated as self-evident and indubitable. Many of the difficulties from which such theories suffer arise from the admission that sense-experience may deceive. Once we admit any gap between experience and knowledge, then we must choose: we can explicitly invoke God, as Descartes did, in order to provide a guarantee against deception; we may collapse into some form of scepticism or idealism; or we must accept that our knowledge is both fallible and discursive but nevertheless objective. Derrida's critique of the metaphysics of presence is difficult to fault; it does *not* follow, as I shall try to show in Chapter 7, that there is no such thing as objective knowledge.

My second reason for taking the 'revolution of language' seriously is political. Whether the social whole is conceived in terms of cause and effect or essence and phenomenon the result is reductionism, in the sense that the 'superstructure' – politics and ideology – is denied any efficacy. Non-economic social phenomena are either the effects of the base or its expressions; in either case, their status is a secondary one and they can be expected to fall in line with the economy. This is a serious question because the history of marxism has shown reductionism to be politically disastrous. In its cause/effect version it prevailed in the Second International; both relations of production and superstructure were conceived as effects of the productive forces. As a result, history was seen as the record of man's unfolding productive powers and social revolutions as phenomena brought ineluctably into being by the requirements of technological progress. As Gramsci put it, the bolshevik revolution was a 'revolution against *Capital*', or rather against the evolutionist and fatalist misreading of Marx involved in this conception of the social whole.

The reductionism of the early Lukács treated class consciousness as the essence of social life. The conditions of revolution were reduced to a changed perception of reality (or rather, a perception which itself changed reality). Relations of production, the capitalist state, the institutions of 'civil society' were all effaced. The result was to be found in the political strategy espoused by Lukács in the early 1920s: the revolutionary party, bearer on the consciousness 'imputed' to the proletariat on the basis of its position in society, could act on its behalf – engaging in stunts designed to galvanise it into action, like the March action of 1921 when the German Communist Party staged a botched insurrection in the hope of rousing the working class from its reformist slumbers. Neither Lukács' 'hegelian' marxism, nor the evolutionist marxism of the Second International (and Stalin), offers an adequate account of the nature of the social whole. Althusser's significance lies in his realisation of this fact. For reasons of his own he wished to accord 'relative autonomy' to the superstructure; in seeking to construct a version of marxism which avoided both the cause/effect and essence/phenomenon model he both drew on, and contributed to, the 'revolution of language'. The result is not less distinctive, or exciting, for being ultimately a failure.

3 Althusser and the Return to Marx

UNFINISHED HISTORY

Althusser has always insisted that the point of his intervention was as much political as theoretical. Very often this insistence is either misinterpreted or ignored. Edward Thompson is a good example of the first response: for him Althusser represents the intellectual culmination of stalinism, the author of a scholasticism completely divorced from both genuine scientific practice and the life and struggles of the working class. Mark Poster, not an especially friendly witness, denies the validity of such an interpretation:

> Far from being a stalinist, Althusser lacked direct political orientation. Throughout the 1960s his theoretical anti-humanism remained a scholastic exercise of reinterpreting Marx's texts, calling for an extreme separation of theoretical practice and political practice and suggesting if anything a political struggle within the Communist Party between the functionaries and the intellectuals. The political import of althusserianism worked to reassert the autonomy of the Communist Party intellectuals against the dominance of the politicians, the same principle that Sartre had advocated since 1946.[1]

It would be a mistake to suggest that the political import of Althusser's writings can be confined to the assertion of the autonomy of theory; however, such an assertion is at the heart of Althusser's enterprise. He joined the French Communist Party in 1948. He was not alone in making this choice: at the Ecole Normale Superièure, where Althusser has studied or taught since the end of the Second World War, 25 per cent of the students were members of the Communist Party in 1945.[2] In 1945–7 the Party, basking in the prestige it had earned in the Resistance and thanks to the feats of Soviet arms, reached a high-point in its popular support. Communist ministers sat in the cabinet. Maurice Thorez, the Party general secretary, assured the *Times* that the French road to socialism would be quite different from the Russian, appealed to coal-miners to 'Produce!', and supported the disarming of the Resistance. Then in 1947 the Communist Parties, previously indispensable as shock-absorbers for the wave of popular radicalism which swept Europe after Hitler's fall, were unceremoniously kicked out of the French, Italian and Belgian governments. The move, carried out with Washington's encouragement, reflected the end of the war-time alliance between Stalin and western imperialism and the onset of the cold war. In France the expulsion of the Communist Party from office coincided with and exacerbated a series of bitter strikes forcibly suppressed by the government and was followed by the general heightening of social and political tensions.

This political upset led to a willingness on the French Communist Party's part to encourage rather than break strikes, to a generalised sectarianism and, most relevant for present purposes, to a drastic change in the Communist Parties' cultural policy, all on orders from Moscow. Whereas previously the French Communist Party had sought to present itself as heir and guardian of the French rationalist and republican tradition, now the dividing line between bourgeoisie and proletariat was sharply drawn within the sphere of intellectual life. This was expressed in the theory of the two sciences, according to which theoretical discourses' ability to reflect reality accurately depended purely on the class interests they embodied. The criterion of class applied both to the human and the natural sciences – most notoriously to genetics, where a 'proletarian' pseudo-science concocted, by Lysenko was imposed by administrative fiat on Soviet geneticists. This decision and the associated campaign against 'bourgeois' mendelian genetics was faithfully implemented by the French Communist Party.[3] (An associated campaign against relativity theory – for relativism! – was dropped when the practical applications of this 'bourgeois' science became plain.) In France the chief exponent of the theory of the two sciences was Laurent Casanova, who was given the job of bringing Communist intellectuals to heel in 1948–9. At a famous meeting at the Salle Wagram on 28 February 1949 Casanova laid down the duties of a Communist Party intellectual: 'Defend in all circumstances and with the most extreme resolution all the positions of the Party . . . cultivate in us love of the Party in its most conscious form: the spirit of the Party'. Another hack, Francois Cohen, declared that 'for a Communist . . . Stalin is the highest scientific authority in the world'. In the sphere of literature Louis Aragon issued the call to 'write the stalinist truth' while Roger Garaudy had this to say about those who did not: 'Every class has the literature it deserves. The big bourgeoisie in decay delights in the erotic obsessions of a Henry Miller or the intellectual fornications of a Jean-Paul Sartre'.[4] (Life is full of ironies. Cohen recently contributed to *Le URSS et nous*, one of the more critical studies of the Soviet Union to have come out of eurocommunism. Garaudy became one of the main Communist exponents of the Christian-Marxist dialogue. The Christians won. He is now a follower of Père Teilhard de Chardin.)

Philosophically the theory of the two sciences was formulated in terms of dialectical materialism. Based on Engels' formulations in *Anti-Duhring* and *Dialectics of Nature*, codified by Stalin, 'the dominant version of dialectical materialism' was, as Althusser put it, 'an ontology of matter'. Engels had extracted from Hegel's *Science of Logic* three principles which he held to be the laws of the dialectic – the transformation of quality into quantity, the law of the interpenetration of opposites, the negation of the negation. These laws underlay, he claimed, all natural and social phenomena, whose mechanisms were held to be merely their specification. Stalin took over these laws, merely dropping the negation of the negation. Applied to the physical sciences, the dialectic bore a suspiciously close resemblance to the romantic philosophies of nature which had flourished in Germany in the early years of the 19th century. Applied to historical materialism, it became a form of evolutionism, in which modes of production succeeded each other as the level of development of the productive forces required. As Althusser said, dialectical materialism had become by the late 1940s 'a practical ideology, sustaining the political ideology of the Party by providing it with the guarantee of the "laws" of the dialectic'.[5] In the political conjuncture following the outbreak of the cold war it proved convenient to the USSR's rulers to give dialectical materialism an aggressive interpretation, attacking 'non-dialectical' discourses as bourgeois. In France, the Communist Party's best-known philosopher, Henri Lefebvre, was forced to make a public self-criticism for 'neo-hegelianism'; his version of the dialectic, under the influence of the young Lukacs, stressed the role of consciousness and had little place for the rehashed *Naturphilosophie* served up by the Party's cultural apparatchiks.[6]

In the introduction to *For Marx* (1965) Althusser recalled the 'delirium', the 'madness' of those years,

> the period of intellectuals in arms, hunting out error from all its hiding places; of the philosophers we were, without writings of our own, but making politics out of all writing, and slicing up the world with a single blade, arts, literatures, philosophies, sciences, with the pitiless demarcation of class – the period summed up in caricature by a single phrase, a banner flapping in the void: 'bourgeois science, proletarian science'.[7]

Althusser's early essays, gathered together in *For Marx*, represent a response to the 'unfinished history' of stalinism. The problems raised by this history were considered at two levels. First there was the deviation underlying the theory of the two sciences – 'theoretical leftism'. The latter expression is an important item in Althusser's conceptual vocabulary and designates the denial of any efficacy to the superstructure and to theoretical discourses. Included in 'theoretical leftism' so defined is not only the attempt to establish a 'class line' in science, but also the hegelian marxism of the 1920s, represented by Lukacs, Gramsci and Korsch, for whom marxist theory was simply the conceptual articulation of the historical experience of the proletariat, its truth-content depending entirely on its contribution to the struggle.[8] Against 'theoretical leftism' Althusser has consistently sought to preserve the specificity and autonomy of theory.

On the other hand, Althusser's early writings reveal a profound dissatisfaction with the state of international communism. While Krushchev's denunciation of Stalin at the Twentieth Congress of the CPSU (1956) had let in some light, it left the main problems unresolved. Denunciation of the 'cult of personality' did not alter the basic structure of Russian society, nor could it explain this structure, while the stress, both in the USSR and the western Communist Parties, on marxism as 'real humanism', and generally the humanist interpretation of Marx encouraged by the discovery of his early manuscripts, seemed to threaten the dissolution of historical materialism into a quagmire of liberalism. Awareness of this danger appeared to underly China's opposition to Moscow's policy of peaceful co-existence with the west. Althusser's sympathies clearly were with the maoist critique of 'krushchevite revisionism'. No doubt his emphasis on a 'return to Marx' in *For Marx* and *Reading Capital* is closely connected to a maoist-inspired desire to slough away the 'revisionist' distortions which concealed the essence of marxism. In particular, the main thrust of these writings was to challenge the evolutionism so characteristic of stalinism. As a former collaborator of Althusser, Jacques Rancière, put it

> *Reading Capital* presented theses which demanded a *political* critique of the Party: the rupture with the evolutionist conception of history, the affirmation of the discontinuity of modes of production, the affirmation that the laws of the dissolution of a structure were not those of its functioning, the radical originality of the problem of the transition, all that led *logically* towards a denunciation of the CP's economism, of the conception of a peaceful road to socialism and of 'true democracy'. The sharp break between modes of production affirmed the necessity of violent revolution.[9]

However, Althusser has never permitted the logical consequences of his theoretical positions to take him beyond the ranks of French communism. His identification with the Communist Party as the organised embodiment of the struggles and aspirations of the French working class appears to be one of the cornerstones of Althusser's politics. Perry Anderson suggests that joining the Party was one of two options open to western marxist theoreticians in the wake of the defeat of revolution in Europe after 1917 and the resulting stalinisation of the Comintern. 'For all these theorists, it may be said that the official communist movement represented the central or sole pole of relationship to organised socialist politics, whether they accepted or rejected it'. Either they joined the Party, retaining a link with the organised working class at the price of political silence, or they retained their political independence, but thereby lost any 'anchorage within the social class for whose benefit theoretical work in marxism alone has ultimate meaning'. Lukàcs and Althusser took the first option, Marcuse and Sartre the second. There followed, whichever horn of the dilemma they chose, the same result – a retreat into a hermetic academic discourse preoccupied with questions of method rather than the problems of economic analysis and political strategy which formed the focus of the classical marxists' writings.[10] This analysis has the merit of going beyond the mere dismissal of Althusser as a stalinist. It is, however, somewhat 'objectivist' – there were marxists, above all from the trotskyist tradition, who sought both 'to develop theory and to unite it with practice, however modest that practice might be, outside the cloisters of orthodox communism.

Nor does it quite capture the peculiarity of Althusser's political preoccupations. He has called his early writings 'the work of a militant trying to take politics seriously in order to think out its conditions, limits and effects within theory itself, trying in consequence to define the line and forms of intervention'. It is the relation between theory and politics that pre-occupies Althusser. His memory of the late 1940s is that of 'intellectuals in arms', not of the CRS (riot police) and pickets fighting it out during the great strikes of that period. His thought is that of an intellectual never able to cross the barrier between theoretical work and the class struggle. Thus he defined the political objective of his early writings as follows: 'to justify the relative autonomy of theory and thus the right of marxist theory not to be treated as a slave to tactical decisions'.[11] The political conclusion Althusser drew from the Lysenko period was that the autonomy of theory had to be defended at all costs. He sought to do so by means of a reinterpretation of Marx which challenged both humanist and evolutionist readings of his thought and which would, he hoped, provide the starting point for an analysis of stalinism. Althusser's theoretical intervention was irreducibly political, but the politics at stake involved in the first instance a declaration of intellectual independence from the Communist Party. The notion of a 'return to Marx', of a reading of the classical texts of marxism designed to liberate its essence from the distortions which it had suffered at the hands of both its adherents and opponents, could not but challenge the 'idea accepted in the Party' that, as Rancière put it, 'the theoretical authority of marxism had been vested in the political authority of the "party of the working class" '.[12] The eccentricity of Althusser's enterprise lay in the fact that he wished to challenge the Communist Party's theoretical authority but not its political authority. His politics were oddly apolitical.

OVERDETERMINATION

The ambiguity of Althusser's political position should not be permitted to obscure the seriousness and originality of his theoretical writing. Many of the main themes of his intervention are outlined in the 1962 essay, 'Contradiction and Overdetermination'. Here he addresses the problem of the relation between Marx and Hegel. His starting point is provided by the metaphors through which Marx and Engels sought to express this relation – as the 'inversion' of Hegel, as the extraction of the 'rational kernel' of the dialectic from its 'mystical shell', as the retention of the dialectical 'method' combined with the rejection of Hegel's idealistic 'system'. But such a separation between form and content is quite foreign to Hegel, for who 'the method is not an extraneous form, but the soul and notion of the content'.[13]

Moreover, Althusser seeks to show that there is an irreducible difference between the marxian and hegelian concepts of totality. The latter is an example of what he will call in *Reading Capital* 'expressive totality' – in other words, all the different aspects of the social formation are mere reflections of some basic principle, some core, some centre which informs the whole. By contrast, within marxism (Althusser takes the example of Lenin's analyses of a particular conjuncture – the

Russian revolution of February 1917) the contradictory relationship constituting a social formation must be conceived as an accumulation of specific determinations each with their own efficacy and autonomy. Factors such as national traditions and political and ideological institutions are not the mere epiphenomena of the economy, passive reflections of the development of the productive forces.

Althusser borrows two concepts, one from psychoanalysis – overdetermination, and the other from Engels – determination in the last instance, in order to articulate the relationship between the economy and the rest of the social formation in marxism. The economy acts on the social formation only indirectly, via a process of interaction with the other instances making up the whole, so that it is only determinant when its effects and those of the other instances coincide to overdetermine the whole, just as the various contradictions within and acting upon the Russian social formation came together to destroy tsarism in February 1917:

> The (economic) 'contradiction'is inseparable from the total structure of the social body in which it is found, inseparable from its formal *conditions* of existence, and even from the *instances* it governs; it is radically *affected by them*, determining, but also determined in one and the same movement, and determined by the various *levels* and *instances* of the social formation it animates; it might be called *overdetermined in its principle*.

Moreover,

> This overdetermination does not refer to apparently unique and aberrant historical situations (Germany, for example), but is *universal*; the economic dialectic is never active *in the pure state*; in History, these instances, the superstructures, etc. – are never seen to step respectfully aside when their work is done or, when the Time comes, as his pure phenomena, to scatter before His Majesty the Economy as he strides along the royal road of the Dialectic. From the first moment to the last, the lonely hour of the last instance never comes.[14]

Before discussing the theoretical import and later career of these propositions, something should be said about their political implications. In the first place they enable Althusser to assert that his two foes – 'economism' and 'humanism' – are variants of the same theoretical structure. The 'economism' of Stalin asserts that both the relations of production and the superstructure are passive effects of the development of the productive forces; the 'humanism' of the early Lukács treats the different aspects of the social whole as mediated reflections of the basic contradiction at its heart: in each case what is involved is an expressive totality in which all the different elements constituting the whole are reducible to some simple principle. This move enables Althusser to bracket the two main strands in marxist philosophy – the evolutionist (Plekhanov, Kautsky, Stalin) and the hegelian (Lukács, Gramsci, Korsch) – as exemplars of the same error. Both roads lead to the same danger – 'theoretical leftism', the denial of any efficacy to the superstructure.

This point leads rapidly to the second. If the social whole is composed of a number of instances each with their own autonomy and effectivity, then a space can be created within which theory can pursue its own goals unencumbered by interference from the Party apparatus. The door is closed (theoretically at least) to zhdanovism. But third, and most important, the notion of overdetermination provides a method on the basis of which to explain stalinism. For overdetermination implies

(1) that a revolution in the *structure* does not *ipso facto* modify the existing superstructure and particularly the *ideologies* at one blow (as it would if the economic was the *sole determinant factor*), for they have sufficient of their own consistency *to survive beyond their immediate life context*, even to recreate, to 'secrete' substitute conditions of existence temporarily; (2) that the new society produced by the revolution may itself *ensure the survival, that is, the reactivation, of older elements* through both the forms of its new superstructures and specific (national and international) circumstances.[15]

In other words, a version of the dialectic which renders due homage to the relative autonomy of politics and ideology can account for the Stalin period in terms of the continued efficacy of bourgeois and even pre-bourgeois elements of the superstructure. But more of this below.

For the moment, let us note the degree to which the 'return to Marx' involved discovering in *Capital* many of the principles we have seen at work in the 'revolution of language'. This is strikingly evident in *Reading Capital*, whose opening essay invokes the three 'masters of suspicion' – Marx, Freud, Nietzsche – and contains a critical discussion of the ' Three H's' – Heidegger, Husserl, Hegel.[16] This is more than a matter of citations – as we shall see there is a definite convergence between many of the theses advanced by Althusser and Derrida.[17] Moreover, Lacan's influence upon Althusser has been profound. Not only did Althusser borrow some lacanian concepts (the imaginary, metonymic causality), as well as, on occasions, the *maitre's* allusive and rhetorical style, but the entire project of the 'return to Marx' appears to have been modelled on Lacan's 'return to Freud'. Just as Lacan seeks to rescue Freud from the misreadings of his followers, so Althusser aims to disengage the basic principles of marxism from their vulgarisation and distortion.[18]

Other influences on Althusser's work have been detected. Perry Anderson writes of 'the systematic induction of Spinoza into historical materialism by Althusser and his pupils'.[19] Yet the 'induction' of a classical philosopher's concepts into a very different body of theory nearly three hundred years after his death is not something that takes place in a vacuum: in what context did Spinoza seem relevant to marxism? We shall have a little more to say about Althusser's 'spinozism' below, and in Chapter 5.

DIFFERENCE

A number of themes in Althusser's writings bring out both his convergence and his disagreements with his contemporaries. First, the theory of overdetermination involved the assertion of the priority of difference. Difference no longer arises from and is resumed back into an original simple unity, as in the hegelian dialectic. Complexity or multiplicity is intrinsic to social formations, it is 'ever-pre-given':

There is no longer any original essence, only an ever-pre-givenness, however far knowledge delves into its past. There is no longer any simple unity, only a structured, complex unity. There is no longer any original simple unity (in any form whatsoever), but instead, *the ever-pre-givenness of a structured complex unity.*

What is 'ever-pre-given' in this 'structured, complex unity'? Practice – or, rather, practices. Althusser's general definition of practice follows Marx's analysis of the labour-process in *Capital* volume 1:[21]

By practice in general I shall mean any process of *transformation* of a determinate given raw material into a determinate *product*, a transformation effected by a determinate human labour, using determinate means (of 'production'). In any practice thus conceived, the *determinant* moment (or element) is neither the raw material nor the product, but the practice is a narrow sense: the moment of the *labour of transformation* itself, which sets to work, in a specific structure, men, means and a technical method of utilising the means.

Practices are multiple: ' "social practice", the complex unity of the practices existing in a determinate society, contains a large number of distinct practices' – Althusser lists economic production, political practice, ideological practice, and theoretical practice.[22]

This theme of the multiplicity and irreducibility of practices is developed further in *Reading Capital*, where Althusser introduces the concept of differential temporality. Hegel's concept of historical time, he argues, follows from his notion of expressive totality. 'Time is just the notion definitely existent, and presented to consciousness in the form of empty intuition'[23] – it is the self-externalisation of the Absolute. It follows that for Hegel time is homogeneous and continuous, and all the different elements of the whole exist in the same time, as epiphenomena of the same essence – thus the different aspects of a historical epoch are mere expressions of the particular form taken by the Absolute Spirit at the time. The concept of overdetermination requires, Althusser argues, a break with 'the hegelian category of the contemporaneity of the *present*':

> It is no longer possible to think of the process of the development of the different levels of the whole *in the same historical time*. Each of these different 'levels' does not have the same type of historical existence. On the contrary, we have to assign to each level a *peculiar time*, relatively autonomous and hence relatively independent, even in its dependence, of the 'times' of the other levels.

Each practice constituting the social whole has its own 'peculiar time and history':

> Each of these peculiar histories is punctuated with peculiar rhythms and can only be known on condition that we have defined the *concept* of its historical temporality and its punctuations (continuous development, revolutions, breaks, etc.).[24]

Althusser's critique of the hegelian expressive totality and assertion of the multiplicity of practices and the differential character of historical times inevitably recall what Derrida has to say about the metaphysics of presence. Derrida indeed explicitly declared of the concept of differential temporality: 'To that . . . I have always subscribed'.[25] Moreover, Althusser undertakes a remarkably similar critique of western metaphysics. In the opening pages of *Reading Capital* he discusses what he calls *'the empiricist conception of knowledge'*. Empiricism is here defined very widely, to include Descartes and Hegel as well as Locke and Hume. Underlying their thought is a 'secular transcription' of 'the religious myth of reading'. This myth in its original form treats knowledge as epiphany or *parousia* – as the revelation of God's presence in the world. Reworked in the scientific revolution of the seventeenth century (its religious origins are still evident in the writings of Bacon and Galileo) the myth retains the notion that knowledge rests upon a complicity between subject and object. The result of knowledge – the concepts it produces – are already there, present in reality as its essence. The subject of knowledge needs only to look, with a properly informed gaze, in order to discover, lurking beneath the appearances, the essence of things. The structure of the real, its division into essential core and inessential surface, renders knowledge possible – its task is to remove the external husk from the inner essence: 'Knowledge is therefore already *really* present in the real object it has to know, in the form of the respective dispositions of its two real parts!'[26]

IDEOLOGY

The pre-established harmony between subject and object means that knowledge takes the form of the *recognition* of a difference (between essence and phenomenon) inscribed in the real. However, unlike Derrida, Althusser offers an account of why and how this structure of recognition should arise. For the closure characteristic of western metaphysics, its reliance upon the complicity of subject and object, arises from the fact that it is produced within *ideology*. Here is the second great theme of Althusser's work. 'Ideological knowledge' is 'a phenomenon of *recognition*':

> In the theoretical mode of production of ideology, . . . the formulation of a *problem* is merely the theoretical expression of the conditions which allow a solution already produced outside the process of knowledge because imposed by extra-theoretical instances and exigencies (by religious, ethical, political or other 'interests') *to recognise itself* in an artificial problem manufactured to serve it both as a theoretical mirror and as a practical justification.[27]

This structure of recognition characteristic of theoretical ideologies is also be found in ideology in general:

> Ideology is a matter of the *lived* relation between men and their world . . . . In ideology men do indeed express, not the relation between them and their conditions of existence, but the *way* they live the relation between them and their conditions of existence: this presupposes both a real relation and an '*imaginary*', '*lived*' relation. Ideology, then, is the expression of the relation between men and their 'world',

that is, the (overdetermined) unity of the real relation and the imaginary relation between them and their conditions of existence. In ideology the real relation is inevitably invested in the imaginary relation, a relation that *expresses a will* (conservative, conformist, reformist or revolutionary), a hope or a nostalgia, rather than describing a reality.[28]

The term 'imaginary' should alert us to the fact that Althusser is attributing to ideology the characteristics of Lacan's imaginary order. Let us recall that for the latter the imaginary pertains primarily to the stage, prior to the child's entry into the symbolic via the Oedipus complex, where it imagines itself to be an autonomous and self-sufficient whole. For Althusser this is precisely what happens in ideology. He develops this thesis in his essay on 'Ideology and Ideological State Apparatuses', where he argues that 'there is no ideology except by the subject and for subjects'. But whereas for Lacan the imaginary is one moment in the constitution of the subject as a self-conscious member of a social, language-using community (and a moment which must be superseded if the perils of psychosis are to be avoided) for Althusser ideology provides the mechanism through which the individual is soldered to the social whole. *'The category of the subject is only constitutive of all ideology insofar as all ideology has the function* (which defines it) of "constituting" concrete individuals as subjects'. It does so by 'interpellating' the individual as a subject: in other words, by treating the individual as an autonomous agent. In this manner the individual is led to believe that he or she is in control of circumstances, that reality exists *for* him or her, rather than grasping the truth, which is that every individual is merely a support of the relations of production. In this fashion, by engendering the illusion in individuals of autonomy and self-sufficiency, by constituting individuals as subjects ideology secures their subjection to the prevailing relations of production:

The reality in question in this mechanism, the reality which is necessarily ignored (*méconnue*) in the very forms of recognition (ideology = misrecognition/ignorance) is indeed, in the last resort, the reproduction of the relations of production and of the relations deriving from them.[29]

This analysis of ideology, together with Althusser's critique of empiricism (in the special sense in which he uses this term) and his insistence on the complex character of the social whole, implies one of his most well-known and controversial theses: *'historical materialism cannot conceive that even a communist society could ever do without ideology'*. Ideology is not a cognitive relation to the world – it is not primarily a set of erroneous beliefs. It is the social practice within which individuals live their relation to their conditions of existence: it provides the framework within which individuals experience the world, and, in doing so, secures the reproduction of the relations of production. 'Human societies secrete ideology as the very element and atmosphere indispensable to their historical respiration and life'.[30]

THEORETICAL PRACTICE

Implicit in this argument is not simply a theory of ideology but an epistemology. The real is not transparent; its essence is not there waiting to be discovered beneath the appearances. Reality is of necessity opaque, a complex of distinct practices which cannot be reduced to some simple essence. Immediate experience, because it encourages us to take the appearances at their face value, is not a guide to the truth, but a lure, enticing us into the realm of the imaginary: 'The truth of history cannot be read in its manifest discourse, because the text of history is not a text in which a voice (the Logos) speaks, but the inaudible and illegible notation of the effects of a structure of structures'.[31] To anticipate some stage of historical development in which reality will become transparent, ideology wither away, is utopian, a surrender to the ideological sphere from which one dreams of escaping.

Several elements are present in this argument. First, Marx's theory of fetishism, according to which the mechanisms of capitalist production are systematically concealed and their phenomenal form distorted because, as a result of the transformation of the social product into commodities exchanged on the market, social relations become relations between things. Secondly, it is at this point that Spinoza first becomes of relevance in an understanding of Althusser. For, according to the latter, Spinoza 'was the first man in the world to have proposed both a theory of history and a philosophy of the opacity of the immediate'.[32] He is here referring to Spinoza's concept of 'knowledge of the first kind, opinion or imagination' whose source is 'individual things represented to our intellect mutilated, confused, and without order', in the form induced by the action of external bodies on our own bodies. It is to be distinguished from knowledge of the second kind, deduced from 'common notions and adequate ideas of the properties of things', and knowledge of the third kind, which 'proceeds from an adequate idea of the formal essence of certain attributes of God to the adequate knowledge of the essence of things', conceiving of the interconnection of nature as a whole. 'Knowledge of the first kind is the only cause of falsity; knowledge of the second and third kinds is necessarily true'.[33]

The notion of 'the opacity of the immediate' in fact goes back to Plato's critique of sense-experience in the *Theatetus* and his distinction between *episteme* (knowledge) and *doxa* (opinion). However, much closer to Althusser were the writings of Gaston Bachelard, his former supervisor. Bachelard developed a philosophy of science based on the thesis that scientific knowledge is constituted at the moment when the theorist breaks with ordinary experience, introducing concepts radically at variance with common sense.[34] This break enables the discourse in question to function autonomously, perfecting its own procedures – notably those of mathematical formalisation – and laying guidelines for experiments, not so as to derive scientific laws from sense-experience but to produce *new phenomena* on the basis of the predictions and laws evolved within the discourse itself.[35]

We find ourselves here confronted with the third of Althusser's main themes – the autonomy of theory. Theoretical discourses are not, as for example Gramsci argued, fully articulated and logically coherent expressions of the world-views of different classes; they form a relatively autonomous practice with its own 'peculiar time and history'. Basing himself on his general definition of practice and on Marx's discussion of the method of political economy in the Introduction to the *Grundrisse*, Althusser analyses theoretical practice as a process of production involving three main elements:

Generalities I, the raw material of the practice, provided by the pre-existing theoretical discourses from which the discourse in question starts; Generalities II, the set of questions, often unstated and only implicit, which provide the discourse in question with its internal unity – what he calls the *problematic* of a discourse; Generalities III, the end-product, the new theories produced by the action of Generalities II on Generalities I. Theoretical practice, then, involved a process of transformation in which the decisive role is played by the theoretical means of production – the discourse's problematic.

Four points should be noted. First, Althusser insists that the process of knowledge takes place entirely in thought. He distinguishes between a discourse's thought-object and its real object. Empiricism's mistake was to confuse the two, claiming that knowledge involves a direct relation between thought and the real. On the contrary, Althusser argues, the starting point is provided by the discourse's thought-object – i.e. by Generalities I, the pre-existing concepts and propositions on which the problematic sets to work. Secondly, this analysis is applicable to both sciences and theoretical ideologies. The difference between the two lies in their problematics: that of a science is constituted by its openness, that of an ideology remains caught within the mirror-structure of recognition, forced to give pre-determined answers to pre-determined questions. The limits of an ideological discourse are set by 'extra-discursive' factors, by the intervention of class interests into knowledge. A science is infinite; its limits are set internally and are constantly overcome in the course of its history. As Alain Badiou put it, 'if science is a process of *transformation*, ideology . . . is a process of *repetition*'.[36] The most important event in the history of knowledge is the rupture through which a science is constituted in opposition to the theoretical ideology which has hitherto prevailed – what Althusser called the 'epistemological break'. Althusser, therefore, believes, unlike Derrida, that it is possible to escape from the closed circle of metaphysics (or ideology) into the open space of science. The third point relates to the question which obviously arises: how do we establish the difference between science and ideology? Althusser is concerned to rule out of order the solution offered by empiricism, which seeks to

guarantee the scientific character of knowledge by resting it
on the complicity of subject and object, so that the principles
of a particular science are derived from the structure of reality
as such. The only criteria of the validity of theoretical
discourses, he argues, are internal to them. 'Demonstration
and proof are the product of certain definite and specific
material and theoretical apparatuses and procedures, internal
to each science'.[37] Fourthly, and finally, theory is a practice.
The old problem of the unity of theory and practice arises
from the failure to grasp this point; it is, as Badiou puts it, a
'problem which has no meaning in post-bachelardian epistemology, where theory itself is originally thought of as a
process of production, that is, as *theoretical practice*'.[38] So
Althusser's epistemology not only serves as a critique of
empiricism; it also enables him to assert the autonomy of
intellectual work from the party.

ANTI-HUMANISM

The last major theme of Althusser's writings is his 'theoretical
anti-humanism'. The obverse of the proposition that the
category of the subject is constitutive of ideology is the claim
that history is a *process without a subject*, whether that subject is
the individual (as in neo-classical economics) or a class (as in
the early Lukács):

> The structure of the relations of production determines the
> *places* and *functions* occupied by the agents of production,
> who are never anything more than the occupants of these
> places, insofar as they are the 'supports' (*Träger*) of these
> functions. The true 'subjects' (in the sense of constitutive
> subjects of the process) are not these occupants or
> functionaries, are not, despite all appearances, the 'ob-
> viousnesses' of the 'given' of naive anthropology, 'concrete
> individuals', 'real men' – but *the definition and distribution of
> these places and functions. The true 'subjects' are these definers
> and distributors: the relations of production* (and political
> and ideological social relations). But since these are
> 'relations', they cannot be thought within the category
> *subject*.[39]

Althusser's anti-humanism takes us back to his first major intervention, the essay 'On the Young Marx', where he argues that since Marx's early writings, notably the *Economic and Philosophical Manuscripts*, are organised around the category of the subject, analysing the alienation of the human essence which develops to its most extreme point in the capital–labour relation, they belong to the realm of ideology, not science. The constitution of the scientific problematic of Marx's maturity, as found in *Capital*, required, therefore, an epistemological break, an event registered in the 'Works of the Break' – *The German Ideology* and the *Theses on Feuerbach*.

The result is a theoretical system of undoubted power and originality, one that responds to the challenge represented by the 'revolution in language' by integrating many of its themes into marxism – above all, the decentring of the subject which we have already seen at work in the writings of Lacan. Althusser's writings represent the most important contribution to marxist philosophy since Lukács' *History and Class Consciousness*. But this comparison may help to indicate the limits and the dangers of Althusser's intervention. Just as Lukács' project foundered as a result of his attempt to reformulate the basic principles of marxism by means of categories derived from neo-kantian philosophy and weberian sociology,[40] so Althusser's enterprise is compromised by some of the concepts most basic to his system.

PROBLEMS

The problems involved in Althusser's position can be summarised under the heading of four 'isms' – *empiricism, pluralism, functionalism, idealism*. As I have discussed the first at some length elsewhere,[41] I shall try to be brief here. Given the relative autonomy of theory and the 'radical inwardness of the criterion of practice for scientific practice', *'by what mechanism does the process of knowledge, which takes place entirely in thought, produce the cognitive appropriation of its real object, which exists outside thought in the real world?'*[42] Althusser must provide an answer to this question: otherwise his insistence on the difference between science and ideology and on the scientific character of marxism is quite meaningless. We see here posed within Althusser's system the first problem posed for marxism by the 'revolution of language' – can dialectical materialism's insistence on the priority of being over thought survive the effacement of the transcendental signified? The form the problem takes here is determined by Althusser's critique of empiricism (broadly defined) – since he has rejected the problematic of guarantees characteristic of traditional epistemology, he cannot found knowledge on the relation between subject and object. It would seem that any general criterion of scientific validity is ruled out by this argument.

Althusser's discussion of this problem in *Reading Capital* concentrates on what he calls the 'knowledge-effect'. This is the specific characteristic of the knowledge process – what demarcates its products from those of ideological, political or economic practice, and it pertains to the internal organisation of the concepts constituting the discourse in question.[43] However, the 'knowledge-effect' is shared by both sciences and theoretical ideologies; the basic question here is that of the difference *within theoretical practice* between science and ideology. In *For Marx* and *Reading Capital* Althusser loads the burden onto the shoulders of dialectical materialism, which he dubs the 'Theory of theoretical practice' – the general theory of scientific and ideological discourses, as opposed to historical materialism, the science of history. 'The proper object of DM [dialectical materialism – AC]', writes Badiou, 'is the system of pertinent differences which at the same time disjoin and conjoin science and ideology'.[44] This appears to give marxist philosophy the status of traditional epistemology, as a science of sciences determining whether or not particular discourses are scientific. This impression is confirmed by a number of passages like the following: in dialectical materialism 'is theoretically expressed the essence of theoretical practice in general, through it the essence of practice in general, and through it the essence of the transformations, of the development of things in general'.[45] It seems, then, that it is the general structure of practice, mirroring in some way that is not explained the essence of 'things in general', that renders possible the determination of the status of theoretical discourses. We seem to be back at 'the empiricist conception of knowledge', with the structure of reality providing the guarantee of the scientificity of discourses.[46]

Althusser has since abandoned this definition of philosophy as the science of sciences; since 1967, he has arrived at a 'new definition', based on Lenin's thesis of partisanship in philosophy, which denies philosophy any cognitive status whatsoever. Philosophy is 'the class struggle in theory', the instance through which the relationship between political and theoretical practice is reflected. Epistemology has been reduced to the status of a region of historical materialism, concerned with the purely factual question of the conditions of production of theoretical discourses.[47] It is not clear how this can be reconciled with Althusser's continued assertion of the scientific character of marxism. We shall consider these matters further in Chapter 7.

The other problems in Althusser's system do not seem to have been affected by developments since the publication of *For Marx* and *Reading Capital*. From the very start Althusser's denial of the possibility of an expressive totality posed a very serious difficulty: how can the thesis that practices are necessarily multiple and irreducible to one another be rendered consistent with *any* notion of social totality? Are we not simply left with the play of difference, which cannot be corralled within an organised structure? Derrida seems to argue, when he associates the concept of totality with that of an immobile centre which both grounds play and neutralises it, confining difference to a subordinate moment within the metaphysics of presence. So, in their own way, argued Althusser's early critics within the French Communist Party, when they accused him of 'pluralism'.[48]

Two concepts developed by Althusser were intended to deal with this problem. The first is that of the structure in dominance. Every social formation, he argues, possesses a structure in dominance, which organises the different practices within it into a definite hierarchy. This hierarchy is in turn determined by the economy, which in particular allocates to a specific instance of the whole the role of dominance within that formation. This, in feudalism politics is dominant, but only because of the nature of the economy in that mode of production. The concept, then, serves two purposes. First, it provides the multiplicity of practices constitutive of a social formation with a definite form, thus avoiding the accusation of pluralism. However, secondly, it enables Althusser to conceptualise the indirect fashion in which the determining role of the economy is exercised. The economy does not directly act upon the social formation; it merely confers a certain structure upon the whole by selecting a particular instance for the dominant role. The concept of structure in dominance provides Althusser with the means to sharpen and give definite shape to the propositions advanced in 'Contradiction and Overdetermination'.

Implied here is a concept of causality radically different from those of classical philosophy. Althusser qualifies the latter as either transitive, involving a linear relationship between discrete objects or events, or expressive, where effects merely reflect a hidden inner essence. The new concept of causality which he puts in their place (in fact, Althusser acknowledges his debt here to Spinoza and Lacan) is that of an absent cause, which exists only in its effects: 'the structure, which is merely a specific combination of its peculiar elements, is nothing outside its effects'.[49] Althusser is here trying to underline the indirect character of economic determination:

> To say that 'the cause is absent' thus means, in historical materialism, that the 'contradiction determinant in the last instance' is *never present in person* on the scene of history ('the hour of the determination in the last instance never strikes') and that one can never grasp it directly, as one can a 'person who is present'. It is a 'cause', but in the dialectical sense, in the sense that it determines *what*, on the stage of the class struggle, is the 'decisive link' which must be grasped.[50]

It is not clear whether this is more than a simply formal solution to the problem of economic determination. Etienne Balibar in his contribution to *Reading Capital* declares that 'a *plurality* of instances must be an essential property of every social structure; ... the problem of the science of society must precisely be the problem of *the forms of variation of their articulation*'. The starting point of the analysis of these forms of variation is the construction of 'a table of the elements of any mode of production'. By permuting the different combinations of these invariant elements – labourer, means of production, non-labourer, relations of production, labour-process – one can arrive at a list of the possible modes of production. Balibar hastens to add that 'this is by no means a *combinatory* in the strict sense, i.e. a form of combination in which only the places of their factors and their relations change, but not their nature'.[51] In other words, Balibar is concerned to distance himself from, say, functionalist sociology, which treats society as composed of a set of discrete factors: overdetermination implies that not simply the place and function, but also the very nature of the different instances is determined by the structure of the whole. But Balibar is here caught in a vicious circle, as André Glucksmann points out: how can modes of production be conceived of as combinations of invariant elements if the character of the elements is determined by the form of the particular combination in which they are inserted?[52] Nicos Poulantzas' first book, *Political Power and Social Class*, one of the most influential texts of applied althusserianism, marks a much more open collapse into structural-functionalism. He analyses 'the political instance of the capitalist mode of production' in isolation, as a discrete factor. The character of the political is determined in straight-forwardly functionalist terms: *'the state has the particular function of constituting the factor of cohesion between the levels of a social formation'*.[53]

The privileged site of Althusser's functionalist tendencies is his theory of ideology. Ideology, according to Althusser, is to be found in all social formations and is, with the state, the means through which the relations of production are reproduced. The inflection given this theory by the later addition of the concept of the ideological state apparatuses (ISAs) – the institutions in which ideology is materialised, where a constant struggle takes place between dominant and dominated classes – does not alter the basic frame of reference. Pluralism and functionalism reinforce each other: every mode of production is a combination of these invariant elements, while ideology fulfills a universal function across the different modes of production. Specific analyses of the institutions embraced under the heading of the ISAs are in a way beside the point, since it is established in advance that they secure the reproduction of the relations of production. Ideology is conceived of as a substance which is secreted in all social formations and transmitted by a variety of institutions.[54]

Finally, there is Althusser's idealism, in particular his tendency to collapse the base into the superstructure. This tendency is most surprising when we consider some of Althusser's arguments. In line with the theory of over-determination, he defines the superstructure as the 'conditions of existence' of the economy and denies that these conditions are reducible to the 'principal' (economic) contradiction. Moreover, within the economy itself,

> *the social relations of production are on no account reducible to mere relations between men, to relations which only involve men, and therefore to variations in a universal matrix*, to *intersubjectivity* (recognition, prestige, struggle, master-slave relationship, etc.). For Marx, the social relations of production do not bring *men alone* onto the stage, but the *agents* of the production process and the *material conditions* of the production process, in specific 'combinations'.[55]

This thesis, that the relations of production involve the distribution of the means of production as well as (and indeed prior to, it could be argued) relations between men, is aimed at the humanist interpretation of the hegelian dialectic, which conceives of society constituted by inter-subjective relations, i.e. forms of consciousness – the classic case being the struggle for recognition between master and slave in *The Phenomenology of Mind*.

Yet this 'theoretical anti-humanism' has not prevented Althusser and his followers from conflating the relations of production with their ideological and political conditions of existence. Thus in his essay on ideology, as Paul Hirst has shown, Althusser equates 'the *relations of production* with the distribution of agents to "places" in the social division of labour. The relations of production are conceived as *relations between agents*' while the latter are equated with subjects.[56] Having first reduced the relations of production to inter-subjective relations, it is a small step to treat the latter as forms of consciousness and thus collapse the base into the superstructure, inverting Marx so that consciousness determines social being.

Precisely such a series of reductions is present in a number of althusserian analyses. Nicos Poulantzas' theory of the new petty bourgeoisie is one example. Poulantzas argues that

> The structural determination of every social class involves its place both in the relations of production, and in the political and ideological relations. This question, however, acquires a quite special significance for classes other than the two basic classes, particularly for the petty bourgeoisie. Since the latter is not at the centre of the dominant relations of exploitation, i.e. the direct extraction of surplus value, it undergoes a polarisation that produces very complex distortions and adaptions of the political and ideological relations in which it is placed.

The petty bourgeoisie embraces a variety of groups caught between workers and capitalists, while the new petty bourgeoisie, created by the changes in the structure of capitalism this century, even includes those who, from the point of view of the relations of production, would be classified as members of the proletariat, since they produce surplus-value, but who 'in their place within the social division of labour ... maintain ideological and political relations of subordination of the working class to capital (the division of manual and mental labour)'.[57] Poulantzas' discussion of the social division of labour in *Classes in Contemporary Capitalism* tends to equate the relations of production and 'ideological and political relations of subordination'; the economy is no longer determinant in the last instance but has been dissolved into the superstructure. We shall discuss this tendency, and its political implications, in Chapters 6 and 8.

A further example of this confusion of relations of production and their ideological and political conditions of existence is provided by Charles Bettelheim's massive study, *Class Struggles in the USSR*. Let us recall that one of the roles that the concept of overdetermination was intended to play was that of a key to the understanding of stalinism. The relative autonomy of the superstructure would serve to explain how Stalin's terror was compatible with a socialist economic base. Bettelheim's book can be taken to be the implementation of this research programme.[58] It accounts for, not merely stalinism but what it claims to be the restoration of capitalism in the USSR, by means of a series of reductions – productive forces to production relations, production relations to superstructure, superstructure to ideology, as I have shown in detail elsewhere.[59]

Similarly, in 'Reply to John Lewis', Althusser discusses the 'Stalin deviation', treating it as the effect of a theoretical error – what he calls the economism/humanism couple. Stalin, you see, identified the construction of socialism with economic growth and technological progress (economism). He therefore ignored the crucial role of the class struggle (humanism). The absurdity of this sort of analysis, which reduces the most important historical process of the century, the Russian revolution and its subsequent degeneration, to mere intellectual history, suggests that it is as much as anything else a product of Althusser and Bettelheim's infatuation with the Chinese cultural revolution (the 'economism' of the 'Bolshevik ideological formation' meant that no attempt was made to carry out a cultural revolution, hence capitalism was restored – QED). Disillusionment with the Chinese, especially after Mao's death and the fall of the Gang of Four, must surely be one of the factors which lay behind Althusser's announcement of the 'crisis of marxism'.

Perhaps 'idealism' is the wrong term to use in describing this element in the thinking of Althusser and his associates. 'Ideologism' might be a better way to put it, since it is ideological relations which tend to assume a central explanatory role in their work.[60] This 'ideologism' has political effects. Althusser's discussion of the superstructure quickly focusses on the ideological state apparatuses – the institutions which sustain the dominance of the ruling class primarily through 'consent' rather than 'force'. This analysis can easily be used to justify a political strategy based upon the assumption that the working class and its allies can win control of the ideological state apparatuses *first* and thereby attain political power without any violent confrontation with the capitalist state machine. Santiago Carrillo invokes this text in support of just such a strategy in his book *Eurocommunism and the State*. And while Althusser and Balibar provide a scrupulous, theoretically impeccable critique of the French Communist Party's abandonment of the formula of the 'dictatorship of the proletariat', it is noteworthy that they distance themselves from Marx and Lenin's insistence on the necessity to smash the bourgeois state machine, preferring to speak instead of its 'reorganisation'.[61] Althusser occupies a space within the political universe of eurocommunism. Left-wing eurocommunism it may be, but eurocommunism it remains nonetheless. His political strategy would appear to differ little from that advocated by Poulantzas in his last book – the 'articulation' of direct democracy and representative democracy, workers' councils and parliament.

The connections between Althusser's 'ideologism' and his political strategy enable us to situate his writings in the history of marxism. In order to understand Althusser, we should compare him to the austro-marxists, the theoreticians of Austrian social democracy in the first three decades of this century. The similarities are striking: although much more closely integrated into a mass party, the theoretical positions of Austro-marxism were initially formulated in the context of a university; heavily influenced by a number of non-marxist theorists – Mach, Weber, the neo-kantians, the austro-marxists sought to present a 'third way' between the vulgar marxism of Kautsky and the revisionism of Bernstein; to do so they offered a reinterpretation of marxist epistemology according to which 'the materialist conception of history and the theory of social progress derive their meaning and their certainty from the concept of socialised men, or as we now understand, the concept of socialised consciousness' (Max Adler);[62] in the revolutionary crisis at the end of the First World War, Otto Bauer, the most politically influential of the austro-marxists, sought to reconcile the opposed positions of bolshevism and social democracy, to combine parliament and soviets.[63] Like the austro-marxists, Althusser's politics can best be described, not as stalinist or reformist, but as centrist, in the sense given the term by Lenin, occupying a position mid-way between the far left and the mass reformist parties. Precisely therein lies his usefulness to the French Communist Party: his presence in their ranks gives a marxist gloss to the steady march towards social democracy.

Vincent Descombes writes of the 'halting of the althusserian enterprise' around 1969.[64] Taken too literally, this statement is inaccurate. Althusser's intervention in Venice in 1977 was not that of someone who had stopped thinking seriously and

critically about marxism. Nor has his thought lost all
continuity – the problem of stalinism continues to dominate
his writings. But the sense of failure is unmistakable. His
original objective – 'to justify the relative autonomy of theory
and thus the right of marxist theory not to be treated as a slave
to tactical political decisions' – was achieved only at the price
of seriously compromising the marxian concept of the social
totality. It is hardly surprising that some of his erstwhile
followers have decided to abandon this concept completely,
conceiving social formations as colligations of discrete practices lacking any necessary structure.[65] In the next chapter I
shall consider an alternative to marxism increasingly popular
on the left, one that starts from some of the same premisses as
Althusser but arrives at very different conclusions.

4 Desire and Power

Signification as play, the irreducibility of difference, the subversion of the subject, the deconstruction of truth – these themes came to dominate French thought in the 1960s and early 1970s. We have seen how even marxism, in the shape of Althusser and his followers, was not immune to their attraction. Necessarily any philosophy which took shape from these themes – a philosophy of difference – could not avoid a confrontation with Hegel. For his was the philosophical system which sought, explicitly and consistently, to interiorise difference within thought, to make difference (in the shape of contradiction) the moving principle of reality and yet, as it were, to sublimate difference into the process of the self-realisation of Absolute Spirit. 'The truth', Hegel wrote, 'is . . . the bacchanalian revel where not a member is sober; and because every member no sooner becomes detached than it *eo ipso* collapses straightaway, the revel is just as much a state of transparent unbroken calm'.[1] The process through which reality differentiates itself, destroying the original self-identity of Being, is also that through which that identity is restored, only now at a fully conscious level. Being as such, the starting point of philosophical thought, is unconscious, inarticulate, indeterminate: it is Nothing. Only when the mute, primordial self-identity is disrupted by negation, thereby introducing difference into Being, setting it in motion, transforming it into a process of Becoming, does the possibility of the self-knowledge of Being arise. But this self-knowledge cannot be realised at the level of first negation, of the original splitting of Being. Here we are in the sphere of Essence, where appearances deceive, where forces external to each other clash without any inner connection, where self-consciousness reflects unhappily upon its estrangement from objective reality. Fortunately, this negation negates itself, giving rise to the comprehension of the process as a whole, to the realisation that the purely external relations characteristic of the realm of Essence are in themselves merely appearances taking on meaning only as different aspects of the coming to self-consciousness of Being. Their essence lies outside them, in the Absolute Idea. The estrangement produced by first negation is *self*-estrangement, a necessary condition if Being is to become self-conscious instead of remaining in its original mute identity, but one that is dissolved once it is grasped for what it is. The Absolute Idea, or absolute knowledge, is precisely this process of self-differentiation and ultimate reconciliation, the recollection (*Erinnerung*, internalisation) of the movement through which it produces itself.

Hegel can, therefore, write both that 'contradiction is the very moving principle of the world' and that 'contradiction is not the end of the matter, but cancels itself'.[2] The introduction of difference into Being does not destroy the latter's self-identity, but serves as an intermediary, permitting its ultimate restoration, enriched because endowed with a wealth of concrete content, and transformed into a system of concepts. Difference is, by contrast, accorded a primordial position in the philosophy of Nietzsche. Hegel had written 'the truth is the whole'.[3] Nietzsche wrote:

> What is the sign of every *literary decadence*? That life no longer dwells in the whole. The word becomes sovereign and leaps out, the sentence reaches out and obscures the meaning of the page, the page gains life at the expense of the whole – the whole is no longer a whole.[4]

Walter Kaufman argues that this description can be applied to Nietzsche himself, to his 'monadologic' style in which 'each aphorism or sequence of aphorisms . . . may be considered as a thought experiment', 'self-sufficient while yet throwing light on every other aphorism'.[5] This is not merely a matter of style, of the fragmented and aphoristic nature of so many of Nietzche's books; his writings both mirror and participate in a reality that is essentially chaotic. Zarathustra speaks for Nietzsche when he says:

Truly, my friends, I walk among men as among the
fragments and limbs of men!
The terrible thing to my eye is to find men shattered in
pieces and scattered as if over a battle-field of slaughter.
And when my eye flees from the present to the past, it
always discovers the same thing: fragments and limbs and
dreadful chances – but no men![6]

The truth may be the whole, but that whole is not a cosmos,
an ordered hierarchy of being, but chaos, chaosmos. The
truth is indeed the bacchanalian revel in which no member is
sober, but no longer does negation of negation heal the
wound left in Being by difference. Dionysus (or Bacchus) is
constantly referred to in Nietzsche's writings, beginning with
The Birth of Tragedy, where, to quote Kaufman, he 'is the
symbol of that drunken frenzy which threatens to destroy all
forms and codes; the ceaseless striving which apparently
defies all limitations; the ultimate abandonment we sometimes
sense in music'.[7] In that book Dionysus is opposed and
subordinated to Apollo, symbol of harmony, order, measure,
but in Nietzsche's later writings Dionysus has become the
dominant figure, a metaphor for reality itself. The universe
possesses no necessary structure, no ultimate identity in
Being; it consists in the endless struggle of opposed forces:
'No things remain but only dynamic quanta, in a relation of
tension to all other quanta: their essence lies in their relation
of all other quanta, in their "effect" upon the same'. However,
the relations between forces cannot be understood mechanis-
tically; concepts such as 'action at a distance' which the theory
of gravity presupposes reveal the inadequacy of physics:

'Attraction' and 'repulsion' in a purely mechanistic sense are
complete fictions: a word. We cannot think of an attraction
divorced from an *intention*. The will to take possession of a
thing or to defend oneself against it and repel it – that, we
'understand': that would be an interpretation of which we
could make use.

The quanta whose relations are exhaustive of reality are
quanta of *power*; their interactions are produced by the *will to
power* innate in each of them:

My idea is that every specific body strives to become master over all space and to extend its force (its will to power:) and to thrust back all that resists its extension. But it continually encounters similar efforts on the part of other bodies and ends by coming to an arrangement ('union') with those of them that are sufficiently related to it: thus they then conspire together for power. And the process goes on.[8]

Reality, then, has no purpose or identity: it is the product of the relations of power subsisting at any one time between a collection of forces; these forces themselves are simply quanta of power, their nature varying depending on the position they occupy within the changing hierarchies of domination and subordination; the will to power itself is not that of a subject, individual, collective or divine, but as Nietzsche puts it a *pathos*, the primordial striving which informs and determines the relations of force. The will to power is a universally applicable concept: human society, morality, thought, are so many configurations of force. Consciousness is merely an effect of a particular relation of forces. 'The assumption of one single subject is perhaps unnecessary; perhaps it is just as permissible to assume a multiplicity of subjects, whose interaction and struggle is the basis of our thought and our consciousness in general'.[9] But there are forces and forces: active forces and reactive forces. The latter, occupying a subordinate position within a given hierarchy of domination, respond by seeking to weaken the force to which they are subordinated. A classic example is Christianity: religion of slaves, of the dominated, who destroyed the materially and spiritually far superior order of ancient Rome, by undermining the morality upon which the latter rested – by the systematic devaluation of the existing world, by postulating another superior, transcendent reality beneath the surface appearances, by the subversion of the aristocratic values of classical antiquity. Metaphysics is but a secularised version of Christian morality: the demotion of empirical reality to the status of mere appearances, beneath which lurks a hidden, ideal essence, the denial of the body in favour of the soul – all this is a reflection of a will to power, that of the reactive forces which destroyed the ancient world, and which Nietzsche now seeks to dislodge from their position of dominance by means of a revaluation of all values.

Most significant from our point of view is that this revaluation involves essentially the affirmation of reality, meaningless and chaotic – 'fragments and limbs and dreadful chances' – as it is. This affirmation leads to a shift in one of the guiding metaphors of Nietzsche's thought; from Dionysus versus Apollo to *'Dionysus versus the Crucified'* (the words with which Nietzsche's last book, *Ecce Homo*, ends). Both are martyred gods – Christ on the cross, Dionysus torn apart by his votaries, but 'the god on the cross is a curse on life, a signpost to seek redemption from life; Dionysus cut to pieces is a *promise* of life: it will be eternally reborn and return again from destruction'.[10]

A PHILOSOPHY OF DIFFERENCE

These features of Nietzsche's philosophy – pluralism, the critique of existing values, the affirmation of chaos – led Gilles Deleuze in his book *Nietzsche et la Philosophie* (1962) to insist on its fundamentally anti-hegelian tendency. Hegel conceives difference as *negative*, as the contradiction which cancels itself, disrupting the identity of Being only as a preliminary to its restoration in the Absolute Idea; thereby the material world is denied any reality except as a manifestation of the Logos. The dialectic is just as much a 'curse on life' as orthodox Christianity. By contrast, writes Deleuze,

> the essential relation of one force to another is never conceived in Nietzsche as an essentially negative element. In its relation to the other, the force which makes itself obeyed does not deny the other or that which it is not, it affirms its own difference and revels in this difference. . . . For the speculative element of negation, of opposition, or of contradiction, Nietzsche substitutes the practical element of *difference*: object of affirmation and of *jouissance*.[11]

Deleuze's significance is in part that, starting from the fundamentally nietzschean position outlined above, he has sought, drawing on a variety of sources ranging from Kant and Bergson to Artaud and Scott Fitzgerald, to develop a comprehensive philosophy of difference. Outlined in two remarkable books – *Différence et Répétition* (1968) and *Logique du Sens* (1969) – this philosophy has acquired, under the impact of May 1968, a more directly political inflection in a collaborative work entitled *Capitalisme et Schizophrénie* undertaken with Felix Guattari, a psychoanalyst, of which one volume – *L'Anti-Oedipe* (1972) – has so far appeared. Discussion of these writings here is necessary because of the convergence of Deleuze's work with that of Michel Foucault. 'Convergence' is perhaps too weak a word to describe the relation between Deleuze and Foucault, one a professional philosopher warrening a bewildering variety of texts, literary, philosophical, psychoanalytic, in order to produce dense, brilliant speculations, the other a historian trained in the quasi-positivist tradition of Bachelard and Cavaillès writing specific analyses of crystalline lucidity drawing largely on contemporary documents. As the 1970s unfolded Deleuze and Foucault came increasingly to be engaged in the same project, pursuing it from different angles, in different directions, in different styles. Deleuze's writings are of particular interest, first, because he is more prepared to make generalisations than the cautious, sybilline Foucault, secondly, because he often provides the philosophical underpinnings of Foucault's historical researches.

Three concepts are of crucial importance to Deleuze – difference, the event, the body. Difference: Deleuze seeks to show how philosophy from Plato onwards has sought to repress difference, the plural, chaotic essence of things, and contain it within a harmonious, unified structure which he calls the structure of *representation*. Deleuze champions a 'transcendental empiricism':

> This empiricism teaches us a strange 'reason', the multiple and the chaos of difference (nomadic distributions, anarchies enthroned). It is always differences which resemble each other, which are analogous, opposed or identical: difference is behind everything, but behind difference there is nothing.[12]

A constant theme in Deleuze's writings is the *nomadic* character of difference. Representation involves the distribution of difference within a pre-determined hierarchy, its subordination to an ordered cosmos, 'a distribution which implies a sharing out of the distributed' and which 'proceeds by fixed and proportional determinations, assimilable to "properties" or limited territories'. Difference is subjected to the law of private property, enclosed within fixed boundaries. Opposed to this is

> a distribution it is necessary to call nomadic ... without property, enclosure or measure (where) there is no longer sharing out of the distributed, but rather distribution of those which arrange themselves in an open, unlimited space.[13]

In *Logique du Sens* Deleuze applies this philosophy of difference to language, drawing, with great skill, on some of the concepts developed by Saussure, Levi-Strauss and Lacan – as well as the writings of Lewis Carroll and the Stoics. Language is to be analysed, not in terms of stable structures or enduring substances, but in terms of *events* – the chance conjunctions of intrinsically meaningless singularities. The event is constitutive of language. The meaning of sentence depends not on the objects it designates, the states of mind it manifests, the conditions under which it is true, but on the sense it expresses. This sense is an event – not a physical state of affairs, but an effect of such states of affairs, incorporeal but dependent on the melanges of bodies which constitute the physical world:

> Melanges in general determine the quantitative and qualitative states of things: the dimensions of a whole, or the heat of iron, the green of a tree. But what we mean by 'to increase', 'to diminish', 'to turn green', 'to cut', 'to be cut', etc., is of quite a different kind: no longer of all the states of things or melanges at the basis of bodies, but of the incorporeal events at the surface, which result from these melanges. *The tree turns green* . . . .[14]

Events, corresponding in language to the infinitive, render possible the indefinite proliferation of words and sentences. A sentence designates some state of affairs; its sense (an event), however, is not referred to, but rather is presupposed as the sentence's condition of existence. In order to speak of this sense, one must use another sentence; the sense *it* presupposes can only be referred to by *another* sentence, and so on to infinity. The regress can only be halted if we presuppose the existence of a 'paradoxical instance', a 'sombre precursor', an 'esoteric word' which refers to its own sense. Relative to such a word the endless proliferation of terms can be halted, or at least stabilised: there are constituted two heterogeneous series, each defined by the differences internal to it, brought into relation to each other by their common relation to the 'sombre precursor'. The contradiction inherent in this term, the violation of the laws of language which it involves, mean that it lacks either identity or fixed position, constantly displaced and concealed within the series it brings into relation. Deleuze here is thinking of Levi-Strauss' 'floating signifier', the term itself lacking meaning which corresponds to the excess of signifiers relative to the signified. The infinite regress involved in sense is Deleuze's own formulation of this excess: the elements of language only organise themselves into two series, each internally differentiated and differing from the other, signifiers and signified, relative to a term which itself is an absurdity, a violation of the laws of sense. Sense derives from 'non-sense'.

Although analysed in *Logique du Sens* as properties of language, the characteristics of events are treated by Deleuze in *Différence et Répétition* as universally applicable: every system of difference involves 'coupling of heterogeneous series; from which derives an *internal resonance* within the system; from which derives a *forced movement* whose amplitude escapes the basic series themselves'.[15] So while both Derrida and Deleuze conceive of language as infinite play, the former deduces from this the claim that we have no access to a reality outside language, a 'transcendental signified', and Deleuze asserts that language shares the structure of reality as a whole – the logic of sense mirrors and is part of the chaosmos.

The concept of disjunctive synthesis is intended by Deleuze to capture the infinite play of difference, the endless proliferation of terms halted only by the relative stabilisations induced by the 'somber precursors'. Lewis Carroll's portmanteau words are one instance of such synthesis:

Take the two words 'fuming' and 'furious'. Make up your mind that you will say both words, but leave it unsettled which you will say first. Now open your mouth and speak. If your thoughts incline ever so little towards 'fuming', you will say 'fuming-furious'; if they turn, by even a hair's breadth, towards 'furious', you will say 'furious-fuming'; but if you have that rarest of gifts, a perfectly balanced mind, you will say 'frumious'.[16]

Disjunctive synthesis is opposed to the hegelian identity of opposites: the latter affirms the difference between two opposed terms only to resume them into an identity which precedes and envelops them. In the case of disjunctive synthesis, however,

Two things or two determinations are affirmed *by* their difference, i.e. are objects of simultaneous affirmation insofar as their difference is itself affirmed, itself affirmative. It is no longer at all a matter of the identity of contraries, as such inseparable from a movement of the negative and of exclusion. It is a matter of a positive distance between differents: no longer to identify two contraries with the same, but to affirm their difference as that which relates them to each other as 'different'.[17]

The role of disjunctive synthesis is performed by 'the somber precursor, this difference in itself, to the second degree, which brings into relation two series themselves different and heterogeneous'.[18]

The significance of Deleuze's analysis of events is threefold. First, certain tendencies involved in the conception of language deriving from saussurian linguistics are taken to their ultimate conclusion. There is no stable resting-point from which meaning derives: language (and indeed, for Deleuze, reality as such) involves the endless play of difference, the proliferation of terms and divergent series to infinity.[19] But, and here Deleuze differs from Derrida, this play is not that of presence and absence – we are not forced to resort to irreducibly metaphysical concepts even when deconstructing metaphysics itself, as Derrida suggests when he envelops difference in differance, both the production of difference

and the necessity of a relation to presence, to the effacement
of difference. For Deleuze difference can be rigorously
conceptualised outside the categories of representation.

Secondly, there are the methodological implications of
Deleuze's analysis of events. It is an error to counter-pose
events (diachrony, history) to structure (synchrony, stasis).
'Structure permits a register of ideal *events*, i.e. an entire *history*
which is internal to it'.[20] A structure is precisely a system
of difference – two heterogeneous series composed of
singularities (events) constituted by the differences between them, themselves brought into relation by a somber
precursor which differentiates the two series from each
other.

Foucault argues that contemporary historians are increasingly adopting a 'serial' method, isolating singularities and the
heterogeneous series they constitute. The claim that historians, for example those around the journal *Annales*, no
longer examine 'the singular event' but rather 'the structures
of long duration' involves a misunderstanding:

> I don't think that the examination of the event and the
> analysis of long duration are inversely related. It seems, on
> the contrary, that it is in drawing as close as possible to the
> grain of the event, in pushing the power of resolution of
> historical analysis right down to price lists, to notarial acts, to
> parish registries, to harbour archives, studied year by year,
> week by week, that one has seen take shape beyond the
> battles, the decrees, the dynasties or the assemblies, the
> massive secular and pluri-secular phenomena. History as it
> is practised today does not turn away from events; on the
> contrary, it endlessly enlarges their domain; it endlessly
> uncovers new layers of them, more superficial or more
> profound; it endlessly isolates new collections of them
> where they are sometimes numerous, dense and inter-
> changeable, sometimes rare and decisive: one goes from the
> almost daily variations of prices to secular inflations. But the
> important point is that history does not consider an event
> without defining the series of which it is part, without
> specifying the mode of analysis appropriate to it, without
> seeking to know the regularity of phenomena and the limits
> of probability of their emergence, without examining the

variations, inflexions and direction of the curve, without wishing to determine the conditions on which they depend.[21]

This method of historical analysis is intended to respect the density and complexity of social life without collapsing into the banalities of positivist historiography. The most outstanding example of such an approach in English is Theodore Zeldin's *France 1848–1945*. It finds its philosophical rationale in Deleuze's logic of sense, which dissolves the apparently stable and definite structures and substances of which the world is composed:

> What is an ideal event? It is a singularity. Or rather it is an ensemble of singularities, of singular points which characterise a mathematical curve, a physical state of affairs, a psychological and moral person.[22]

Thirdly, this philosophy of the event has an epistemological dimension. Events are 'surface-effects'; their meaning is not an essence concealed beneath them, but consists in their differential relations to other events. Deleuze is concerned to displace the opposition between essence and phenomenon constitutive of the philosophy of representation since Plato, who reduced empirical reality to good or bad copies (icons or simulacra) of an original model, the Idea.[23] For Deleuze, 'everything is become simulacrum', for a simulacrum is precisely a copy in which all relation to the original is denied, 'a demoniac image, denuded of resemblance': 'the simulacrum is difference in itself, as (at least) two divergent series on which it plays'.[24] It is from this standpoint that Deleuze quotes Paul Valery approvingly: 'there is nothing deeper than the skin'.[25] There is nothing behind difference, only the endless proliferation of terms, divergent series brought into relation by a term which is itself what Deleuze calls *le dispars*, difference in itself, a disjunctive synthesis which relates them only by affirming their difference.

The surface, however, even if freed from the identity to which representation seeks to reduce it, remains only an effect, an attribute of physical states of affairs. It is a result, and indeed a result which can crack, collapsing back into its foundation, or allowing this foundation to rise to the surface. 'Nothing is more fragile than the surface'.[26] Beneath lies the undifferentiated, the formless, the indeterminate. Here all is flux, a confused melange of fragments:

> Everything is body and corporeal. Everything is melange of bodies, and in the body, interlocking, penetration. . . . A tree, a bed-post, a flower, a walking-stick thrust across the body; always other bodies penetrate our body and co-exist with its parts.[27]

The organisation of language into signifiers and signified collapses once the distinction between body and language, foundation and surface, which subtended it has been sub-verted. The result is *language without articulation*. In the chaos beneath the surface 'every word is physical, affects the body immediately'; 'it breaks into pieces, decomposes into syllables, letters, above all consonants, which act directly on the body, penetrating it and murdering it'.[28] This strange and terrible world of grunts and cries, of 'fragments and limbs and dreadful chances' is the world of the unconscious; it is also the world of schizophrenia.

In *L'Anti-Oedipe* Deleuze and Guattari explore this world beneath the surface. Here they consider it less in contrast to language, but in its own right, as a system of difference sharing the same structural properties as language, notably that of disjunctive synthesis. The unconscious is, for them, essentially *desiring production*:

> It functions everywhere, sometimes without stopping, sometimes discontinuous. It breathes, it sweats, it eats. It shits, it kisses. What a mistake to have said *the* id [*ca* means both 'it' and 'id' in French – AC]. Everywhere there are machines, not at all metaphorically: machines of machines, with their couplings, their connections. An organ-machine is wired up to a source-machine: one emits a flux, which the other cuts.

The unconscious, then, in Nietzsche's words, is a 'multiplicity of subjects', or rather of 'desiring machines'. Thus under-stood, it corresponds to the very early stages of sexual development, where the child is a bundle of fragmentary drives oriented on 'part-objects' – a thumb, a nipple and so on. For Lacan this stage is already one of alienation, defined by the child's expulsion from his mother's body at birth, the beginning of a process in which lack is finally accepted with the resolution of the Oedipus complex. Deleuze and Guattari wish to challenge the identification of desire with lack, with an endless metonymic process in which satisfaction is impossible because it would involve the negation of individuality, the restoration of the immediate unity of child and mother in the womb. For them, the drives, fragmentary and oriented on fragments, are the authentic core of human reality. Desire is inherently positive and productive. It is not the nostalgic striving for a lost unity, but a binary process which 'does not cease to effectuate the coupling of continuous fluxes and essentially fragmentary and fragmented part-objects'. The unconscious is a system of 'desiring machines', of the chance conjunctions of fragments – for example, a breast and a mouth – in which one acts as or produces a flux and the other cuts the flux. These roles are not fixed: an element which produces the flux in one relation may cut it in another. Thus 'the binary series is linear in all directions. . . . Desire causes to flow, flows and cuts'.[29]

However, desiring production contains within it a third element, apart from the binary relation of flux and cut constituting desiring machines. Machines may always break down, while the binary conjunctions of desire are still a form of organisation, of articulation. The 'body without organs' is the point at which production breaks down, articulation ceases, death within life:

> Flows of energy are still too connected, part-objects still too organic. But a pure fluid, free and without cut, flowing across a full body. Desiring machines make us an organism; but at the heart of this production, in its very production, the body without organs allows itself to be thus organised, to have no other organisation, or no organisation at all. . . .: 'No mouth. No tongue. No teeth. No larynx. No oseophagus. No stomach. No womb. No anus.' The automata stop and allow the unorganised mass which they articulate to rise. The full body without organs is the unproductive,

the sterile, the unborn, the unconsumable. Antonin Artaud discovered it, there where he was, without form, without figure. Death instinct, such is its name.[30]

Artaud (the words quoted by Deleuze and Guattari in the passage above are his) invoked the concept of a body without organs to close the gap introduced into Being by articulation, both linguistic and physical. As Derrida points out, he thereby ran the risk of collapsing into the metaphysics of presence, escaping from difference into 'full presence, non-difference: simultaneously life and death'.[31] Deleuze, by contrast, seeks here to be exploring the implications of his philosophy of difference. The contrast he draws in *Logique du Sens* between the incorporeal events at the surface and the chaotic melanges of bodies below can only be a relative one: both are systems of difference in which singular points are organised into series.[32] However, the nature of these singularities depends on their differential relations with the other terms composing each series. This is, as Pierre Veyne puts it, 'a nietzschean philosophy of the primacy of relation: *things exist only by relation*'. The identity things possess is conferred upon them by the relations of difference into which they are organised. Prior to these relations there exists 'an entirely *material* universe, composed of prediscursive referents which are virtualities still without face'.[33] 'Material' here has the sense in which Plato and Aristotle would have used it: matter as the raw material of the universe, in itself an 'unorganised mass' until form is conferred upon it. The body without organs is this 'without-foundation' subtending difference – 'the excessive and the unequal, the interminable and the incessant, the informal'. Deleuze here quotes a discussion of death by Maurice Blanchot, death not as something personal, the limit of my existence,

> not the irreversible passage beyond which there is no return, for it is that which is never completed, the interminable and the incessant. . . . Time without present, with which I have no relation, that towards which I cannot fling myself, for in (it) *I* do not die, I am deprived of the power to die, in (it) *one* dies, one does not cease and does not finish dying.[34]

The limiting point of difference is the pure undifferentiated flux which it presupposes and to which it gives temporary shape within the heterogeneous series it organises. The death instinct, with which Deleuze identifies the body without organs, is not, as Freud suggested, a principle in eternal conflict with the pleasure seeking libido, Thanatos against Eros, but rather a tendency towards a chaos so perfect, so pure, so complete that in it all differences, all articulations are effaced.

The body without organs does not, however, simply envelop difference in pure flux. It provides the surface upon which difference is organised, across which the heterogeneous series spread in all directions. The elements composing any series, whether physical, psychic, linguistic or social, are intensities, 'the property of intensity being to be constituted by a difference which relates it to other differences'.[35]

> Where do these pure intensities come from? They come from two preceding forces, repulsion and attraction, and from the opposition of these two forces. Not that the intensities are themselves in opposition to each other and equilibrate around a neutral state. On the contrary, they are all positive starting from the intensity $= 0$ which designates the body without organs.[36]

The body without organs, then, is the zero degree of difference. As such, it 'serves as the surface for the entire process of production of desire', the chaotic raw material to which the heterogeneous series give shape and across which they spread. Pure flux, the undifferentiated chaos at the heart of reality, it does not form an articulated whole:

> The body without organs is produced as a whole, but in its place, in the process of production, besides parts which it does not unify and does not totalise. . . . The whole does not co-exist with the parts, it is contiguous with them.

The body without organs is totality, not as organised cosmos, but as undifferentiated surface, which does not envelop difference, reducing it to identity within the structure of representation, but subtends it:

> Basically, part-objects and body without organs are one and
> the same thing, one and the same multiplicity. . . . The body
> without organs is the matter which fills space to such and
> such a degree of intensity, and part-objects are these
> degrees, these intensive parts which produce the real in
> space starting from matter as intensity = 0.[37]

To begin with, therefore, the concept of the body without
organs is intended to give Deleuze's philosophy of difference
a sharper profile, highlighting the plural and anarchic character of reality, its refusal to be corralled into any harmonious
structure.

Accordingly, and in line with a vitalism implicit in all
Deleuze's writings (his debt to Bergson is evident and acknowledged) desiring production is held to be constitutive of reality
as such: 'There is no longer man or nature, but uniquely (the)
process which produces one in the other and couples
machines'. The idealistic character of this statement is somewhat qualified by the fact that for Deleuze desire is merely one
system of difference among others, sharing the same *formal*
properties as physical, biological, social and literary systems.
The identity of the various aspects of reality depends upon
their common structure as heterogeneous series of singular
points brought into relation by a sombre precursor, spread
out upon an undifferentiated surface. Deleuze's is a structuralist vitalism. The particular isomorphism which preoc-
cupies Deleuze and Guattari in *L'Anti-Oedipe* is that between
the social and the psychic. Social and desiring production are,
they argue, identical in nature, differing only in regime. The
marxist distinction between base and superstructure is beside
the point: desiring production is as much part of the base as
social production. The *socius*, the social body, plays the same
role as representation; it seeks to contain the nomadic
distribution of difference within fixed boundaries and an
ordered hierarchy, to 'code' the fluxes of desire. This process
of 'territorialisation' takes place on a surface, 'a full body
determined as *socius*':

> This can only be the body of the earth, or the despotic body,
> or capital. It is of it that Marx says: it is not the product of
> labour, but it appears as its natural or divine presupposi-

tion. . . . It attaches itself to all production, constituting a surface where the forces and agents of production distribute themselves, so successfully that it appropriates the surplus-product and attributes to itself the whole and the parts which seem now to emanate from it as from a quasi-cause.[38]

Within social production the body without organs plays the role of a fetish – the earth, the despot, money, an essentially unproductive agency to whom the powers of social and desiring production are attributed, thereby serving to contain difference, desire, within fixed boundaries. The productivity of desire is transposed onto a passive element on the basis of which society is organised into a structured whole and the flux of desire imprisoned.

Finally, the body without organs is the object of history – not in the sense of a self-identical, organised totality whose properties are uncovered by historical analysis. Rather it is the matter of history, the shapeless, undifferentiated flux in which both 'man' and 'nature' find their reality, and which acquires form only within systems of difference. One such system, or collection of systems, is social practice. Foucault writes:

The body is the inscribed surface of events (traced by language and dissolved by ideas), the locus of a dissociated self (adopting the illusion of a substantial unity), and a volume in perpetual disintegration. Genealogy, as an analogy of descent, is thus situated within the articulation of the body and history. Its task is to expose a body totally imprinted by history and the process of history's destruction of the body.[39]

It is the 'articulation of the body and history' which forms the focus of Foucault's recent work. To this let us now turn.

KNOWLEDGE AND POWER

Foucault, unlike Deleuze, has been quite well served by English translators and commentators.[40] I shall, therefore, merely seek to isolate some of the main lines of his argument, rather than its detail. *The Archaeology of Knowledge* (1969) arguably represents a turning point in his intellectual development, the text in which Foucault reflects upon the methodological problems raised by his earlier studies, but also lays the foundation for his later writings. In a series of books – *Madness and Civilisation, The Birth of the Clinic, The Order of Things* – published in the 1960s Foucault had examined the conditions of production of certain theoretical discourses – psychiatry, clinical medicine, the human sciences. In no case had he treated the history of sciences as the unfolding of truth, the teleology of pure reason; both *Madness and Civilisation* and *The Birth of the Clinic* isolate the institutional conditions for the emergence of the discourse under consideration – for example, the physical confinement of those described as mad. His concern was not so much epistemological – the evaluation of discourses relative to some norm of truth, as archaeological – the discovery of the conditions under which certain discourses became possible, while others were excluded:

> Quite obviously, such an analysis does not belong to the history of ideas or of science: it is rather an inquiry whose aim is to rediscover on what basis knowledge and theory became possible; within what space of order knowledge was constituted; on the basis of what historical *a priori*, and in the element of what positivity, ideas could appear, sciences be established, experience be reflected in philosophies, rationalities to be formed, only, perhaps, to dissolve and vanish soon afterwards.[41]

In *The Order of Things* this 'historical *a priori*' is called the *episteme* and functions as an autonomous theoretical structure, rather like the althusserian problematic, determining how we perceive the world and identify, classify and organise its elements. One reason for Foucault's dissatisfaction with this concept was that it treated discourse as somehow isolated from politics:

What was lacking in my work [in the 1960s – AC] was this

problem of the 'discursive regime', of the effects of power proper to the play of statements. I confused it much too much with systematicity, with theoretical form or something like a paradigm.

As in the case of Althusser, one constant preoccupation of Foucault's work is the relation between theory and politics; and, like Althusser, the starting point for this reflection was the Lysenko affair and the French Communist Party's championing of proletarian science:

> When I was studying in the years 1950–55, one of the great problems which posed itself was that of the political status of discourse and of the ideological functions it could serve. It wasn't exactly the Lysenko business which dominated, but I believe that around this disgraceful affair which remained for such a long time ignored and carefully concealed, a mass of interesting questions were raised. Two words will sum them all up: power and knowledge.[42]

Whereas, however, Althusser responded to the Lysenko affair by constructing a philosophy of difference which enabled him to assert the autonomy of theoretical practice from politics, Foucault has progressively come to deny knowledge any identity of its own, reducing it to an effect of power. The first stage in this progress is represented by *The Archaeology of Knowledge*. Here Foucault confronts the problem of the 'historical *a priori*'.

He resolves discourses into their constituent elements – statements. These are deleuzian events – singular points organized into heterogeneous series.[43] The unity of a discourse does not derive from its real object

> 'Words and things' ['Les mots et les choses' – the original title of *The Order of Things* – AC] is the entirely serious title of a problem; it is the ironic title of a work that modifies its own form, displaces its own data, and reveals, at the end of the day, a quite different task. A task that consists of not – of no longer – treating discourses as groups of signs (signifying elements referring to contents or representations) but

as practices that systematically form the objects of which they speak.

Nor does a discourse acquire its identity from a subject:

> Discourse is not the majestically unfolding manifestation of a thinking, knowing, speaking, subject, but, on the contrary, a totality in which the dispersion of the subject and his discontinuity with himself may be determined. It is a space of exteriority in which a network of distinct sites is deployed.[44]

The 'author' of a text is neither autonomous nor creative but occupies a subordinate place within a given discursive practice: 'The subject (and its substitutes) must be stripped of its creative role and analysed as a complex and variable function of discourse'.[45]

Statements are *rare*. Out of the infinity of logically and grammatically well-formed sentences only certain statements are uttered. The problem of archaeology is to determine the conditions which permit (or require) certain statements to be uttered and exclude the utterance of others. This is a very different method from interpretation, the organised 'suspicion of language' to which Foucault referred in his paper 'Nietzsche, Freud, Marx' quoted in Chapter 2. There is no hidden meaning, no 'unsaid', beneath what is actually said, a repressed discourse which it is our task to bring to the surface.[46] For Foucault, as for Deleuze, 'nothing is deeper than the skin'. All that offers itself for analysis is a multiplicity of statements organised in a field of dispersion. Discourse is, quite simply, 'the totality of things said'. The task of archaeology

> presupposes that the field of statements is not described as a 'translation' of operations or processes that take place elsewhere; . . . but that it is accepted, in its empirical modesty, as the locus of particular events, regularities, relationships, modifications and systematic transformations; in short, that it is treated not as the result or trace of something else, but as a practical domain that is autonomous (although dependent), and which can be described at its

own level (although it must be articulated on something other than itself)'.[47]

This 'something other than itself' is what Foucault calls non-discursive practice. A discursive practice is

a body of anonymous, historical rules, always determined in the time and space that have defined a given period, and for a given social, economic, geographical, or linguistic area, the conditions of operation of the enunciative function.

The relation between discursive and non-discursive practices is neither expressive (the structure of clinical medicine, say, mirroring that of early capitalism) nor causal (the development of industrial capitalism necessitating the birth of the clinic); Foucault argues that in the early nineteenth century political practice opened up new fields of objects to medicine, accorded to the doctor the sole position of enunciator of the discourse in question, and allocated to medicine a determinate social role.[48] Non-discursive practices, therefore, play an intimate role in determining the character of discursive practice, 'the conditions of operation of the enunciative function'. As Karel Williams puts it,

In the *Archaeology* the non-discursive is directly used to define the discursive. Relations between objects and so forth are between (anterior) heterogeneous elements ('institutions', techniques, social groups, perceptual organisations, relations between various discourses) which are not directly given in discourse.[49]

Foucault's emphasis on the autonomy of discourse is, therefore, slightly misleading. If what is said now becomes an object of analysis in its own right, its rules of formation refer us to the institutional complexes upon which discourses are articulated.[50]

From the *Archaeology* onwards Foucault's attention comes to centre on the articulation of discursive and non-discursive. His inaugural lecture at the College de France, *L'Ordre du Discours* (1970), is concerned to isolate the principles determining the 'rarefaction' of discourses, the rules of formation of statements. Already power-relations are coming to be conceived as exercising a productive role in shaping discourses: 'each discursive practice implies a play of prescriptions that designate its exclusions and choices'.[51] But the decisive step came in *Discipline and Punish* (1975). Deleuze places this book in the context of Foucault's distinction between discursive and non-discursive. *Discipline and Punish* raises two new questions:

> 1. since there is no resemblance, no correspondence, no isomorphism between the two forms, since there is no economic causality, nor semantic determination, nor structural homology, is there something which functions as (their) common immanent cause? 2. And how are the arrangement, the adjustment of the two forms, their mutual penetration assured in a variable manner in each precise case? . . . Foucault's conception of power is going to play the principal role in the answer to these questions.[52]

The 'common immanent cause' of both discursive and non-discursive is what Deleuze calls the 'diagram', Foucault 'power-knowledge'. The traditional opposition between power and knowledge must be displaced:

> There is no power-relation without the correlative constitution of a field of knowledge, nor any knowledge that does not presuppose or constitute at the same time power-relations. These 'power-knowledge' relations are to be analysed, therefore, not on the basis of a subject of knowledge who is or is not free in relation to the power-system, but, on the contrary, the subject who knows, the objects to be known and the modalities of knowledge must be regarded as so many effects of these fundamental implications of power-knowledge and their historical transformations.[53]

The implications of these assertions can only be established once we have examined the conception of power advanced in Foucault's recent writings. The fascination that the term 'power' had for Parisian intellectuals in the 1970s did not arise simply from a logical progression, in Foucault's case from *episteme* to discursive practice and then to power-knowledge; to a large part it is a product of 1968. The events of 1968 raised the question of power in a restricted sense – not so much that of the confrontation between a mass movement and a disintegrating state apparatus (as in Russia 1917, Portugal 1975, Iran 1978–9), the 'classical' form of revolution in this century, but in the sense of a global challenging of the relations of power specific to particular sectors of society. Students challenging the authority relations characteristic of the universities and *thereby* the existing structure of society as a whole were a representative case. In the case of intellectuals this process of 'contestation' inevitably raised the question of the relation between the 'autonomous' procedures specific to their discipline and the power-relations governing the institutions within which they worked. Not simply, therefore, fighting power where one stood, but also 'power-knowledge'. Moreover, orthodox marxism was unavailable to conceptualise this new form of struggle – apparently concerned exclusively with the question of political power rather than the power-relations immanent to every aspect of social life, embodied by the Communist Party, which betrayed the movement, identified (especially after the appearance of *The Gulag Archipelago*) with the cruelty and barbarity of stalinism. Nor did the most sophisticated version of marxism improve much on the official original. As Vincent Descombes put it:

> Althusser could not maintain his thesis on the nature of the Soviet system (a socialist infrastructure supporting a non-socialist superstructure) except at the price of contenting himself with a naive and idealist notion of power. Naiveté which became evident with the events of 1968.[54]

Foucault's debt to 1968 as the model and inspiration of his analysis of power is evident and acknowledged.[55] Archaeology has become genealogy, in the nietzschean sense – a method of historical analysis which discovers 'at the historical beginning of things . . . not the inviolable identity of their origin . . . (but) the dissension of other things', which 'seeks to re-establish the various systems of subjection: not the anticipatory power of meaning, but the hazardous play of dominations'.[56] However, power is not to be conceived as it is (according to Foucault and Deleuze) within the marxist tradition – as the property of a class, localised in a state apparatus, subordinated to the economy, functioning by repression or ideology – denying or deceiving.[57] Power is not a substance, but a relation – or rather a multiplicity of relations immanent and omnipresent in the social body, in 'the apparatuses of production, families, small groups, institutions'. Power is not something negative – it does not function merely to repress classes and individuals formed anterior to it in the process of production. Rather it is directly productive – shaping the relations constituting the social, forming human bodies into individuals and allocating them to their places within these relations. Moreover, 'relations of power are at once intentional and non-subjective'. They involve, not the global strategy imposed on the social whole by a despotic Leviathan, but local tactics adopted often with a lucidity, a lack of hypocrisy which overturns the marxist problematic of a state power whose repressive functions are masked by ideology. Finally, 'where there is power, there is resistance'. Relations of power 'can only exist in function of a multiplicity of points of resistance: these play, in the relations of power, the role of adversary, of target, of support, of prize to be taken. These points of resistances are present everywhere in the network of power'.[58]

Discipline and Punish is the first work of this new historical method. It analyses the emergence, at the turn of the eighteenth and beginning of the nineteenth centuries, of a 'disciplinary society'. This process is typified by the transition from one form of punishment to another – from the literal pulverisation of the criminal's body in the spectacular public executions of the Ancien Regime, a drama designed to symbolise the 'super-power' of the monarch but also carrying with it the danger that the crowd might rescue the condemned man, to his confinement within prison, where he is subjected to norms which do not simply govern his conduct, but determine his very nature as an individual:

> The historical moment of the disciplines was the moment at which an art of the human body was born, which was directed not only at the growth of its skills, nor at the intensification of its subjection, but at the formation of a

relation that in the mechanism itself makes it more obedient as it becomes more useful, and conversely. What was then being formed was a policy of coercions that act upon the body, a calculated manipulation of its elements, its gestures, its behaviour. The human body was entering a machinery of power that explores it, breaks it down and rearranges it. A 'political anatomy', which was also a 'mechanics' of power was being born; it defined how one may have a hold on others' bodies, not only so that they may do what one wishes, but so they may operate as one wishes, with the techniques, the speed and the efficiency that one determines. Thus discipline produces subjected and practised bodies, 'docile' bodies.[59]

This process, through which bodies are subjected to power, is also the process through which subjects are constituted. Francois Ewald writes of this 'political investment of bodies':

> To occupy a body, to invest it, is to *animate* it. . . . To animate a body is to '*mobilise*' it, i.e. to invest it to endow it with a will, to give it a consciousness. For a body has need of a soul to live, and to produce.[60]

Here we again find Deleuze's body without organs – inchoate matter of history, which takes shape only within definite relations of power. The subject accorded a sovereign role by philosophy since Descartes is here demoted to the status of an effect produced by the disciplines: 'Discipline "makes" individuals; it is the specific technique of a power that regards individuals both as objects and as instruments of its exercise'. Power, then, does not act upon pre-formed individuals, containing them through repression or deceiving them by means of ideology – it creates them. The human sciences as a discursive practice become possible only with the emergence of the form of 'power-knowledge' characteristic of the disciplines: they participate in the process through which the subject is created as an object both of study and of action. The prison is only the 'concentrated and austere figure of all the disciplines', it merely exemplifies 'the general form of an apparatus intended to render individuals docile and useful, by means of precise work upon their bodies' to be found also in 'factories, schools, barracks, hospitals'.[61] Society can only be understood on the model of the prison.

Two general consequences follow from this method of analysis, exemplified in *Discipline and Punish*, most fully presented in *Le Volonté de Savoir* (1976), the introduction to a projected (but apparently subsequent abandoned) six-volume history of sexuality. The first is epistemological, or perhaps it would be better to say, following Francois Ewald, 'anti-epistemological'. As he puts it, 'according to the principle of political anatomy, a science is incapable of finding within itself its own conditions of possibility. The conditions of a science . . . must be sought in the transformation of relations of power'.[62] The rarity of statements derives from the particular 'diagram' of 'power-knowledge' within which they are produced. Paradoxically, the isolation of a space within which discourses may be analysed has led to the dissolution of discourse into power. The 'will to truth', the pursuit of an absolute truth independent of all spatio-temporal conditions, is itself a determinate form of the will to power, possible only within definite relations of power.[63] In its place we have what Nietzsche called 'perspectivism'. This doctrine is much stronger than relativism. The latter asserts that all points of view are to be judged of equal value in depicting reality; preferences between them can be determined only on the basis of criteria other than that of a theory's truth-content – for example, pragmatic grounds of utility. But relativists tend not to give up the notion of *some* criterion on the basis of which one prefers a given theory over another, or that of an objectively existing reality. Foucault and Deleuze go much further. They can be taken to claim that *each theory creates its own reality*. Rejecting Leibniz's monadology, which conceives of things as 'points of view', but ones that converge, 'points of view on the same town', Deleuze opts for Nietzsche and perspectivism:

> With Nietzsche by contrast, . . . another town corresponds to each point of view, each point of view is another town, the towns are united only by their distance and resound only by the divergence of their series, of their houses and streets. And always another town in the town.[64]

Involved here is partly the epistemological thesis (which we shall discuss further in Chapter 7) that the objects to which a discourse refers are constituted in and by that discourse. However, Foucault and Deleuze support a stronger claim. Knowledge is always constructed within and on the basis of power-relations. Power creates the objects of knowledge not only within discourse but as *real objects*. The subject, organising principle of the human sciences, is not an illusion induced by ideology but the really existing effect of certain relations of power. Power produces reality, or, as Deleuze puts it, '*a diagram never functions to represent an objectivised world*; on the contrary, it organises a new type of reality'.[65]

This position does not, however, imply that (historical) reality is merely the actualisation of thought. Theories have efficacity as programmes for the production of reality; but whether the theories have their intended effects depends on the political technologies in which they are materialised, techniques of power which are always localised in their field of operation. A programme may be realised in quite a different form from that which was intended – Foucault gives the example of the utilitarian theories of penal reform, based on a calculus of pleasure and pain, which led to an unexpected result, the disciplines. Global strategies of power arise from the interaction of programmes and technologies, rather than being the work of some malevolent, omnipotent Leviathan.[66] Moreover, according to Foucault's 'rule of the tactical poly-valence of discourse', the same statement can be used for quite different ends – depending on 'who speaks, his position of power, the institutional context in which he finds himself placed'. Discourse is not the uncontested property of power; it is the site of a perpetual struggle in which strategies of resistance as well as strategies of power are pursued.[67]

The second consequence of Foucault's conception of 'power-knowledge' is a new form of political practice. Marxism, with its concentration on the struggle for political power located in the state apparatus, is dismissed. Hence the admiration of Foucault and some of his followers for André Glucksmann's recent books, where marxism is shown to be, in Francois Ewald's words,

extraordinary instrument of power, incredible principle of

production of concentration camps and production of camps as apparatus of production, formidable principle of delusion, of obliteration, of interdiction, of exclusion and of death.

That this evaluation of the 'marxist "power-knowledge" '[68] is shared by Foucault himself is confirmed by his extravagantly approving review of Glucksmann's *Les Maitres Penseurs*, where he writes:

Stalinism was the truth, 'rather' naked, admittedly, of an entire political discourse which was that of Marx and of other thinkers before him. With the Gulag, one sees not the consequences of an unfortunate error but the effect of the most 'true' theories in the order of politics. Those who hoped to save themselves by opposing Marx's real beard to Stalin's false nose are wasting their time.[69]

Stalinism, then, is the logical culmination of marxism, of a political discourse which identifies power with the state and social liberation, therefore, with the capture of the omnipotent state machine.[70]

Foucault's alternative analysis, which denies any unique location to power, conceiving it as a multiplicity of relations co-extensive with the social body within which resistances are omnipresent, implies the rejection of any unique and unified agency of social change. Instead of the struggle of the working-class for self-emancipation we have a plurality of resistances as irreducibly multiple as the relations of power themselves. The thesis of the omnipresence of resistances is, in a sense, a consequence of the nietzschean axiom that '"will" can of course operate only on "will"'[71] – the interactions constitutive of reality are those of clashing quanta of *power*, one of which at ony one time prevails, although its dominance is always under threat from the subordinated quantum. It follows 'that where there is power, there is resistance and that however, or rather equally, the latter is never in position of exteriority in relation to power'.[72]

If resistance then takes place always within a given power-relation, and power relations are always localised, then the notion of any final, decisive struggle fought out between two more or less cohesive social forces ('the last fight' to which the Internationale invites us) must be ruled out. What we are left with is spelled out rather more clearly by Deleuze and Guattari than by Foucault. As we have seen, the function of the *socius* in *L'Anti-Oedipe* is to code the flux of desire, to contain and canalise it within a definite framework. Capitalism is the limiting point of this process, since here the flux is decodified, it is no longer tied, for example, to a definite territory, but only at the price of evacuating desiring production of all concrete content, 'axiomatising' the flux – reducing it to flows of an abstract quantity, value, money. Leaving aside the plausibility or otherwise of this analysis, which involves the identification of social production and the mechanisms of the unconscious as of essentially the same nature, we should note the position of schizophrenia in this analysis. For Lacanian psychoanalysis the psychoses, of which schizophrenia is one species, arise from the failure of the subject to accede to the symbolic order through a successful resolution of the Oedipus complex. The subject cannot distinguish between its mental images, the signifiers organised into language at the level of the symbolic and the real order distinct from and independent of thought and language. Experience for the psychotic is an inarticulate chaos in which words, images, real objects cannot be distinguished, no longer form separate series, act directly upon each other. This is the world beneath the surface described by Deleuze and Guattari, the world of desiring production. They argue that the experience of the schizophrenic, precisely because he has not entered the order of the symbolic where the flux of desire is coded, organised, controlled, more accurately reflects the nature of reality. 'Schizophrenia is the universe of producing and reproducing desiring machines, the universal primary production as "essential" reality of man and nature.' The task of the revolutionary is to free the flux of desire from all codification, from all territorialisation. From this point of view, 'the schizo is not a revolutionary, but the schizophrenic process ... is the potential for revolution'.[73]

This analysis reinforces the conception of a plurality of localised struggles engaged in unending resistance to equally localised technologies of power. The fragmentation, the difference, inherent in desiring production rules out the pos-

sibility of a centralised struggle for power. Discussing 'the re-
inforcement of the structures of confinement' by the French
state, Deleuze says:

> Against this global policy of power, we initiate localised
> counter-responses, skirmishes, active and occasionally pre-
> ventive defences. We have no need to totalise that which is
> invariably totalised on the side of power; if we were to move
> in this direction, it would mean restoring the representative
> forms of centralism and a hierarchical structure. We must
> set up lateral affiliations and an entire system of networks
> and popular bases.[74]

Hence the importance of the concept of the nomad for
Deleuze, Foucault and their collaborators. In *Difference et
Repetition*, as we have seen, Deleuze opposes the nomadic
distribution of difference which escapes all limits and boundaries to the enclosure of difference within the identity of the
concept characteristic of representation. This analysis has
acquired an increasingly political value: the nomad includes
those social forces which resist power, not through a strategy
centred on the seizure of state power, which would result only
in the reproduction and intensification of oppression, but
through localised subversion, through escaping the boundaries imposed by power. Examples would be schizophrenics,
gypsies, gays, feminists. Deleuze and Guattari ask in their
latest book: 'What have nomads done? They have invented a
machine of war against the state apparatus, (that is) completely different from the state apparatus'.[75]

This position is clearly related to Marcuse's thesis that
under late capitalism it is not the working class, but marginal
social groups – youth, unemployed blacks etc. – which constitute the only revolutionary force. But the 'nomadology' of
Foucault, Deleuze, Guattari, Donzelot[76] and others is formulated within a very different theoretical framework from
Marcuse's, one that posits the omnipresence within the social
body of relations of domination and subordination. Such a
proposition seems to presuppose the nietzschean doctrine of
the will to power as 'the *primordial fact* of all history'

Everywhere one enthuses, even under scientific disguises,

about coming states of society in which there will be 'no more exploitation' – that sounds to my ears like promising a life in which there will be no organic functions. 'Exploitation' does not pertain to a corrupt or imperfect or primitive society: it pertains to the *essence* of the living thing as a fundamental organic function, it is a consequence of the intrinsic will to power which is precisely the will to life.[77]

The most consistent version of a philosophy of difference formulated in post-war France has led, therefore, to an 'anarcho-nietzscheanism' which denies the possibility of both objective knowledge and social emancipation.

As much as Nietzsche these writers recall some of the thinkers of the 1840s – Stirner, Proudhon, Herzen – who detected in any theoretical generalisation traces of the hegelian absolute, stressing instead the uniqueness and particularity of the different aspects of an infinitely variegated reality, who saw in the concept of man a secularised version of that of God, who dismissed struggles for political power as attempts to substitute one master for another. The difference lies in the fact that Foucault and Deleuze have substituted for the individual subject, whose sovereignty and substantial unity Stirner and company not only retained but took to new extremes, a 'multiplicity of subjects'.[78] The first systematic presentation of historical materialism occurs in Marx's and Engels' critique of Stirner, *The German Ideology*. Was Stirner right after all? Is marxism in reality a marriage of ancient theology and modern totalitarianism, as the *nouveaux philosophes* claim? Hopefully, the rest of this book will answer these questions.

5 Difference and Contradiction

COLLETTI AND HEGEL

'Our entire epoch, whether by logic or by epistemology, whether by Marx or by Nietzsche, is trying to escape Hegel'.[1] These words of Foucault are easily understood in the light of the last three chapters. From the standpoint of a philosophy of difference, which insists on the priority of multiplicity, which denies the possibility of a simple essence at the origin of things – 'the true substantive, substance itself, is "multiplicity"', writes Deleuze,[2] Hegel, because his system envelops difference in the Absolute Idea, is the enemy who must be defeated, must be destroyed. This is the rationale of the anti-hegelianism which informs the writings of Foucault and Deleuze.[3] Similar considerations underly the anti-hegelianism of otherwise widely differing versions of marxist philosophy.[4] The difference is, however, that anti-hegelian marxists such as Althusser have, on the whole, sought to retain the notion of the social formation as an articulated whole, while Foucault and Deleuze have rejected it – the only concept of totality in their writings is that of the chaotic, undifferentiated, non-totalising body without organs. We have seen how Althusser's attempt to reconcile multiplicity and totality in radically non-hegelian terms failed. In this chapter we shall begin considering another such attempt – that offered by the Italian marxist school of Galvano Della Volpe, notably in the form popularised by Lucio Colletti – because the errors they commit, in their interpretation of both Hegel and Marx, provide us with access to Marx's solution of the problem.

Colletti's recent writings have involved a critique of the concept of 'internal contradiction' used by most marxist philosophers. The thesis that there are contradictions inhe-

112

rent in reality conflates, he argues, two quite distinct concepts, one materialist and scientific, the other idealist and speculative. The first is 'real or "non-contradictory" opposition': 'Here everything is different. . . . Each of the opposites is real and positive. Each subsists for itself . . . (in) a relation of mutual repulsion'. On the other hand, in ' "contradictory" or dialectical opposition' each of the two terms involved is the negation of the other and exists, not in its own right, but by virtue of its relation to the other.[5] The assertion that the latter form of opposition is to be found in reality as well as thought is a formula for the effacement of matter. For opposition is here conceived along the lines of *logical* contradiction, the assertion of a proposition and its negation (p and −p). The terms of a contradictory opposition do not exist – they negate each other. Therefore, to assert, as Hegel does, that 'all things are *contradictory in themselves*' is to deny the existence of things as positive, self-subsistent entities. Which of course he does; the contradictory nature of finite things, established through first negation and negation of negation, provides the process through which the Absolute Idea constitutes itself – 'the absolute is just because the finite is self-contradictory opposition – just because it is *not*'.[6]

The difficulty comes, Colletti argues, when marxists attempt to construct a materialist dialectic on the same premiss as Hegel's – that 'all things are *contradictory in themselves*'. In *Marxism and Hegel* he is concerned to show that one cannot couple dialectical contradiction and materialism – the dialectics of matter leads to its dissolution. Hegel, far from offering the 'critical', 'revolutionary', 'scientific' method which Marx and Engels celebrated, was the author of a system of Christian metaphysics aimed directly at the understanding, the faculty which according to Kant grounds the hypothetico-deductive and empirical methods of the sciences, setting in its place a romantic, intuitive reason identical both with God and with the sum of reality.

The only materialist conception of opposition, Colletti argues, is that of real opposition, which respects the multiplicity and the irreducibility of finite things. Della Volpe in his *Logic* traces the genealogy of materialism properly understood, from Aristotle's critique of Plato to Marx's of Hegel (in the 1843 *Critique of Hegel's Doctrine of the State*) via Galileo and

Kant (the latter is the author of the distinction between 'real' and 'contradictory' opposition). In a manner often strikingly similar to Deleuze's 'reversal of platonism' Della Volpe accuses Hegel of denying the discrete, finite things given in sense-experience anything but a merely negative status as the products of confused and contradictory thought. Material-ism, by contrast, 'is meaningless unless it can be constituted while respecting the empirical, i.e. while fully respecting the positivity of content – multiplicity, matter'. Marx's method, accordingly, is that of a *'moral galileanism'* ('moral' in the slightly obsolete sense of 'pertaining to the human and social') involving the observation of phenomena, the generalisation of these observations into hypotheses and further experimen-tation.[7]

There is a sense in which Della Volpe and Colletti are right and a sense in which they are wrong. Implicit in much of what they have to say is an argument which is never clearly stated. A version of this argument is offered by Karl Popper in his article 'What is Dialectic?', but it is valid despite these anti-marxist credentials.[8] It goes as follows. The principle of non-contradiction, which prohibits the assertion of a proposi-tion and its negation – in symbolic terms, $-(p.-p)$ – is an essential presupposition of a materialist epistemology. For it is an elementary logical truth that a contradictory proposition $(p.-p)$ entails every other proposition. To assert $p.-p$ is, therefore, to assert everything and thereby to deny oneself the possibility of delimiting any determinate state of affairs. For *omnis determinatio negatio est*. Specifying any determinate entity – be it a table, a proposition, an inertial system, a number or a social formation – involves specifying what it is *not*, drawing limits around things. But, since to affirm a contradiction is to affirm everything, denial of the principle of non-contradiction removes the ability to specify and delimit things. This might not matter if our experience were of a formless, viscous chaos lacking any order or stability, but since our initial impression (itself no doubt theory-laden) is of a relatively stable and structured reality the principle of non-contradiction is an essential item in our conceptual armoury.

This argument is fine as far as it goes, which is not very far. For acceptance of the principle of non-contradiction does not in itself entail acceptance of materialism, at least in the sense of the thesis that there exists a reality prior to and independent of thought which the latter in some way merely reflects (this is how materialism will be understood in this book). The entities which may be given definite shape by virtue of the principle of non-contradiction could be Berkeley's ideas instead of physical objects. Indeed, it is not clear that Hegel simply rejected the principle of non-contradiction. The Absolute Idea as such is not contradictory – it is its determinate embodiments which are found to contain contradiction within themselves and thereby pass over into a new shape. Contradiction cancels itself and, through negation of negation, restores identity, now involuted and rendered concrete in contrast to the mute identity in which it originated. The principle of non-contradiction alone cannot provide a rationale for a materialist epistemology.

More fundamental, however, is the misreading of Hegel perpetrated especially by Colletti. It is, of course, perfectly true that Hegel's system is designed to provide an adequate conceptual foundation for Christian revelation. There is that famous passage at the beginning of *The Science of Logic*:

Logic . . . is to be understood as the System of Pure Reason, as the Realm of Pure Thought. *This realm is the Truth as it is, without husk in and for itself.* One may therefore express it thus: that this content *shows forth God as he is in his eternal essence before the creation of Nature and of a Finite Spirit.*[9]

It is an error to suppose that the method of the Logic thus conceived can be separated from its content: 'the form is the indwelling process of the concrete content itself'.[10] Indeed, in the conclusion of *The Science of Logic*, Hegel shows that the method of Logic is identical with the Absolute Idea, which is nothing other than the process of immediate identity splitting itself up and then reconciling its divisions through negation of negation. Colletti, by emphasising the Christian-metaphysical aspects of the hegelian dialectic, provides a valuable corrective to those who have this century read Hegel through Kant and Heidegger, reducing the Absolute Idea to a metaphor for human consciousness,[11] as well as to those marxists who believe that certain universal 'laws of the dialectic' can be derived from Hegel as the foundation for the methods of the sciences (Engels' *Dialectics of Nature* is a prime example of this approach).

From this point of view the hegelian dialectic may be seen as a modern version of a very old philosophical programme – the attempt, dating back at least to the neo-platonists, to show that God did not simply create the world, but is identical with his creation. However, Hegel cannot be understood merely as a modern edition of neo-platonism, 'the German Proclus' as Feuerbach called him.[12] In particular, to present Hegel as an irrationalist and anti-scientific philosopher, as Colletti does in *Marxism and Hegel*, is seriously to misrepresent the significance of his philosophy. Its distinctive character derives from the fact that Hegel attempts to establish the identity of God and the world as the outcome of a rational process of discursive knowledge. Hegel aims many of his most biting polemics against those of his contemporaries, notably Schelling, who argue that the presence of God in his creation, and therefore the unity of reality, can be apprehended only through immediate knowledge, through some simple intuitive act:

> To pit this single assertion, that 'in the Absolute all is one' against the organised whole of determinate and complete knowledge, [as Schelling does – AC] or of knowledge which at least aims at and demands complete development – to give out the Absolute as the night in which, as we say, all cows are black – that is the very *naiveté* of emptiness of knowledge.

The Phenomenology of Mind, by contrast to the irrationalism of Schelling and the romantics, is the 'attempt to justify the claim of science to be a conceptual process'.[13]

To establish by rational means the identity of God and the world necessitated a transformation of existing notions of rationality. Knowledge cannot be conceived of as immediate – as the direct contact of subject and object, what Bertrand Russell called 'knowledge by acquaintance'. The early chapters of the *Phenomenology* are designed to show that even the simplest sense-experiences contain mediation – relation to others – within them. In particular, they involve conceptual connections. But the notion of logic to be found in traditional metaphysics treats concepts as essentially abstract.

Universals are conceived as abstract; the particulars which instantiate them and which they subsume are outside the universals. 'What makes this Universality abstract is the fact that mediation' – the concrete particularity and connectedness making up the reality which thought seeks to know – 'is only condition, or is not posited of itself'.[14] Because thought is unable to take the mediation characteristic of reality within itself, mediation itself is conceived of as external – thought cannot show the inner connections between the different aspects of reality.

The abstract character of universality is reflected in the methods Hegel claims to be characteristic of the sciences. Here a body of thought is conceived of as a deductive system in which the propositions composing it are derived from a set of basic axioms. The problem arises of how these axioms are themselves established. If they themselves are the results of another deduction, then we find ourselves in an infinite regress in which the axioms of *that* deduction must themselves be justified; alternatively, if we wish to halt the regress it seems that we can only do so by invoking immediate knowledge – some intuitive act which founds deductive reasoning. However, Hegel argues, there is a way out of this dilemma, for

> these forms of proposition, of consecutive proof, etc., do not in this form apply to that which is speculative as though the proposition were before us here, and the proof were something separate from it; for in this case [that of speculative as opposed to metaphysical logic – AC] *the proof comes with the proposition*. The Notion is a self-movement, and not, as a proposition, a desire to rest; nor is it true that the proof brings forward another ground or middle term and is another movement; for it has this movement in itself.[15]

Hegel is seeking to develop a new form of rationality, an *immanent rationality*, in which 'the proof comes with the proposition', i.e. the propositions constituting a particular discourse are established in the course of the exposition of that discourse, rather than depending on some set of axioms whose rationale lies outside the discourse in question. We shall have something to say about the contemporary relevance of this notion of rationality in Chapter 7. For the moment let us concentrate on Hegel's treatment of thought as the Notion, containing within itself the mediation and motion characteristic of reality rather than merely reflecting them from outside. This treatment involves the counterposition to the abstract universal of the concrete universal, in which the connections through which the particulars are woven together are shown to be rational and thereby mediation is brought within thought. The concrete universal as unity of universal and particular is individuality. It is here crucial to note that the concrete universal involves not only mediation, but subjectivity. Hegel argues that the distinctive philosophical contribution of Christianity was to introduce the principle of subjectivity: God is not simply the impersonal, neo-platonic, One – he individuates himself and acquires personality through the Incarnation, the Word becoming Flesh. Negation of negation is not simply the reconciliation of opposition, the restoration of the self-identity of Being; or rather it is these things only by virtue of being also subjectivity. The essence of subjectivity is precisely the unfolding of the dialectic. Subjectivity arises only with the awareness of a self distinct from the rest of reality; first negation is the self-estrangement which arises from the subject's awareness that his identity arises only from alienation from the rest of the world, which is the Other to his Self; but in second negation the world is saved for the self through his cognition (in philosophy) of the identity of subject and object, Self and Other, in the Absolute Idea. Therefore,

> the transcendence of the opposition between the Notion and Reality, and that unity which is the truth, rest upon this subjectivity alone. – The second negative, the negative of the negative, . . . is this transcendence of the contradiction, but is no more the activity of an external reflection than the contradiction is: it is the innermost and most objective moment of Life and Spirit, by virtue of which a subject is personal and free.[16]

Hegel's attempt to develop a new form of rationality does not, therefore, make the dialectic any less idealist. Rational thought in its fullest sense, the concrete universal, shares the structure of subjectivity, or rather is that structure. The realms of Nature and Spirit (the latter including individual mental life, society, art, religion and philosophy) are determinate developments of a conceptual structure articulated at the level of Logic, 'God as he is in his eternal essence'. But something of great import should be noted here. Hegel's famous remark that 'everything depends on grasping the ultimate truth not as Substance but as Subject as well'[17] should not be taken simply in the sense in which it is normally understood – to Plotinus' One and Spinoza's Substance must be added the principle of subjectivity. It can also be understood as prescribing an alteration in our concept of subjectivity. Descartes conceived the subject as a finite substance created by and dependent upon an infinite substance, God. But for Hegel the subject is no longer the stable and enduring substratum of change but a relation, a movement.[18] The subject is the process through which the identity of thought and the world is established. Its character as subjectivity derives from the *structure* of this process, the passing of immediate identity into otherness and mediation and its ultimate restoration. To paraphrase Marx, for Hegel the subject is a relation, not a thing. 'In its essential nature the truth is subject: being so, it is merely the dialectical movement, this self-producing course of activity, maintaining its advance by returning back into itself'.[19] The truth is subject because the dialectical movement is teleological, not in the sense that it pursues a goal outside itself, but in that it describes a circle – the process returns to its starting point, the original, simple identity of Being, now enriched by all the concrete determinations developed within it: 'the science is seen to be a circle which returns upon itself, for mediation bends back its end into its beginning or simple ground'.[20]

FETISHISM AND THE LOGIC OF CAPITAL

An understanding of these characteristics of the hegelian dialectic – the attempt to establish the identity of God and his creation by means of a concept of immanent rationality, the dependence of the latter concept on the proposition that 'the truth is subject' and the transformation of the subject into a set of structures forming a self-complicating circle – is indispensable if any discussion of the presence of hegelian categories in Marx's writings is to be fruitful. That such categories are present, even in the works of Marx's maturity such as *Capital*, is not contested, even by anti-hegelian marxists. Colletti's discussion of the problem is especially interesting.

Colletti, at least in his more recent writings, cannot accept Della Volpe's qualification of Marx as the 'Galileo of the moral world', for

> The contradictions of capitalism – from the contradiction between capital and wage-labour to all the others – are not, for Marx, "real oppositions", . . . i.e. objective but "non-contradictory" oppositions, but are *dialectical contradictions* in the full sense of the word.

The contradiction between use-value and value inherent in the commodity-form, for example, is not a 'real opposition' between two independent forces. The contradiction is internal to the commodity and arises from the fact that social labour is split under capitalism into abstract labour (the source of value) and private labour (the source of use-value). When the two aspects of the commodity assume autonomous and independent form with the sale of goods on the market the possibility arises that some use-values will go unsold and thereby the social labour employed in their production has been wasted. The unity of the two aspects of the commodity is reasserted in crises, where firms that produced goods that went unsold go into liquidation and the workers they employed are sacked. Dialectical opposition therefore develops into real opposition, while its inner unity is restored in crises. The presence of a concept of internal contradiction in *Capital* is, Colletti argues, reconciled with Marx's 'moral galileiansm' when we recall that for Marx the capitalist mode of production is a 'topsy-turvy reality' in which the producers are alienated from their labour and its products, where social relations take the form of relations between things, the exchange of commodities on the market governing the process of production. '*So the theory of alienation and the theory of contradiction are now seen as a single theory – one which embraces and encompasses within itself the theory of value*'. Marx is both scientist and philosopher, the heir of political economy and its critic, author of a scientific analysis of capitalism and of a philosophical critique of alienation.[21]

Colletti's argument involves an interpretation of *Capital* which is shared by many other marxists, both hegelian and anti-hegelian – namely, that the structure of *Capital* can be understood only in terms of the theory of fetishism.[22] It is an interpretation supported by many passages in *Capital* which argue that the dislocation between the surface appearance of the capitalist mode of production and its inner mechanisms derives from the fetishism of the commodity, where 'the relationships between the producers, within which the social characteristics of their labours are manifested, take the form of a social relation between the products of labour'.[23] Althusser adopts the same view:

> '*Capital* ... exactly measures a distance and an internal dislocation in the real, inscribed in its *structure*, a distance and a dislocation such as to make their own effects themselves illegible, and the illusion of an immediate reading of them the ultimate apex of their effects: *fetishism*.[24]

This interpretation of *Capital* conceives of capitalist relations of production as a structure which in its very functioning conceals its basic mechanisms. This process of self-occultation is no illusion – as Marx puts it, 'to the producers ... the social relations between their labours appear as what they are, i.e. ... as material relations between persons and social relations between things'.[25] It is intrinsic to the functioning of the capitalist mode of production that the process of production is governed by the exchange of the products of labour on the market. The effect, however, is that to the agent of production, whether capitalist or worker, the surface appearance of the system is one in which the social determinants of commodity production are no longer evident. Thus,

> The actual process of production, as a unity of the production process and the circulation process, gives rise to new formations, in which the vein of internal connections is increasingly lost, the production relations are rendered independent of one another, and the component values

become ossified into forms independent of one another.[26]

One example of such 'new formations' is the 'trinity formula', according to which the source of value is the purely technical contribution of the three 'factors of production' – capital, land and labour – to the process of production; the origin of value in socially necessary labour-time is here completely lost.

This reading of *Capital*, shared by so many different schools, reduces the structure of capitalism to a structure of *representation*, in which the system functions both to present itself to, and conceal itself from, the individual subject. Althusser indeed picks on the term *Darstellung* (as in the '*presentation* of value as exchange-value') and calls it 'the key epistemological concept of the whole marxist theory of value', one that shows how the capitalist mode of production functions as an 'authorless theatre'.[27] A theatre is the place where a play is presented to an audience, even if the play has no author and the production so functions as to deceive the audience. The concept of *Darstellung* and the theory of fetishism bear a close relationship to the hegelian Doctrine of Essence, Book II of *The Science of Logic*, where Being splits itself in two, into hidden essence and surface phenomena. The stage of Essence is that of the duplicity of Being, of Being appearing to and deceiving itself within the dual structure of essence and appearance. To reduce *Capital* to this structure is to reduce it to a theory of ideology, an explanation of why the agents of production are deceived as to its working, rather than an analysis of the laws of motion of capitalism. It is not to uncover two Marxs, the scientist and the philosopher, but to dissolve one into the other, transforming Marx into the theorist of the unhappy consciousness of man under capitalism. We have uncovered here an additional reason for Althusser's 'ideologism': it is an easy step from seeing *Capital* as the explanation of why consciousness is deceived, to reducing the social to the ideological. Leaving aside the inadequacy of the theory of fetishism even as an account of ideology,[28] it is necessary to present an alternative interpretation of the structure of *Capital*. This interpretation is most fully developed in Roman Rosdolsky's commentary on the *Grundrisse*, *The Making of Marx's 'Capital'*, a work which, despite certain weaknesses, is of fundamental importance for an understanding of Marx's economic writings,[29] but is also to be found in a less developed form in Isaak Rubin's *Essays on Marx's Theory of Value*. For the interpretation of *Capital* as an analysis of fetishism, apart from its idealist implications, is seriously misleading as to the structure of *Capital*.

Marx assumes as axiomatic that every mode of production involves some mechanism for securing the distribution of social labour to the different branches of production. The law of value is the form taken by that mechanism under capitalist relations of production.[30] The capitalist mode of production is a system of *commodity* production. Essentially this means that the process of production is under the direction of a set of autonomous but interdependent units of production (for example, firms). Each unit of production cannot provide for its own needs (for raw materials, means of production and of course the consumption goods necessary to reproduce the workforce) out of its own production; it can only secure the use-values it requires by exchanging its own products on the market. It follows that the concrete labour carried out in a given unit of production (the specific activity involved in producing machine tools, shoes or rockets) is not directly social labour; whether it meets some social need in proportion to the overall requirements of society is not established directly, since there is no mechanism to enable society to determine collectively what shall be produced and in what quantities. Whether a given concrete labour is social labour can be established only via the market and the only way in which the social need for a use-value can be determined in these circumstances is through the exchange-ratios between different goods (their exchange values or prices). The fluctuations of relative price record the shifting balance of supply and demand of particular commodities. If a commodity is produced in excess of the social need for it, it will go unsold and its market price will fall. Units of production whose products are not in demand or are priced uncompetitively, will cease producing and their workforce will be transferred elsewhere.

The process of exchange reduces the particular productive activities carried out in different units of production to portions of abstract social labour. Once use-values have been rendered universally exchangeable, the determination of their exchange-ratios depends not on their particular characteristics but on the amount of abstract social labour involved in their production. Marx regarded the distinction between abstract social labour and concrete private labour as one of his most important innovations.[31] Crucial in the process of reducing particular concrete labours to portions of abstract social labour is competition – if two units produce the same commodity then the unit producing under more efficient conditions will drive the other out of business. What counts is *socially necessary* labour – private labour is only abstract social labour if it produces in the average conditions prevailing in the industry concerned. The value of a commodity is the socially necessary labour time required to produce it. Exchange-value, or relative price, is the form taken by value on the market.

The first great separation definitive of the capitalist mode of production, then, is that between the different units of production. The distribution of social labour to the different units of production is secured only through the exchange of the products of labour on the market. The theory of fetishism must be seen in this light; it is a subordinate feature of a theory whose task it is to account for the distribution of social labour under capitalism. But capitalism is a system of *generalised* commodity production, above all in the sense that labour-power, the ability to engage in productive activity, is itself a commodity. This situation arises from the second great separation, that of the direct producer from the means of production. Marx's theory of surplus-value follows directly from the analysis of this situation, and we do not need to rehearse it in great detail here: labour-power is sold to the owner of the means of production in exchange for a wage; as the ability to work, it is also the power to create value; it follows that if the value of labour-power is less than the value created during a given working day, the difference may be appropriated by the owner of the means of production as surplus-value. The second separation characteristic of capitalism, therefore, opens to view the internal structure of the unit of production, showing it to involve an antagonism between the owner of the means of production and the direct producer. In so far as the units of production involve the extraction and accumulation of surplus-value they are *capitals*.

So far we have followed the argument of *Capital* Volume 1:
the analysis of the commodity is logically prior to that of the
capital-relation; the commodity can be conceived of as existing (and has existed) without capitalism, whilst the reverse is
not true. However, only where capitalist relations of production prevail can the entire product of labour take the form of
commodities, because only where the direct producer is
separated from the means of production and therefore
unable to meet his own needs does the mass production of
consumer goods for the market become possible. The labour
theory of value does not involve positing, even as an 'ideal
type', a stage of simple commodity production where production is entirely for the market but there are no capitalists.[32]

A further misunderstanding of *Capital*, which is closely
linked to the tendency to accord central importance to the
theory of fetishism, is to interpret the value-relations analysed
in Volume 1 as a hidden essence manifested in the deceptive
surface phenomena of circulation (Volume 2) and of the
system as a whole (Volume 3). This 'fundamentalist' interpretation has a ready answer to the criticisms of *Capital* made in
the last few years by neo-ricardian economists: any attempt to
question the internal coherence of Marx's discourse or its
empirical corroboration founders on the critics' failure to
distinguish between essence and appearance.[33] A similar
interpretation underlies the recent critique of *Capital* by
Anthony Cutler, Barry Hindess, Paul Hirst and Athar Hussain. The discourse of *Capital* is an 'essentialist' one in the
sense that 'the general conception of object in the epistemology under the sign of which *Capital* is written is that of an
entity the effects of which are given in its concept'. The
capitalist mode of production as conceptualised by Marx is an
essence which must of necessity perpetuate itself in whatever
concrete circumstances in which it is placed. The essence by
virtue of its nature manifests itself in the phenomena. It
follows that the phenomena are themselves of no interest.
'Thus the concept of the structure of definite capitalist
economies is impertinent, a non-problem, if all capitalist
economies can be considered as exemplars of an essentially
common structure, the capitalist mode of production'.[34]

Now while this interpretation is applied by Cutler and his
collaborators to the relation between *Capital* and the concrete

exemplification of the capitalist mode of production (CMP) in definite social formations, there is no reason why it should not be imputed to the structure of *Capital* itself, so that the process of circulation of capital (analysed in Volume 2) and the unity of production and circulation (Volume 3) are seen as inessential phenomena concealing the value relations below. However, this interpretation is false. Marx's analysis of the capitalist economy involves distinguishing between two irreducible levels – 'capital in general' and 'many capitals'. The sphere of 'capital in general' is dealt with in *Capital*, volume 1 and the first two parts of volume 2. '*Capital in general*, as distinct from the particular capitals', Marx writes, appears

> *only as an abstraction*; not an arbitrary abstraction, but an abstraction which grasps the specific characteristics which distinguish capital from all the other forms of social wealth – or modes in which (social) production develops. These are the aspects common to every capital as such, or which make every specific sum of values into capital.[35]

The 'aspects . . . which make every specific sum of values into capital' are the social relationships involved in the separation of the direct producer from the means of production and the consequent purchase and sale of labour-power, relationships which transform the labour process (the production of use-values) into the process of self-expansion of capital (the production of value and surplus-value). The sphere of 'capital in general' is then, above all, that of the capitalist production process, analysed by Marx in *Capital* Volume 1 as the unity of labour-process and valorisation-process, where the production of use-values is subordinated to the self-expansion of value. The differences between individual capitals (their size, organic composition, efficiency, market-share, products etc.) are irrelevant from the standpoint of 'capital in general' since it is concerned with 'the aspects common to every capital'. The analysis of the production process can, therefore, be made on the assumption that commodities exchange at their values since the possibility of the systematic divergence of value and price becomes relevant only when differences between individual capitals are taken into account.

The sphere of 'many capitals', by contrast, is that of

competition, and *Capital*, volume 3 is devoted to its analysis. The necessity for the distinction between 'capital in general' and 'many capitals' is inherent in the labour theory of value, since the latter depicts a situation in which social production is controlled by a set of autonomous but interdependent capitals:

> Since value forms the foundation of capital, and since it therefore necessarily exists only through the exchange for *counter-value*, it thus necessarily repels itself from itself. A *universal capital*, one without alien capitals confronting it, with which it exchanges . . . is therefore a non-thing.[36]

The introduction of 'many capitals' as a problem of analysis implies a modification of some of the propositions developed in *Capital*, volume 1. Competition, both in the sense of the battle for markets between different firms in the same industry and in the sense of the flow of money-capital from less profitable to more profitable sectors, leads to the formation of the general rate of profit. Commodities can no longer exchange at their values, but instead fluctuate around their modified values or prices of production, which presuppose a redistribution of surplus value effected by the equalisation of the rate of profit. The transformation of value into price of production is, therefore, an effect of competition. This conclusion does not contradict the labour theory of value but completes it, since, as we have seen, the basic axioms of the theory imply the existence of 'many capitals'.[37] 'Competition merely *expresses* as real, posits as an external necessity, that which lies within the nature of capital'.[38]

However, the passage last cited should not be taken to imply that competition is a mere epiphenomenon of 'capital in general'. On the contrary, the reverse is true: 'The influence of individual capitals on one another has the effect precisely that they must conduct themselves as *capital*'.[39] The tendencies analysed by Marx in volume 1 as inherent in the accumulation of capital – notably the rising organic composition of capital which finds expression in the tendency of the rate of profit to fall – become operative only by virtue of competition. Thus Marx shows that the tendency towards technical innovation which underlies the rising organic composition of capital is the result of the pressure of competition – firms introduce changes in the conditions of production which will enable them to under sell their competitors and at the same time realise a surplus-profit.[40] Indeed, the very accumulation of capital itself arises not from the capitalists' greed or will to power[41] but in the structure of mutual compulsions inherent in the process of competition: if a given capital does not reinvest the surplus-value extracted from its workers in order to expand production and render it more efficient its competitors will drive it out of the market. The labour theory of value essentially involves competition conceived of as a coercive process which enforces the laws of capitalist production upon individual capitals.

The organisation of the discourse of *Capital* around the distinction between 'capital in general' and 'many capitals', therefore, follows from the specification of the two great separations characteristic of the CMP – those between the units of production and between the direct producers and the owners of the means of production, the antagonisms between capitals and between capital and labour. Only here the order is reversed: 'capital in general' before 'many capitals'. The conceptual priority of 'capital in general' arises from the fact that here the analysis involves determining those 'aspects common to every capital as such, or which make every specific sum of value into capital'. Before analysing 'many capitals' one must first understand what 'capital' is. The analysis of 'capital in general' is more than a generic definition of 'capital', however; it determines the limits of individual capitals' behaviour. The specific mechanisms of competition analysed in volume 3 – the equalisation of the rate of profit, the division of profit into profit of enterprise, interest and rent etc. – involve the redistribution of surplus-value created in the process of production. The limits to competition between capitals is set by the common source of the profits each firm seeks to maximise at the expense of its fellows – the exploitation of the working class. The surplus-value extracted from the whole working class forms a pool whose contents are shared out among capitals through competition:

> In each particular sphere of production the individual capitalist, as well as the capitalists as a whole, take direct part

in the exploitation of the total working class by the totality of the capitalist class and in the degree of that exploitation, not only out of general class sympathy, but also for direct economic reasons. For, assuming all other conditions . . . to be given, the average rate of profit depends on the intensity of exploitation of the total sum of labour by the total sum of capital.

At the same time, individual capitals seek to raise the productivity of labour in their own firms and thereby to realise an extra profit:

> Here, then, we have a mathematically precise proof why capitalists form a veritable freemason society *vis-a-vis* the whole working class, while there is little love lost between them in competition among themselves.[42]

The dependence of competition between 'many capitals' upon the relations of exploitation analysed at the level of 'capital in general' does not nullify the former. *Capital* does not trace the manner in which a simple essence (value) is both manifested and concealed, but uncovers a complex structure involving levels which are both interdependent and irreducible.

STRUCTURE AND CONTRADICTION

The establishment of the fact that the relations constitutive of the capitalist mode of production form a multiplicity returns us to the question posed at the beginning of this chapter. How are we to conceive of a totality which involves determinations that are not reducible to one another yet form a structured whole? Let us recall that Althusser tried to answer this question in part through the concept of structural causality, where the whole is a spinozist immanent cause, the structure nothing other than the relation of its different effects. The implications of this concept for our understanding of contradiction are spelled out, not by Althusser, but by two of his collaborators, Étienne Balibar and Pierre Macherey.

Balibar discusses the marxian law of the tendency of the rate of profit to fall, which he understands (rightly, as we shall see below) as involving a series of contradictory effects which both cause the general rate of profit to fall and counteract the tendency for it to do so.[43] Balibar claims that this discussion clarifies 'the true status of contradiction in Marx. Marx defines the terms between which there is a contradiction as *'the contradictory effects of a single cause'*. He continues:

> This definition also includes the limitation of the role of contradiction, i.e. its situation of *dependence* with respect to the cause (the structure): there is only a contradiction between the effects, the cause is not divided in itself, it cannot be analysed in antagonistić terms. Contradiction is therefore not original, but derivative. The effects are organised in a series of particular contradictions, but the process of production of these effects is in no way contradictory.[44]

Macherey attributes this doctrine, that 'contradiction is . . . not original, but derivative', to Spinoza, for whom things were contradictory only when conceived from the standpoint of their mere existence, as distinct objects repelling and attracting each other in an endless and contingent causal chain. From the standpoint of their essence, as grasped through knowledge of the third kind, *amor intellectualis Dei*, they are simply aspects of the single Substance, *Deus sive Natura*.[45]

We seem here to be discussing contradiction in the sense of real rather than dialectical opposition – the repulsion of opposites not their identity. It is not obvious, however, that adding to real opposition the notion of a non-contradictory cause helps very much to clarify matters. Spinoza's conception of existence and essence pertains, at least on Macherey's interpretation, to the distinction between the two higher kinds of knowledge; ordinary deductive reasoning (knowledge of the second kind) conceives of reality as the endless concatenation of cause and effect, involving relations of real opposition, while it is the shift to *scientia intuitiva* (knowledge of the third kind) which enables us to grasp reality as the expressions of a non-contradictory essence which exists only in the act of expression. If Substance itself is not a simple essence, since its expressions are multiple (the attributes of God are infinite), there is no determinate relation between these expressions, except that of sharing the same structure. No wonder that Deleuze has been able to give a quasi-nietzschean interpretation of Spinoza in which Substance becomes the chaotic play of its effects.[46]

Is the choice, then, between pluralism, which preserves multiplicity at the price of structure, and 'dialectical materialism', which imputes to reality a structure – dialectical or contradictory opposition – whose function can only be to subsume difference into the Idea? Let us first recall that contradiction performs this latter function in Hegel by cancelling itself and that this is possible because of the teleological and circular structure of the dialectic, whose end is implicit in its beginning, the first and final terms being immediate identity, one mute and simple, the other enriched and restored. In the light of the discussion of *Capital* in the preceding section it seems to me undeniable that Marx employs a concept of contradiction that is both stronger than mere real opposition and yet non-teleological and non-reductionist.

Consider the two great separations constitutive of capitalist relations of production. Each is antagonistic: the capitalist exploits the worker and the latter resists his exploitation; capitals compete with each other. The terms of the antagonism do not make sense outside their relation: Marx often insists that wage-labour and capital are each inconceivable without the other; more generally, Althusser and Poulantzas in their later writings argue that the class struggle is anterior to classes, i.e. that classes take shape only within their antagonistic mutual relations; while 'a *universal capital*, one without alien capitals confronting it, ... is ... a non-thing'. So we are not dealing here with a real opposition in the sense of a relation of mutual exclusion between essentially distinct and independent entities, but of a relation whose terms are constituted by virtue of their mutual antagonism.

However, the terms of these antagonisms are not thereby effaced, nor the outcome of their struggles determined in advance. There is, first, no simple essence from which they originate – the two separations are treated by Marx as providing the starting point of his analysis. In Althusser's terms, multiplicity or difference is ever-pre-given. The first two parts of *Capital* Volume 1 deal with, respectively, commodities and money and the essence of the capital-relation; it is only in Part VIII that Marx turns to discussing some historical conditions of the emergence of capitalist relations of production, and here again he concentrates upon class *struggle*, and in particular the expropriation of the direct producers.

Secondly, these contradictions (which have, it should by now be clear, nothing to do with a denial of the principle of non-contradiction) do not imply any necessary outcome of the struggles to which they give rise. This statement is controversial, but must be insisted on – the analysis of *Capital* does not imply that proletarian revolution is inevitable. Thus, the discussion of the tendency of the rate of profit to fall in *Capital* Volume 3, Part III makes quite clear that this tendency involves counteracting principles some of which are intrinsic to its nature (for example, the cheapening of the elements of constant capital):

> The same influences which produce a tendency in the general rate of profit to fall, also call forth countereffects, which hamper, retard and partly paralyse this fall.

The 'internal contradictions of the law' are expressed in crises, which 'are always but momentary and forcible solutions of the existing contradictions. They are violent eruptions which for a time restore the disturbed equilibrium'. Crises achieve this result chiefly through 'the periodical depreciation of existing capitals', which removes the less efficient capitals from the scene, thereby enabling the more efficient ones to expand and reorganise production, and through mass unemployment, which forces workers to accept worse wages and conditions. The depreciation or devalorisation of capital is 'one of the means immanent in capitalist production to check the fall of the rate of profit and hasten accumulation of capital-value through formation of new capital' but in doing so it 'disturbs the given conditions within which the process of circulation and reproduction of capital takes place, and therefore is accompanied by sudden stoppages and crises in the production process'.[47] There is no tendency inherent in capitalist relations of production for the economy to break down irreperably; *crises* are inevitable but these are 'violent eruptions which for a time restore the disturbed equilibrium'; or, as Trotsky put it, 'capitalism does live by crises and booms, just as a human being lives by inhaling and exhaling'.[48]

Finally, as we have seen, the antagonistic relations form a structured whole. The contradictions between competing capitals presuppose the contradiction between capital and labour but are not reducible to it. The structure of *Capital*, therefore, involves a multiplicity of determinations which display a definite order. The error of Althusser and his followers was, that by treating contradiction as derivative, i.e. as extrinsic to the structure of the whole, they reproduced the opposition between simple essence and chaotic difference. The most serious effect is to render class struggle external to the relations of production; this is most obvious in the case of Nicos Poulantzas' distinction in *Political Power and Social Classes* between structures and practices, where the class struggle pertains to the latter. The possibility of social revolution, of the overthrow of a particular set of relations of production and their replacement by another, is external to these relations. It is true that Althusser later wrote, in the context of the thesis that 'the class struggle is the motor of history', of '*the primacy of contradiction* over the *terms* of contradiction', but this proposition was expressed in terms of a voluntarist conception of the class struggle, as we shall see in the next chapter, and has not been developed further.[49] Here, by contrast, the class struggle is intrinsic to the relations of production; the two antagonisms constitutive of capitalism include that between capital and labour on the basis of which their struggle develops. This position does not involve a relapse into the hegelian marxism of the early Lukács, where the different determinations of capitalist society are treated as mediated forms of the contradiction between capital and labour, since here, as we have argued at length, the sphere of 'many capitals' is not a phenomenal expression of 'capital in general'. Indeed, there are further determinations of capitalist relations of production – notably the state – which may be only conceptualised on the basis of the 'capital-in-general'/'many capitals' couple but which are again not reducible to it: we shall discuss these matters further in Chapters 6 to 8.

These remarks do not amount to a 'theory' of contradiction. Indeed, it is not clear what such a theory would involve.

Certainly, contradiction as here conceived would not be readily applicable to nature. Nevertheless this discussion may help to clarify the nature of Marx's argument in *Capital* and the sense in which it involves a materialist dialectic. The most basic concept produced within Marx's discourse is that of *relations of production*. *Capital* is essentially an analysis of capitalist relations of production. Our discussion of contradiction indicates that these relations are constituted by certain antagonisms which relate primarily, although not exclusively, to the relations of exploitation characteristic of a given mode of production, and that these antagonisms are irreducible to each other, display a definite order and determine the nature of the social forces involved in that mode of production and of the conflicts between them, even if they do not predetermine any particular outcome to these conflicts.

MARX AFTER HEGEL

There are two obvious difficulties to this account, which are closely related. One is that my interpretation of *Capital* implies that its structures are radically non-hegelian. How, then, does one explain the presence of hegelian categories in *Capital*? Secondly, the claim that Marx's concept of contradiction is non-teleological conflicts with the fact that so much of classical marxism posits the inevitablity of socialist revolution.

Taking these points in order, it is very difficult to assign a unique cause underlying Marx's very diverse use of hegelian categories. His writings are full of hegelian terminology and references, and it seems that he regarded Hegel's system as providing a unique conceptual resource, an initial definition of the landscape from which one started in discussing particular problems (notably those relating to the national question and the analysis of precapitalist social formations), even if the point of arrival was often very different from that of departure. In *Capital* itself, however, Marx's main interest in Hegel was methodological. His economic writings, notably *Theories of Surplus-Value*, contain extended discussions of the ways in which the internal construction of his predecessors' theoretical discourses precluded any adequate solution of the problems posed by political economy. Notable in this respect was their treatment of *abstraction*. Thus the vulgar economists (whose most notable representatives were Nassau Senior and Samuel Bailey, two of the precursors of neo-classical economics) claimed simply to be describing the visible workings of the capitalist economy, eschewing abstraction *tout court*; they therefore concentrated on the exchange-ratios of goods on the market, refusing to see these relations as involving the equalisation of social labour, and accepted the trinity formula as an adequate account of the determination of wages, prices and profit. On the other hand, the classical economists, above all Ricardo, who were prepared to employ the method of abstraction in order to uncover the internal mechanisms of the capitalist economy and thereby developed the labour theory of value, failed to offer any adequate account of the manner in which these intrinsic relations gave rise to the surface phenomena described by the vulgar economists, assuming that the two were directly identical.

Marx, for example, criticises Ricardo for assuming as an axiom of his system that there is a general rate of profit, i.e. that returns on capital in different branches of production have been equalised, since it follows from this proposition that, if conditions of production are not uniform, commodities cannot exchange according to the socially necessary labour-time involved in their production:

> Instead of *postulating* this *general rate of profit*, Ricardo should rather have examined how far its *existence* is in fact consistent with the determination of value by labour-time, and he would have found that, instead of being consistent with it, *prima facie*, it *contradicts* it, and that its existence would therefore have to be explained through a number of intermediary stages, a procedure which is very different from merely including it under the law of value.[50]

One could paraphrase Marx's criticism as follows: Ricardo conceives of value as an abstract universal, lacking mediation and concrete content. The result is that the various determinations of the capitalist economy are merely included under the law of value, treated as its phenomenal expressions, without themselves being explained in terms of it. Hence the glaring contradiction (seized on at once by Ricardo's critics – Torrens, for example) between the labour theory of value and the assumption that returns on capital are equalised. The labour theory of value can be rescued only if value is treated as a concrete universal, containing internal differentiation within itself, indeed necessarily differentiating itself, giving rise to 'many capitals' and the determinations of competition which apparently contradict the law of value but in reality complete it: 'conceptually, *competition* is nothing other than the inner *nature of capital*, its essential character, appearing in and realised as the reciprocal interaction of many capitals with one another, the inner tendency as external necessity'.[51]

Marx's treatment of value as a concrete universal, whose validity can be established only 'through a number of inter- mediary stages', is closely related to his description of his method as that 'of rising from the abstract to the concrete'.[52] This method is reflected in the structure of *Capital*: the process of production is examined first, in isolation from the rest of the economy, and on the assumption that commodities exchange at their value; then, in Volume 2, the process of circulation is treated in isolation, and on the same assumption; it is only in Volume 3 that the process as a whole, the unity of production and circulation, the sphere of 'many capitals' is treated and the assumption dropped. This approach presup- poses the priority of production over consumption and distribution.[53] It also involves a notion of scientific proof as internal to the discourse in question remarkably similar to Hegel's claim that 'the (speculative) proof comes with the proposition'. Marx dismissed the objection that Chapter 1 of *Capital* Volume 1 does not prove the labour theory of value:

> All that palaver about the necessity of proving the concept of value arises from complete ignorance both of the subject dealt with and of scientific method.... Science consists precisely in demonstrating *how* the law of value asserts itself. So that if one wanted at the very beginning to 'explain' all the phenomena that seemingly contradict the law, one would have to present the science *before* the science.[54]

In other words, the law of value cannot be established outside the discourse of *Capital* and its continuations; it cannot be justified by deduction from some higher-order principle, conceptual analysis of the term 'value' or induction from observation. Its proof is inseparable from its discursive exposition.

The difficulty with Marx's use of hegelian categories should be obvious here. Hegel's assertion that proof is internal to the speculative Logic is one aspect of a more general thesis, namely that the course of the dialectic describes a circle. The process through which the immediate identity of Being is cracked open and given determinate content is also that through which it is shown to be the sum of reality, so that all mediation is absorbed within it:

> Each step in the progress of further determination in advancing from the indeterminate beginning is also a rearward approach to it, so that the two processes which may at first appear to be different (the regressive confirmation of the beginning and its progressive further determination) coincide and are the same. The method thus forms a circle.[55]

Hegel's notion of immanent rationality is part of his general programme of showing that all the definite determinations of reality are aspects of the Absolute Idea, itself the immediate unity of Being enriched and restored as absolute negativity, the destruction of all finite being. Can Marx disengage the concepts of internal proof and of the concrete universal from the speculative and idealist roles they play in Hegel's system?

An examination of *Capital* suggests that Marx secured a considerable degree of success in 'escaping Hegel'. While the hegelian echoes are considerable, the structure of *Capital* cannot be assimilated to that of the *Logic*. Thus, the latter work forms a triad – Being (immediate identity), Essence (externalisation and self-estrangement) and Notion (restoration of identity as inner connection = the Absolute Idea). *Capital*, by contrast, starts with the inner connection (value), and its subsequent development shows how 'the vein of internal connection is increasingly lost' in the form it takes in the determinations of competition (see the passage quoted above pp. 122–3). Most of Marx's borrowings from Hegel come from Book I of the *Logic*, the Doctrine of Being, where Hegel shows how attempts to analyse reality in terms of the surface connection between things and their quantitative aspects is inadequate without positing some internal structure, which gives rise to the Doctrine of Essence. It should be obvious that this argument would be an attractive one to Marx in his polemics against the vulgar economists' attempts to reduce value to a purely quantitative relation expressed in goods' exchange-ratios.

Marx's borrowings from Hegel, however, in the absence of any explicit critique, have their effect on the construction of his discourse. The theory of fetishism is one example. Here Marx transposes a methodological choice – to start one's analysis of the capitalist economy from the quantitative relations between commodities rather than from, as in the case of Smith and Ricardo, the relations of distribution, or, as in Marx's case, the relations of production – into the necessary effect of capitalist social relations. The step would be an easy one for Hegel, since for him the movement of thought is also the process through which thought realises itself, creating an objective world counterposed to the subject; for Marx, however, it is a retreat into idealism. Similarly, in the *Grundrisse*, where the hegelian influence is most evident, Marx tends to treat capital a bit like the Absolute Idea, as a relation which necessarily realises itself. As Edward Thompson observes,

> In the *Grundrisse* – and not once or twice, but in the whole mode of presentation – we have examples of *unreconstructed* hegelianism. Capital posits conditions '*in accordance with its immanent essence*', reminding us that Marx had studied Hegel's Philosophy of Nature, and had noted of 'the Idea as nature' that 'reality is posited with immanent determinateness of form'. Capital posits this and that, and if we are to conceive of capital*ism* ('the inner construction of modern society') it can only be as 'capital in the totality of its relations'.[56]

This picture, while to a large degree valid for the *Grundrisse*, does not fit *Capital* and *Theories of Surplus-Value*. There Marx is very careful to establish the determinations of the capitalist economy not as logically implicit in the concept of value and of capital[57] but on the basis of these concepts through a series of 'intermediary stages'. For example, in the *Grundrisse* Marx tends to treat the relation between 'capital in general' and 'many capitals' as that between the Absolute Idea and its externalisation in Nature; the result is that the determinations of competition become estranged, inessential, phenomenal expressions of 'capital in general'. In *Capital*, by contrast, Marx devotes much attention to developing the articulations relating the creation of surplus-value in the process of production to the sphere of competition, notably those 'intermediary stages' involved in the circulation process – the three circuits of capital, the turnover of capital and the reproduction of the aggregate social capital.

Hegelian forms of argument, however, persist within *Capital*. Most notable is Chapter 32 of *Capital* Volume 1, 'The Historical Tendency of Capitalist Accumulation'. Here Marx analyses the trajectory of the capitalist mode of production in terms of a hegelian triad. The starting point is 'private property which is personally earned, i.e. which is based, as it were, on the fusing together of the isolated, independent working individual with the conditions of his labour'. This is negated by the primitive accumulation of capital, where the direct producer is expropriated and there arises 'capitalist private property, which rests on the exploitation of alien, but formally free, labour'. 'But capitalist production begets, with the inexorability of a natural process, its own negation. This is the negation of the negation' – socialist revolution, which is the result of 'the centralisation of the means of production and the socialisation of labour' brought about by 'the action of the immanent laws of capitalist production itself'.[58]

Let us note that Marx does not make the claim that the economic breakdown of capitalism is inevitable; nor, as we saw is Marx's theory of crises a theory of collapse. But Chapter 32 of *Capital* does assert that the proletarian revolution is inevitable, arising 'with the inexorability of a natural process'. This statement is not justified by any detailed argument in *Capital* or elsewhere. Its roots, surely, lie in the teleological structure of the hegelian dialectic, with its three moments necessarily passing over into each other – immediate identity (petty production), self-estrangement (capitalism), identity restored and enriched (socialism). Here lies the answer to the second question posed at the beginning of this section: the notion, so prevalent in marxist thought, that the socialist revolution is inevitable arises from the transposition into historical materialism of the hegelian dialectic. For the latter involves the proposition that the outcome of the process is implicit in its starting point. It follows that any individual moment of the process is in itself of little significance, since it counts only insofar as it contributes to the total process ('the truth is the whole'), but the outcome of that process is pre-determined – it has been settled in advance by the structure of first and second negation. In so far as marxism shares the structure of Hegel's speculative Logic (and it is possible to do so without making explicit programmatic statements about the 'dialectics of nature'), with its circular, teleological structure, it is in constant danger of falling into a vulgar evolutionism, in which a series of modes of production succeed each other 'with the inexorability of a natural process'.

The result is well described by Walter Benjamin in the first of his 'Theses on the Philosophy of History':

> The story is told of an automaton constructed in such a way that it could play a winning game of chess, answering every move of an opponent with a countermove. A puppet in Turkish attire and with a hookah in its mouth sat before a chess board placed on a large table. A system of mirrors created the illusion that this table was transparent on all sides. Actually, a little hunchback who was an expert chess player sat inside and guided the puppet's hands by means of strings. One can imagine a philosophical counterpart to this device. The puppet called 'historical materialism' is to win all the time. It can easily be a match for anyone if it enlists the services of theology, which today, as we know, is wizened and has to be kept out of sight.[59]

This picture is not unfamiliar: it can be applied to Kautsky, Plekhanov and the marxism of the Second International, to Stalin and his followers, to orthodox trotskyism, all of which conceive revolution as the inevitable outcome of the historical process. Theology becomes teleology, immanent in history. Nor are the 'classics' free from this evolutionism. To take Marx and Engels themselves, apart from the example already cited, there is their well-documented tendency to conceive of revolutionary consciousness as the inevitable result of a linear process that takes the working class from economic struggles to the seizure of power; to imagine that national differences will be effected by the development of the world economy; to predict that the oppression of women will be decisively undermined by the involvement of women in wage-labour.[60]

The contradiction in Marx is not, as Colletti believes that between the philosopher and the scientist, but that arising from the co-presence within the same discourse of a secularised theology deriving from Hegel and of a mode of analysis that is, as we have seen, radically non-teleological in the manner in which it conceptualises relations of production. Therefore Althusser is completely justified in arguing that marxism must criticise and reject the teleological structure of the hegelian dialectic and replace it with that of 'a process without a subject' in which history has no pre-determined origin or outcome,[61] even if his version of the dialectic is defective. In the following chapter we shall attempt to clarify the concept of relations of production before, in Chapter 8, discussing the uses of this concept in dealing with the problems of contemporary marxist theory.

6 Relations of Production

No discussion of historical materialism in Britain today can avoid confrontation with the arguments of two recent contributions to the subject – *Pre-Capitalist Modes of Production* by Barry Hindess and Paul Hirst and *Karl Marx's Theory of History* by G. A. Cohen. Both books are in their way highly ambitious attempts to state the basic concepts of historical materialism from opposed standpoints and in very different idioms – the first a key-work of post-althusserian marxism heavily influenced by the 'revolution of language' sketched in Chapter 2 of this volume, in retrospect a stepping stone to the authors' openly 'revisionist' 'auto-critique', *Mode of Production and Social Formation*, the second defending 'an old-fashion historical materialism', very close to Kautsky and Plekhanov, applying 'those standards of clarity and rigour which distinguish twentieth century analytical philosophy'.[1] I cannot hope here to match the authors' scope or their capacity for detailed argument, but shall merely attempt to elucidate Marx's concept of relations of production and draw out its consequences.

Let us start by considering the following much-quoted passage from *Capital* volume 3, one of Marx's most important definitions of relations of production:

The specific economic form, in which unpaid surplus-labour is pumped out of the direct producers, determines the relationship between rulers and ruled, as it grows out of production itself and, in turn, reacts upon it as a determining element. Upon this, however, is founded the entire formation of the economic community which grows out of the production relations themselves, thereby simultane-

ously its specific political form. It is always the direct
relationship of the owners of the conditions of production
to the direct producers – a relation always naturally corresponding to a definite stage in the development of the
methods of labour and thereby its social productivity –
which reveals the innermost secret of the entire social
structure, and with it the political form of the relation of
sovereignty and dependence, in short, the corresponding
specific form of the state.²

Let us note some of the elements of this statement. Relations
of production are relations of exploitation – 'the specific
economic form in which unpaid surplus-labour is pumped out
of the direct producers'. Secondly, the social formation as a
whole – 'the entire social structure' – and in particular 'the
specific form of the state' can be understood only in terms of
these relations. Thirdly, these relations 'always naturally'
correspond 'to a definite stage in the development of the
methods of labour and thereby its social productivity'.

The third element poses the problem of the nature of the
'correspondence' between production relations and productive forces. To begin with, what are the productive forces?
Marx's only extended discussion of this concept is in *Capital*,
volume 1, where he analyses the labour-process, 'purposeful
activity aimed at the production of use-values':

It is the universal condition for the metabolic interaction
between man and nature, the ever-lasting nature-imposed
condition of human existence, and it is therefore independent of every form of that existence, or rather it is common
to all forms of society in which human beings live.

'The simple elements of the labour-process are, (1) purposeful activity, that is work itself, (2) the object on which that work
is performed, and (3) the instruments of that work'.³ Althusser's general discussion of the concept of practice, which is
based on Marx's analysis of the labour-process, draws out one
very important aspect of this analysis, namely that it conceives
production as a process of transformation in which a raw
material is worked up into a use-value by means of the
combination of 'work' and 'the instruments of that work'. It is

an emphatically materialist conception of production, in which heterogeneous elements are brought together in order to transform nature. A second aspect which Althusser brings out is that the productive forces should not be conceived of as an unorganised collection of the elements listed above but rather as a structured combination of these elements, what he calls the 'technical relations of production'.[4]

This discussion has not, however, clarified the nature of the relation between the productive forces thus understood and the relations of production. In what sense do the latter 'correspond' to the former? The traditional answer offered by evolutionist marxism, whether of the Second International or of the (stalinist) Third International, is that there is a linear causal chain linking the productive forces, the relations of production and the ideologico-political superstructure. This claim is to be found in Kautsky and Stalin, it can claim some support in Marx's (1859) Preface to *A Contribution to the Critique of Political Economy* and is defended at length by G. A. Cohen. Cohen is concerned to justify two claims:

(a) The productive forces tend to develop throughout history (the Development Thesis).
(b) The nature of the production relations of a society is explained by the level of development of its productive forces (the Primacy Thesis proper).[5]

Now the problem with the second thesis is that of how to determine the 'level of development' of the productive forces independently of the relations of production. The obvious answer to this question, would seem to be that this level is given by the level of productivity of labour. But to establish the productivity of labour for a social formation as a whole rather than any specific productive activity poses the problem of how to aggregate different use-values and different concrete labours and to compare them over time. We are interested in the relation between the total social labour and the total product of labour. But what measure can we adopt to arrive at these sums? In capitalism the problem is solved practically because the equivalence of different concrete labours and different use-values is established through the process of competition, as we saw in the last chapter. But this is not a measure that abstracts from the relations of production – on the contrary. Moreover the critique of neo-classical economics by Piero Sraffa and his followers has shown that there is no neutral technique for aggregrating the different use-values composing capital without invoking social relations (in this case those of distribution – in particular the rate of interest). Cohen attempts to get round this problem as follows:

> The development of the productive forces may be identified with the growth in the surplus they make possible, and this in turn may be identified with the amount of the day that remains after the labouring-time required to maintain the producers has been subtracted.[6]

In what way this measure can possibly be regarded as independent of the relations of production is beyond me. Can the ratio between necessary and surplus labour be defined without reference to the relations of production? Surely not. It is not simply that Marx states, as is well-known, that 'the determination of the value of labour-power contains a historical and moral element',[7] it is that the level of necessary labour and hence the size of the surplus-product cannot be established without reference to (1) whether or not the direct producers own and control the means of production, (2) if not, the nature of their relation to those who do own the means of production, (3) the balance of forces between exploiters and exploited at any given time.

Cohen, therefore, cannot get off square one, and the detailed elaboration of his argument is undermined by the defects involved in its most basic concepts. The other principal claim which he advances, namely, the development thesis, in conjunction with the proposition that 'a given level of productive forces is compatible only with a certain type, or certain types, of economic structure' and the primacy thesis, entails the proposition that 'forces select structures according to their capacity to promote development'.[8] Social revolutions, it seems, merely register the subterranean development of the productive forces. The 'standards of clarity and rigour' Cohen applies to marxism merely serve to highlight the inadequacy of one version of marxism.

Perhaps, however, this version is Marx's, as Cohen claims.

Here we need to distinguish between what the discourse of *Capital* in strict logic permits Marx to claim and the sweeping generalisations he sometimes offers. As we saw in the last chapter, Marx's theory of crises does not imply the inevitable breakdown of capitalism, nor does he offer any alternative mechanism which will bring about proletarian revolution 'with the inexorability of a natural process' (nor does Cohen: on the basis of his two theses he merely posits the inevitability of revolution without attempting to determine, even in the most general terms, the conditions of its occurrence). The 'primacy thesis', as stated by Marx, for example in the 1859 Preface, reflects in part the presence of hegelian categories in his discourse, and the consequent tendencies towards evolutionism which we discussed in the previous chapter. It also reflects the influence of Adam Smith and the Scottish historical school, who conceived of the different stages of historical evolution as the effects of different forms of the division of labour. Now 'the division of labour' is an ambiguous concept: it can be taken to denote either social or technical relations, either relations of production or forms of cooperation in the labour-process – or both together. In *The German Ideology*, the first explicit development of the main propositions of historical materialism, Marx, under the influence this earlier 'materialist interpretation of history', tends to equate social and technical relations.[9] It is not surprising that this work contains many of the most emphatic formulations of the 'primacy' thesis.

In *Capital*, by contrast, Marx conceives of the relations and forces of production as forming an articulated whole. Thus the capitalist process of production is the unity of labour-process and valorisation-process (i.e. process of the self-expansion of capital) in which the latter is dominant. Hindess and Hirst are right to argue that the relations of production are 'the primary element in the concept of mode of production' since

> the concept of a determinate labour-process is sufficient to define a technical differentiation of functions between the agents of production, but it is impossible to deduce a determinate division of social labour from these functional differences.[10]

Modes of production can be distinguished only on the basis of the relations of production they involve. The forces of production are not an independent variable and can be determined only on the basis of the social relations within which they are organised. Those, such as Sebastiano Timpanaro, a philologist much in vogue among some British marxists in recent years, who interpret Marx's materialism as involving the primacy of physical and biological factors in social life, are regressing to the reductive materialism of d'Holbach and La Mettrie. The distinctive nature of Marx's discourse, wherein its originality lies, derives from the concept of the relations of production which are *both* social and material, as we shall see.

None of this should be taken to license the inversion of the 'primacy thesis', namely the dissolution of the productive forces into the relations of production. Charles Bettelheim's *Class Struggles in the USSR*, for example, seeks to prove that the construction of socialism is possible *independent* of the level of development of the productive forces. It is true that Marx showed that the transformation of the labour-process involved in the establishment of mass manufacturing industry depended upon the 'formal subsumption of labour under capital' – i.e. the establishment of capitalist relations of production.[11] But it does not follow that any set of relations of production is compatible with any form of organisation of the labour-process – feudal social relations with assembly-line production – nor that (to turn to the case discussed by Bettelheim) the transition to socialism may take place in grossly unfavourable material conditions. Bettelheim, in seeking to provide theoretical and empirical justification for maoism of cultural-revolution vintage lapses into radical idealism and voluntarism quite alien to Marx.[12] If the level of development of the productive forces cannot be determined independently of social relations it nevertheless acts as a constraint upon or stimulus to changes in the relations of production. The relation of correspondence between forces and relations of production does not involve the causal primacy of either term but rather their mutual presupposition.

RELATIONS OF PRODUCTION

These remarks should suffice to absolve Marx of any charge of technological determinism. The concept of relations of production involves a transformation of the concepts of the economic and of the social. Of the economic, since for Marx the labour-process as the purely technical process of producing use-values, always takes place within a set of social relations. Of the social, since it is 'the specific economic form, in which unpaid surplus-labour is pumped out of the direct producers' which 'reveals the innermost secret of the social structure'. Let us now seek to clarify further the concept of relations of production.

Some passages in Marx, especially his discussions of fetishism, encourage us to conceive of social relations in general and the relations of production in particular as inter-subjective relations, as 'social relations between men'. That this is not the case, and that relations between individuals presuppose a prior relation between individuals and the means of production should be clear from the following passage, where Marx is criticising those like John Stuart Mill who conceive of the distribution of income as the primordial social reality:

> Before distribution can be the distribution of products, it is: (1) the distribution of the instruments of production, and (2), which is a further specification of the same relation, the distribution of the members of the society among the different kinds of production. (Subsumption of the individuals under specific relations of production.) The distribution of products is evidently only a result of this distribution, which is comprised within the process of production itself and determines the structure of production. To examine production while disregarding this internal distribution within it is obviously an empty abstraction.[13]

This passage is highly important. First, it asserts the priority of production over distribution and consumption. Secondly, it rejects the technical conception of production as the labour-process *tout court* (such a conception is shared by both classical and neo-classical economics; the difference between these two schools depends on whether they take the distribution of income or the exchange-ratios of goods as the starting point for economic analysis) – production treated in isolation from the *social relations* of production is 'an empty abstraction'. Thirdly, these relations involve essentially an 'internal distribution', namely, the distribution of the means of production, and, following from this, the 'subsumption of the individuals under specific relations of production'.

Packed into this notion of 'subsumption' is, I think, two elements. First, it involves the concept presupposed by the labour theory of value of the mechanism necessary in any mode of production determining the allocation of social labour to various productive activities – 'the distribution of the members of the society among the different kinds of production'. The subordination of this mechanism to the distribution of the means of production serves to rule out any interpretation of the law of value as a purely technical mechanism independent of social relations.[14]

Second, this 'subsumption' involves the constitution of social classes. The nature of classes in a given social formation depends upon their antagonistic relation, which itself is determined by the distribution of the means of production, 'the direct relationship of the owners of the conditions of production to the direct producers'. It is this 'internal distribution' involved in the process of production itself which determines the mode of appropriation of surplus-labour in the social formation concerned and thereby the nature of class relations in that society. This interpretation implies acceptance of the traditional marxist definition of class as depending essentially on the individual's relation to the means of production. This definition has come under much attack in recent years both from althusserian marxists such as Nicos Poulantzas and humanist marxists such as Edward Thompson, who have argued that ideological and political determinations should be included in the definition of class. We saw in Chapter 3 the arbitrary and subjectivist conclusions this position led Poulantzas in his discussion of the 'new petty bourgeoisie'. More generally, as Frank Parkin pointed out, 'the introduction of political and ideological criteria do not have the effect of rounding out the preceding analysis so much as displacing it altogether',[15] of setting the marxist theory of classes loose from any anchorage in production relations and thereby effacing the demarcation between marxism and weberian sociology, which explains class relations by means of power relations. Nor does the traditional marxist approach entail economic reductionism. As G. A. Cohen puts it,

> We are at liberty to define class, with more or less (if not, perhaps, 'mathematical') precision, by reference to production relations, without inferring, as Thompson says we are then bound to do, that the culture and consciousness of a class may be readily deduced from its objective position within production relations.[16]

The core-element of the concept of relations of production involves the mode of appropriation of surplus-labour and the 'internal distribution' of the means of production corresponding to it. Hindess and Hirst's discussion in *Pre-Capitalist Modes of Production* is very helpful. They argue that every mode of production, even primitive communism, involves the existence of surplus-labour, but that classes arise where the distribution of the means of production involves the separation of the direct producers from the means of production and therefore the appropriation of surplus-labour by the owners of the means of production. This separation depends upon, not the legal property rights of the owners of the means of production, but their effective possession of these means. In the feudal mode of production, where the labour-process is in the first instance under the control of the direct producers, the landowner's legal title to the land endows him with the right to exclude the direct producers from his property; whether he succeeds in translating this 'right of exclusion' into effective possession, i.e. sufficient control of the process of production to appropriate the surplus-product, depends upon a process of class struggle where the landowners' access to the means of ideological and political domination is of crucial importance in reinforcing the legal title. In the capitalist mode of production, by contrast, the capitalist is in effective possession of the means of production because, not only is he legal owner, but also the labour-process can take place only under his control, given that only he is in a position to bring together workers and means of production in the appropriate quantities.[17]

It follows that this well-known passage from *Capital* can be accepted only with qualification:

> In all forms in which the direct labourer remains the 'possessor' of the means of production and the labour conditions necessary for the production of his subsistence, the property relationship must spontaneously appear as a direct relation of lordship and servitude, so that the direct producer is not free.... Under these conditions the surplus-labour for the nominal owner of the land can only be extorted from them [the direct producers – AC] by other than economic means.[18]

This passage should not be taken to imply, as Perry Anderson argues, that 'the "superstructures" of kinship, religion, law or the state necessarily enter into the constitutive structure of the mode of production in pre-capitalist social formations'.[19] Hindess and Hirst's formulation seems closer to Marx's general approach, since it stresses the explanatory primacy of the relations of production: '*The feudal economy supposes the intervention of another instance* [i.e. the state – AC] *in order to make the condition of feudal exploitation possible*'. However,

> the political/legal instance is limited in its intervention to the determination and defence of property rights in land. The subsumption of the direct producer [under feudal relations of exploitation – AC] has been derived only in the first instance from the monopoly ownership of the land, from the *right of exclusion*. Subsumption rests on economic control.[20]

The danger of Anderson's formulation is that it conflates feudal (and other pre-capitalist) relations of production with their ideological and political conditions of existence, rather than explaining the nature, form and mode of operation of these conditions on the basis of the relations of production.

This discussion is important because of the persistent tendency in recent marxist work to identify the relations of production with political and ideological relations of domination. This interpretation, designed to rescue marxism from evolutionism, succeeds in doing so only at the price of evacuating its specific content. It is subscribed to by otherwise very diverse schools.

First, there is the 'capital-logic' approach, originating in Germany and represented in Britain especially by the work of John Holloway and Sol Picciotto. A distinctive feature of this school is the application of the theory of fetishism to the analysis of the capitalist state. 'It is a peculiarity of capitalist society', Holloway and Picciotto write, 'that social relations appear not as what they are (relations of class domination), but "assume a fantastic form different from their reality"'.[21] One case of such a 'fantastic form' is the capitalist state, which assumes an autonomy from the economy because here the appropriation of surplus-labour is secured, not by 'extra-economic means', i.e. direct coercion, as in feudal social formations, but by means of the exchange of commodities. Hence the fragmentation of social relations into the economic and the political:

> The economic and political should not be seen as the base which determines the political superstructure, but rather the economic and political are both forms of social relations, forms assumed by the basic relation of class conflict in capitalist society, the capital relation; forms whose separate existence springs, both logically and historically, from the nature of that relation.

'The "logic of capital"', therefore, 'is nothing but the expression of class struggle in capitalist society'.[22] A rather similar view is taken by the Italian 'workerist' school, which tends to conceive of the totality of social life as a reflection of the conflict between capital and labour within the process of production.[23]

Nicos Poulantzas, in his last book, *State, Power, Socialism* moves close to this position. No doubt motivated by awareness of the 'formalism' of *Political Power and Social Class*, its tendency to conceive of modes of production as differing combinations of invariant elements,[24] and perhaps influenced by the 'capital-logic' school, Poulantzas came to see the solution to the problem of economic determination as involving the equation of relations of production and relations of domination. This is already implicit in his claim in *Classes in Contemporary Capitalism* that ideological and political criteria enter into the determination of classes. It is explicitly stated in his last book, where, deeply influenced by Foucault, Poulantzas includes under 'relations of power' both 'economic exploitation' and 'political-ideological domination and subordination' and even asserts that *'relations of power do not exhaust class relations* and may go a certain way beyond them'.[25]

Interestingly, Edward Thompson, self-appointed hammer of the althusserians, adopts a rather similar approach in *The Poverty of Theory*. He argues that in the *Grundrisse*, and to some extent in *Capital*, Marx constructed an 'anti-Political Economy' sharing the same premisses as classical political economy, and in particular conceiving the economy as a self-reproducing mechanism. The result is a tendency to conflate mode of production and social formation, capital and capitalism, the failure by most of Marx's followers to grasp that 'the whole society comprises many activities and relations (of power, of consciousness, sexual, cultural, normative) which are not the concern of political economy, which have been *defined out of* political economy, and for which it has no terms'. *Capital* 'remains a study of the logic of capital, not of capitalism, and the social and political dimensions of the history, the wrath, and the understanding of the class struggle arise from a region independent of the closed system of economic logic'. The defects of Marx's discourse opened the door to stalinism and to 'althusserianism, . . . stalinism reduced to the paradigm of theory'. Thompson's alternative is a marxism based upon the empirical study of society as whole, which finds a place for experience, for struggle and for 'the moral and affective consciousness' – all the elements excluded by *Capital* and by orthodox marxism.[26]

Andre Glucksmann goes much further. He argues that workers' resistance is absent from *Capital*, which 'deals with management strategy and it alone'. This approach reflects the totalitarian will to power secreted within marxist discourse:

The image of the industrial hierarchy [in *Capital* – AC],

involves a strategic project, not a descriptive truth, it does
not seek to correspond to reality, it seeks to make reality
correspond to it by reducing to infinity workers' resistance.

Glucksmann's proof of this claim?

> By describing the domination of the earth and of man as if it
> were accomplished and completed, by decreeing 'all power
> to capital' as absolute law of the 'old world', Marx puts into
> orbit the stake of the epoch: all power.[27]

Gluksmann's ravings, which would make earlier theorists of
totalitarianism such as Karl Popper and J. L. Talmon blench,
are endorsed by Foucault and his associates. Thus Francois
Ewald describes *La cuisiniere et le mangeur des hommes*, in which
Glucksmann deduces the Gulag from Plato and Marx, as a
confirmation of the 'theses of *Discipline and Punish*'. He goes on
to argue that relations of power subsume relations of production:

> The despotism of capital cannot be explained by its exclu-
> sive need for surplus-value, no more than by the resistance
> of the exploited, since the workshop is already and indissoci-
> ably disciplinary, since it presupposes and effectuates the
> setting in place of this new technology for investing and
> subjecting bodies; subjection which is thus not the effect of
> capital, but which the capitalist mode of production, in-
> versely, presupposes.

In other words,

> Relations of power are constitutive of the mode of produc-
> tion, far from being an effect; they are its heart; and if the
> infrastructure of capitalist society is certainly situated at the
> level of production, the latter is more political than
> economic.[28]

So, far from the disciplinary society being a production of the
development of capitalism, as some passages in *Discipline and
Punish* might lead one to suppose,[29] capitalist relations of
production presuppose the disciplinary technology of power.

CLASS STRUGGLE AND CRISIS

Now of course it is true that relations of production *involve* relations of power. Marx writes that 'in the society where the capitalist mode of production prevails, anarchy in the social division of labour and despotism in the manufacturing division of labour mutually condition each other' and that 'capitalist direction' of the production process, even if in content it partially arises from the technical necessities involved in any labour-process, 'in form . . . is purely despotic'.[30]

It is, however, a serious error to seek to *reduce* the relations of production to relations of power. The position of authority enjoyed by capital is not somehow the primordial fact to be grasped in analysing the capitalist mode of production. On the contrary, this position derives from the 'internal distribution' of the means of production 'which is comprised within the process of production itself and determines the structure of production'. The fact that capital is dominant within the process of production rises from the capitalists' effective possession of the means of production and the workers' resulting need to sell their labour-power to capital. Marx takes some trouble to show how the extraction of surplus-value within the process of production not only valorises capital but also ensures that the worker remains propertyless. 'The worker always leaves the process in the same state as he entered it – a personal source of wealth, but deprived of any means of making that wealth a reality for himself':

Capitalist production therefore reproduces in the course of its own process the separation between labour-power and the conditions of labour. It thereby reproduces and perpetuates the conditions under which the worker is exploited. It incessantly forces him to sell his labour-power and enables the capitalist to purchase labour-power in order that he may enrich himself . . . it produces and reproduces the capital-relation itself; on the one hand the worker, on the other the wage-labourer.[31]

Furthermore, the 'despotism' within the factory and the 'anarchy' of competition are not merely two juxtaposed and unrelated aspects of the capitalist mode of production. The particular imperatives which govern the capitalist process of production are enforced upon individual capitals through competition. As we saw in Chapter 5, 'the influence of individual capitals on one another has the effect precisely that they must conduct themselves as *capital*'.[32] The drive to accumulate, indeed the drive to extract surplus-value itself, arise from the fact that individual capitals must match and strive to surpass the levels of productivity reached by their rivals or risk seeing themselves forced out of business. Therefore,

> the inner law enforces itself through their competition, their mutual pressure upon each other, whereby the deviations are mutually cancelled. Only as an inner law, *vis-a-vis* the individual agents, as a blind law of Nature, does the law of value exert its influence here and maintain the social equilibrium of production among its accidental fluctuations.[33]

It is essential to grasp the irreducible role of the sphere of competition, of 'many capitals' in ensuring that individual capitals assume the characteristics of 'capital in general', if we are to avoid either essentialism or nietzscheanism. In the first case, the drive to accumulate is made true of capital by definition (this is the style of argument according to which this or that tendency is 'contained' in the concept of capital). In the second, the drive to accumulate is merely a manifestation of the primordial will to power.

The issue can be brought into sharper focus if we consider its implications for the theory of crises. The 'capital-logic' school, in line with their tendency to treat 'many capitals' as the mere phenomenal expression of 'capital in general', claim that economic crises are the product of the struggle between capital and labour. Thus Holloway and Picciotto write that 'the tendency of the rate of profit to fall ... is merely the economic expression of a process of class struggle'.[34] This sounds very revolutionary, as does the similar statement by Poulantzas that 'the falling tendency [sic] is ultimately nothing but the expression of popular struggles against exploitation'.[35] These claims can only mean something like the following: workers' resistance to exploitation causes a fall in the rate of surplus-value and hence the rate of profit, and it is this rising share of workers in the national income which underlies economic crises.[36]

Leaving aside the empirical evidence for this theory, which is limited,[37] it is clear that it is quite different from Marx's. He writes:

> The tendency of the rate of profit to fall is bound up with a tendency for the rate of surplus-value to rise, hence with a tendency for the rate of labour-exploitation to rise. Nothing is more absurd, for this reason, than to explain the fall in the rate of profit by a rise in the rate of wages, although this may be the case by way of an exception. . . . The rate of profit does not fall because labour becomes less productive, but because it becomes more productive. Both the rise in the rate of surplus-value and the fall in the rate of profit are but specific forms through which growing productivity of labour is expressed under capitalism.

The same increase in the productivity of labour which reduces the portion of the working day devoted to replacing the value of labour-power and thus increases the rate of surplus-value (the ratio of surplus-value to variable capital) also increases the organic composition of capital and thereby causes the rate of profit (the ratio of surplus-value to total capital) to fall. The impulse behind rising labour productivity is provided by competition, which forces individual capitals to innovate or die.[38]

Of course this theory is not without its difficulties, which have caused much controversy in recent years.[39] It is clear, however, that any explanation of crises in terms of rising wages and a falling rate of exploitation can find little justification in *Capital*. In volume 1 of that work, Marx argues, against Ricardo and his followers, that 'the rate of accumulation is the independent, not the dependent variable; the rate of wages is the dependent, not the independent variable'. Furthermore, 'the general movements of wages are exclusively regulated by the expansion and contraction of the industrial reserve army' which in turn depends on the process of capital accumulation, in particular the tendency for the organic composition of capital to rise, expelling workers from production, and the cyclical movements of boom and slump.[40] Therefore, from Marx's standpoint, as Rosdolsky puts it,

> it is simply not the case that labour and capital represent two autonomous powers, whose respective 'shares' in the national product merely depend on their respective strengths; rather, labour is subject to the economic power of capital from the outset, and its 'share' must always be conditional on the 'share' of capital.[41]

More generally, it is an error to suppose that Marx treated the class struggle as the primordial phenomenon of social life. 'The history of all hitherto existing society is the history of class struggles', states the *Communist Manifesto*,[42] but this should not be taken in the sense given it by Althusser in the early 1970s, namely, 'the class struggle is the motor of history'.[43] The class struggle is not the *explanans* but the *explanandum*, it is the phenomenon which itself requires explanation, not the principle in terms of which explanations are made. The task of historical materialism is to uncover the objective determinants of the class struggle – namely, the relations of production, and in particular the distribution of the means of production, on which the mode of appropriation of surplus-labour depends. While it is of course true that 'exploitation is already class struggle', as Althusser puts it,[44] it is more than that, since its nature is determined by this 'internal distribution' within the process of production. To return to the case in point, Marx's theory of crises serves to specify the complex objective conditions – not only the relations of exploitation but the competitive struggle between capitals – which provide the objective framework within which the struggle between capital and labour unfolds, not to reduce all social relations to mere expressions of this struggle.[45] Workers' struggles may intensify economic crises and make their resolution more difficult, they do not cause them. The tendency on the part of so many contemporary marxists to make the class struggle the determining element of the historical process is a form of voluntarism, which accords primacy to the autonomous wills of the classes concerned. It reminds one of what Spinoza said about the freedom of the will – that it was 'the asylum of ignorance'. Evolutionism and voluntarism are branches of the same reductionist tree.

A LITTLE SOCIOLOGY

The dangers involved in according primacy to relations of power are most obvious in the case of Foucault and his school. In so far as their genealogical method involves treating the whole of reality as a manifestation of the will to power, as Deleuze has argued from *Nietzsche et la Philosophie* onwards and as Francois Ewald explicitly asserts – 'there is nothing in the material or immaterial order which is or can be foreign to power'[46] – it rests upon anthropomorphic and idealist premisses. Nietzsche seems to have intended the concepts of the will to power and the eternal recurrence of the same (which denies the possibility of either an origin of things or an end of history) as at least in part scientific hypotheses to remedy the defects of the purely mechanical explanations characteristic of the physical sciences of his day.[47] In Deleuze's case especially they have become metaphysical cornerstones of a romantic philosophy of life.

Even if we simply treat the concept of power as it is understood by Foucault as a hypothesis to guide historical studies, the heuristic of a research programme, difficulties cannot be avoided.[48] Consider Deleuze's discussion of the 'diagram' of 'power-knowledge'. It is, he says, an 'abstract machine', 'immanent in the social field', which 'can only effectuate its function in concrete machines which give forms to this function, and can only work over its material in concrete machines which shape this material into qualified substances'. Examples of concrete machines in the disciplinary diagram are schools, prisons, etc.

> Power, relations of power are everywhere in this network. Power dilates throughout the abstract machine, it contracts in every concrete machine. In the social field, it assures at the same time the reciprocal differentiation and adjustment, the heterogeneity and the correlation of forms of content and of expression, of pregnant material systems and dominant enunciative regimes, of non-discursive and

discursive formations, of fields of perception and of knowledge.[49]

It is difficult not to see the 'diagram' as a concept akin to
Kant's transcendental unity of apperception, an instance itself
outside experience which must however be presupposed,
since it renders our experience both of an objective world and
of our own inner life possible. Analogously, the 'diagram' is
the transcendental unity of the social body, determining the
form taken by individual power-relations ('concrete
machines') and rendering possible certain forms of knowledge.[50] One problem is then how to avoid transforming
power from a multiplicity of relations into a unified substance
ramifying itself in the different aspects of social life, in the
way that, according to Kant, metaphysics committed the
'paralogisms of pure reason', treating the transcendental
unity of apperception as, not the necessary presupposition of
experience, but the soul, a substance accessible within experience. Foucault and Deleuze, in treating 'power-knowledge' as
an 'abstract machine' dilating and contracting throughout the
social field, seem to have fallen into just such a metaphysical
paralogism.

Nor is it evident how historical change, in the sense of the
transition from one 'diagram' to another, takes place. Foucault
writes of the disciplines 'infiltrating' the earlier power-
relations,[51] but that is all. The picture he and his collaborators
imply without explicitly stating is that of a molecular process
of change in which a multiplicity of individual actions, often
involving consequences quite different from those intended,
interact to cause reorganisations and transformations of
'power-knowledge'. All this is rather like Karl Popper's
methodological individualism, which involves the principle of
the unintended consequences of individual actions. If the
agents of change differ – power-relations, not subjects – and
there is no 'hidden hand' guiding the process, Foucault like
Popper agree in treating social change as irreducibly
piecemeal.

Foucault also shares Popper's suspicion of collective action
designed to end exploitation and oppression once and for
all – in other words, of socialist revolution. For any action that
goes beyond the mere resistance of power to seek to overturn

it can only result, if successful, in a new 'diagram', one perhaps worse than the old. Hence Foucault's endorsement of Glucksmann – marxism, because its objective is social revolution through the conquest of political power, can only arrive at the Gulag. As Peter Dews points out, Foucault's claim that power is coextensive with the real in conjunction with his identification with the oppressed, his hostility to the status quo, 'leads inevitably towards the *Nouvelle Philosophie* conception of a pure essence of rebellion, which is neutralised as soon as it sets itself any positive goal'.[52]

At best this implies libertarianism, although libertarianism without any real basis or positive values. Foucault does write that 'against the apparatus of sexuality' which is one aspect of the modern 'power-knowledge' one must counterpose 'the body and its pleasures'.[53] Perhaps he has in mind Deleuze and Guattari's desiring production, in terms of which they judge specific regimes of social production.[54] If so, it seems as if an ahistorical essence somehow outside the supposedly all-pervasive relations of power is being posited. In that case, Foucault is merely re-instating the old utopian theme of the natural man whose instincts are repressed by civilisation – as they said in 1968, beneath the paving stones, the beach.[55] But if we do not take talk of the 'body and its pleasures' too seriously, then Poulantzas' questions are unanswerable: 'if power is always already there, ... *why should there ever be resistance? From where* would resistance come, *and how would it even be possible?*'[56]

Similar problems do not arise in Marx's case. Let us note first that he does not write workers' resistance out of *Capital*. On the contrary, 'the struggle between capital and the wage-labourer', he asserts, 'starts with the existence of the capital-relation itself'. Various forms of that struggle are analysed in *Capital* Volume 1, notably that leading to the limitation of the working day, 'the product of a protracted and more or less concealed civil war between the capitalist class and the working class'.[57] Workers' resistance is intrinsic to capitalist relations of production because these relations involve and depend upon exploitation, the extraction of surplus-labour from the direct producers. Here is a good example of how antagonisms are constitutive of the relations of production in class society – class struggle is inherent in the relations of production because they are relations of exploitation. Furthermore, Marx outlines the bases upon which workers' resistance takes place. The process of competition and the constant transformations of the labour-process it involves socialises the workforce, drawing it together in large units of production, and bringing into being a web of close connections between different productive activities – creating, in other words, what Marx calls 'the collective worker'. This process is also that through which the capitalist mode of production constantly tends to shift from the extraction of absolute surplus-value (based on lengthening the working day) to that of relative surplus-value (based on increasing the productivity of labour) – it is a process of increased exploitation as well as technological change. Workers are driven to resist this exploitation, but in particular forms – those dictated by the character of the labour-process, based on collective action and organisation. We shall have more to say about this in Chapter 8.

At worst Foucault's genealogy involves the reactionary neo-liberalism of Glucksmann and company – an irrationalist version of the identification of marxism and totalitarianism long ago made by Popper, Hayek and others. Most likely, however, is neither of the extremes – neither anarchism nor liberalism – but simply academicism. Foucault dismisses Derrida as the founder of a 'little pedagogy'.[58] But has he not himself fathered a 'little sociology'? Already his disciples are busy producing empirical studies of particular institutions – penal justice, the family, psychiatry, etc. No doubt these have their value. But is this what historical knowledge is to be reduced to? History does not become less theological (or less boring) if Benjamin's dwarf ensures the triumph of, not the level of development of the productive forces, but Power.

The superiority of marxism in the sense defended in this book over foucauldian genealogy seem to me evident. The concept of the relations of production, and the more definite concepts which may be constructed starting from it, offer a means to uncover the objective determinants of different struggles. Foucault, by making power and social relations co-extensive, not only rules out the possibility of genuine emancipation, but must ultimately rely upon an idealist metaphysic of the will to power. Furthermore, it is possible to suggest a crucial experiment between the two research programmes. Stalinism provides Foucault's heuristic with most of its attractions: the Gulag is both the logical culmination of marxism and the case it cannot explain. Many marxists have conceded half the argument by claiming that at the present stage of its development historical materialism cannot account for the Soviet Union. I shall try to show in Chapter 8 that there exists an analysis of the Soviet social formation which denies that the latter is socialist and is derived from the basic propositions and arguments of *Capital*. If I am right, then Foucault has very little to offer us compared with marxism.

THE LONELY HOUR OF THE LAST INSTANCE

One final issue needs to be considered in this chapter – the problem of economic determination or, as it is sometimes called, of base and superstructure. We have already seen how Althusser sought to accord relative autonomy to politics and ideology, leaving the economy determinant only 'in the last instance'. Followers of eurocommunism in Britain have used his arguments as part of a struggle against what they choose to call 'economism'. This term has long ceased to have the definite political meaning given it by Lenin, for whom 'economism' referred to tendencies which denied the proletariat its own autonomous political objectives, restricting it to the improvement of its material condition within the framework of capitalism. Today opposition to 'economism' has come to involve the adoption of a political strategy centred on the capture of the existing state apparatus rather than its destruction. The autonomy of the politico-ideological superstructure ceases to be relative and becomes absolute: thus Anthony Cutler, Barry Hindess, Paul Hirst and Athar Hussain claim that any attempt to account for social processes in terms of relations of production is 'economism'.

Rather than follow Althusser and his disciples down this road, I wish to reject their conceptualisation of the mode of production as a complex whole the nature of whose constituent elements – economic, political and ideological practice – does not change from one mode of production to another. One of the merits of the 'state-derivation' debate among German marxists has been to highlight the fact that the separation of the social whole where capitalist relations prevail into distinct and apparently autonomous instances is a *problem*, something which requires explanation, rather than a characteristic of all social formations (as the althusserians tend to assume). Thus, according to the 'capital-logic' school the existence of the capitalist state as a unified apparatus apparently independent of 'civil society' is to be explained by the fact that the distribution of social labour and the extraction of surplus labour is, in this mode of production, effected by the purchase and sale of commodities.[59] It is, therefore, illegitimate for Poulantzas to argue that a 'relatively autonomous political instance' is an invariant element of all (class) modes of production. As Ernesto Laclau puts it,

> What happens is that the separation between the economic and political has not been verified in modes of production prior to capitalism and, therefore, the discrimination between economic and non-economic factors is an artificial operation which projects onto the previous mode of production a type of social rationality existing under capitalism.[60]

The concept of relations of production, understood as the distribution of the means of production and mode of appropriation of surplus-labour is prior to that of the different 'levels' or 'instances' that a given mode of production may involve. Prior in the discursive sense that the nature of the relations of production explains the internal organisation of the mode of production. It is, therefore, an error to identify the relations of production with the economic 'base'; on the contrary, the distinction between 'base' and 'superstructure' is not an invariant one – it is specific to certain modes of production and must be explained in terms of the relations of production defining them. Therefore, to write of ideological, political and economic conditions of existence of a given mode of production as if the former were external to the latter, as Hindess and Hirst do, is to invite a collapse into pluralism, i.e., into the denial of the explanatory primacy of the concept of relations of production. Which is, of course, what happened in their case.[61] The nature of the conditions of existence (at least in the sense of those normally included under the heading of the 'superstructure') of a given set of relations of production can be understood only on the basis of these relations.

This does sound like the wildest reductionism. And indeed the version of this argument to be found in the 'capital-logic' school *is* reductionist. For example, Simon Clarke writes:

> *The economic, political and ideological are forms which are taken by the relations of production.* Political and ideological relations are as much relations of production as are strictly economic forms of the social relations within which production takes place.[62]

Now either this is merely a verbal solution to the problem of economic determination, by dubbing the whole of the social formation relations of production, or it is reductionist. Indeed, the 'capital-logic' school tends, via the theory of fetishism, to effect a double reduction – of 'many capitals' to 'capital in general', and then of the social totality to 'capital in general'. All aspects of social life are treated as phenomenal expressions of the contradiction between capital and labour.

The relation between production relations and ideological/political/economic can no more be reduced, however, to that between phenomenon and essence than the relation, internal to the capitalist economy, between 'capital in general' and 'many capitals'. Because the relations of production determine the internal organisation of a mode of production – its form of articulation – it does not follow that this form is a mere deceptive surface appearance. To take the case of capitalism: the decisive characteristic of this mode of production is not that the state is autonomous here, but that the *economy* is. In other words, in the CMP the relations of production assume the form of an autonomous, self-regulating economy. The reasons for this are two fold: first, the appropriation of surplus-labour here takes the form of the purchase and sale of commodities, so that the extraction of surplus-value takes place automatically within the production process rather than requiring, as in the case of feudalism, the 'external' intervention of the nominal owner of the means of production to transform the labour-process into a process of exploitation;[63] second, the relation between the differing units of production and the distribution of labour and means of production across different sectors are secured through the purchase and sale of commodities and flows of money. The emergence of an autonomous state apparatus is merely the correlate of the autonomisation of the relations of production, disrupting the apparently 'organic' imbrication of economy and politics characteristic of pre-capitalist social formations (although, as we saw above, this imbrication is something that must be explained, not asserted).

This separation of the mode of production into distinct 'instances', although specific to capitalism and explicable only in terms of capitalist relations of production, is not the phenomenal expression of these relations. It is the form of articulation of the social whole peculiar to the capitalist mode of production. To describe it as phenomenal is to suggest (if the essence/phenomenon distinction is taken seriously) that those practices separated from the relations of production under capitalism – the superstructure – are somehow inessential. In reality, the contrary is true: the reproduction of capitalist relations of production would be impossible without the existence of a unified state apparatus monopolising the means of coercion. Poulantzas is right, therefore, to argue in *State, Power, Socialism* that '*the political field of the state* (as well as the sphere of ideology) *has always, in different forms, been present in the constitution and reproduction of the relations of production*'.[64] Maurice Godelier, drawing on his anthropological studies, argues that forms of articulation of social formations will vary according to the relations of production prevailing within them. In hunter–gatherer societies '*relations of kinship serve as relations of production*'. Therefore,

> the distinction between infrastructure and superstructure is not a distinction between institutions and instances, but between functions. It is only in *certain societies*, and *particularly in capitalist society, that this distinction between functions becomes a distinction between institutions*.[65]

We need to drive from marxism the idea of the economy as a substance acting on another substance, the superstructure, as well as that of the economy as an essence reflected in all the different aspects of social life. The corner-stone of historical materialism is the proposition that social formations are to be explained in terms of the relations of production prevailing within them. This is the thesis of the *explanatory primacy* of the relations of production. The concept of a particular set of relations of production provides the starting point for the analysis of given social formations. It forms the basis on which more definite concepts are constructed, rather like the way in which the concepts of the commodity, use-value, value, money, labour-power, etc., provide the starting point for the construction of the more concrete concepts and propositions of *Capital* Volumes 2 and 3. As in the case of the theory of value, our knowledge of specific modes of production and social formations involve a number of 'intermediary stages' irreducible to this starting point. Although this argument requires some clarification, which it will receive in the next chapter, I believe that it offers the basis of a non-reductionist version of the proposition on which Marx's basic claim to originality rests. It is the character of the *social* relations governing the *material* process of transforming nature – 'the direct relationship of the owners of the conditions of production to the direct producers' –and not the state, forms of consciousness or even the level of development of the productive forces 'which reveals the innermost secret of the entire social structure'. But before further clarification can be given to this statement we will have to desert the *terra firma* of historical materialism for the stormy waters of epistemology.

7 For and Against Epistemology

THE DENIAL OF IMMEDIATE KNOWLEDGE

One of the implications of the 'revolution of language' discussed in Chapter 2 was that our relation to reality is irremediably discursive. There is no such thing as the immediate, direct, intuitive contact between subject and object which for so many philosophers since Aristotle has provided the foundation of our knowledge of the world. Knowledge by acquaintance is a myth, all knowledge is knowledge by description, mediated, organised in discourse, connecting with 'things' only through 'words'. It is worth noting that this thesis is not specific to French philosophy – in some version it would be accepted by many English-speaking philosophers and therefore is not entailed merely by the particular theory of language originating from Saussure.

Ian Hacking has suggested that seventeenth century and contemporary English-speaking philosophy 'have the same structure but different content'. Where once ideas mediated between subject and object, now sentences play the same role:

> Ideas were once the objects of all philosophising, and were the link between the cartesian *ego* and the world external to it. Connections between ideas were expressed in mental discourse, and formed representations of reality in response to changes in the ego's experience and reflection. In today's discussion, public discourse has replaced mental discourse. . . . Sentences appear to have replaced ideas.[1]

This contrast is much too simple (as Hacking indeed acknowledges).[2] The 'revolution of language' has not simply substituted one intermediary between subject and object for another, leaving unchanged the two terms connected. The conception of language shared by figures as diverse as Levi-Strauss, Lacan, Derrida, Deleuze, Althusser, Barthes and Kristeva, is that of an autonomous process that is unhinged from reality (the 'floating' of the signifier, the 'sliding' of the signified under the signifier, the absence of any 'transcendental signified' prior to discourse) and which organises and at the same time cracks open the subject, reducing it to the status of a subordinate agency of this process, rather than the autonomous source of meaning.

There are analogies to this change in our conception of the nature and role of consciousness outside France. Ludwig Wittgenstein argued that it is impossible to construct a private language, a code accessible only to the individual subject himself; language is irremediably public and social and the description of private sensations is parasitic upon the observation of behaviour. Here again the cartesian subject is cracked open and drawn into a realm of discourse that transcends and exceeds it.[3]

I am especially concerned in this chapter with the epistemological implications of this changed understanding of the relation between thought and reality. In other words, what effect does the thesis that our knowledge is inherently discursive have on the rationality of the sciences? The commonplace notion of science is one that holds it to depend on the empirical character of the discourse in question – on the degree to which it is based on observation and experiment (this notion is, we should note, one shared by some marxists, for example, Della Volpe and Colletti).[4] But if all our knowledge is discursive, then this is true of the empirical data which supposedly lies at the foundation of the sciences. This data consists, not of 'hard' experiences somehow beyond discourse, but of *reports* of observations and experimental results that are recorded and stored in some discursive form (writing, film, magnetic tape etc.). There is no 'experience' which somehow closes the gap between discourse and the world. Karl Popper, a philosopher widely regarded as the author of a ruggedly empirical theory of the sciences, acknowledged this: the potential falsifiers of scientific theories are, according to him, basic *statements*, i.e. discursive entities, which describe observations, not the raw observations themselves.[5]

David-Hillel Ruben, in an interesting attempt to state and defend a materialist theory of knowledge, suggests that the denial of immediate knowledge is a 'banality', and his general discussion concentrates on the thesis that 'there is an objective realm, i.e. *some* objects essentially independent of all human activity' which thought merely reflects.[6] The weakness of his account is that it fails to take into consideration the following implication of the denial of immediate knowledge, which makes it very far from a 'banality'. If we are to avoid the neo-kantian doctrine that reality is essentially unknowable (and it is clear that Ruben would wish to avoid this conclusion), then it would seem that we require some method for determining whether which of two theories is a more accurate reflection of reality. But the denial of immediate knowledge closes off the possibility of any access to reality independent of discourse.

Just how damaging a point this is, is brought home by the late Imre Lakatos, the most outstanding of contemporary philosophers of science. He points out that once we admit that the 'empirical basis' of theories consists of 'factual' *statements*, then the 'falsificationist' model of science offered by Popper, according to which a theory is scientific only if it is falsifiable – i.e. if it contradicts certain 'empirical' basic statements, cannot be sustained:

> *No factual proposition can ever be proved from an experiment.*
> Propositions can only be derived from other propositions, they cannot be derived from facts: one cannot prove statements from experiences – 'no more than by thumping the table'. . . . If factual propositions are unprovable then they are fallible. If they are fallible then clashes between theories and factual propositions are not 'falsifications' but merely inconsistencies. . . . The demarcation between the soft, unproven 'theories' and the hard, proven 'empirical basis' is non-existent; *all* propositions of science are theoretical and, incurably, fallible.[7]

If an experimental result contradicts a higher-order theory then it is always admissible to save the theory by, for example revising the theories which determine our interpretation of the result. In this case, therefore, 'the clash is not "between theories and facts" but between two high-level theories: between an *interpretative* theory to provide the facts and an *explanatory* theory to explain them'. So, 'it is not that we propose a theory and Nature may shout NO; rather, we propose a maze of theories, and Nature may shout INCON-SISTENT'.[8]

CRITICS OF EPISTEMOLOGY

It is but a short step from the denial of immediate knowledge to questioning the possibility of *objective* knowledge. The objectivity of theoretical discourses depends upon the degree to which they approximate to the truth, where 'truth' is understood in its traditional sense as *adequatio rei et intellectus*, the correspondence of reality and thought. If we have no direct access to reality, how can we establish which, if any, of a set of competing theories is closest to the truth? Many contemporary philosophers have concluded that we cannot. This is part of the point of Derrida's critique of the 'transcendental signified'. Foucault and Deleuze's 'perspectivism' leads them in the same direction. The closest parallel to these thinkers in the English-speaking world is the 'epistemological anarchism' or 'dadaism' of Paul Feyerabend, for whom the very notions of science and truth represent a denial of the essential freedom of the human spirit, while T. S. Kuhn claims that the history of the sciences is that of a succession of incommensurable paradigms, conceptual frameworks each of which organises experience and guides experimentation without being intrinsically superior to its predecessors or successors.[9] Epistemology as a discipline is undermined by the rejection of objective knowledge, since it is a normative activity, evaluating discourses from the standpoint of their relation to the truth rather than merely concentrating on the historical question of the conditions under which they are produced. In other words, it is concerned with what Kant called 'the question of right (*quid juris*)' rather than 'the question of fact (*quid facti*)'.[10] In this chapter I wish to argue that both objective knowledge and therefore epistemology are possible *despite* the denial of immediate knowledge. I shall do so in the first instance by examining the arguments advanced *against* epistemology by Barry Hindess and Paul Hirst.

Epistemologies, they argue, typically distinguish between discourse and its objects. The latter is the real, or part of the real, yet its structure is such that it may be represented in discourse. Conversely, there is a particular level of discourse which has a privileged relation to the real. In the case of empiricist epistemologies this level is that of the basic statements which record observations. In the case of rationalist epistemologies, of which the prime example cited by Hindess and Hirst is *Reading Capital*, it is the internal structure of the discourse, its problematic. Discourses which are incompatible with this privileged level – for the empiricists metaphysical statements which cannot be empirically verified or falsified, for Althusser theoretical ideologies – must be rejected as unscientific. Only those statements compatible with the privileged level of discourse offer access to the real.

Hindess and Hirst argue that such an approach is untenable. It leads to 'an indefensible dogmatism in which predetermined conclusions govern our treatment of theoretical discourse'.[11] Furthermore, the denial of immediate knowledge implies that there is no realm of objects which exists prior to and independent of discourse but whose nature is such that they are representable in discourse:

> What is specified in theoretical discourse can only be conceived through that form of discourse (or another, critical or complementary discourse); it cannot be specified extra-discursively. The question of the 'reality of the external world' is not the issue. It is not a question of whether objects *exist* when we do not speak of them. *Objects of discourse do not exist.* The entities discourse refers to are constituted in and by it.[12]

This thesis – that 'the entities discourse refers to are constituted in and by it' – seems to derive from W. V. O. Quine's claim that our ontology consists in the entities presupposed by the sciences.[13] Following Russell, Quine argues that every definite description (for example, 'the King of France is bald') may be analysed into a statement of the following form: 'There is something which is the King of France and is bald and there is nothing else that is the King of

France and is bald'. Extending this analysis to the universal propositions of the sciences, Quine argues that 'to be assumed as an entity is, purely and simply, to be reckoned the value of a variable'. The variables in question are 'something', 'nothing', 'everything'; so, in the above example, 'the King of France' is a value of the variable 'something':

> We are convicted of a particular ontological presupposition if and only if, the alleged presuppositum has to be reckoned among the entities over which our variables range in order to render one of our affirmations true.[14]

The attraction of Quine's approach for Hindess and Hirst is that it does not treat ontology as designating a realm of being independent of discourse, but instead treats the objects referred to in discourse as entities constructed within and dependent upon discourse.

Having set discourse loose from its anchorage in the real, Hindess and Hirst go on to argue that there are no rational criteria which enable us to choose between discourses, although they may be examined from the point of view of their purely logical properties – their internal consistency and implications. However, the structure of discourses depends, not on any form of organisation internal to them such as Althusser's problematic or their relation to the real, but on the intervention of extra-discursive practices. So, for example,

> The order of discourse in the analysis of social relations and the connections between them is not given in the order of social relations themselves: it is a consequence of definite political ideologies and specific political objectives. The discursive primacy accorded to economic relations in marxism and more generally in socialist discourse cannot be conceived of as an effect of the ontological structure of reality. On the contrary it is an effect of a definite political ideology and a definite political objective, namely, the objective of a socialist transformation of capitalist relations of production.[15]

Thus theoretical ideology, in the sense given it by Althusser of a discourse governed by extra-discursive interests, has come to drive science out of the sphere of theoretical practice. Hindess and Hirst are to some extent reacting to their own hyper-rationalist excesses. In *Pre-Capitalist Modes of Production* they examine various analyses of pre-capitalist modes of production purely from the standpoint of their consistency with the marxist problematic:

> If the concept [of a pre-capitalist mode – AC] can be constructed in accordance with the general concept of mode of production then it is a valid concept of the marxist theory of modes of production. Otherwise the concept has no validity in terms of marxist theory.[16]

But there is more at stake than Hindess and Hirst's embarrassment at their youthful vagaries. In many cases epistemologies do function in the manner they describe, ruling out those discourses which do not conform to a certain pre-ordained pattern. For example, Ernst Mach rejected the general theory of relativity because it was incompatible with his epistemology, according to which reality is composed of simple, functionally related elements directly accessible in experience.[17] Closer to home, dialectical materialism in its traditional form is potentially a Science of Sciences banning discourses incompatible with it, since it characterises reality as possessing a certain basic structure which is exemplified in nature, history and thought. 'Diamat' was invoked to sanction lysenkoism and the assault on mendelian genetics, on the grounds that all theoretical discourses must conform to the 'laws of the dialectic'. Here we have what Dominique Lecourt calls 'a *normative* conception of the relationship between marxist philosophy and the sciences – a conception one of the logical conclusions of which is indeed the absurd theory of the "two sciences" '.[18] There is, as Lecourt points out, a weaker version of 'Diamat', which no longer demands that all discourses obey its prescriptions, but merely treats scientific discoveries as 'illustrations' of the 'laws of the dialectic', so that, for example, the complementarity principle in sub-atomic physics 'confirms' the unity of opposites. Here dialectical materialism ceases to be much of a threat and becomes instead banal, 'an evening-class philosophical pastiche', as Colletti put it.[19]

Lecourt (and Althusser) wish to reject the notion of epistemology as a normative discipline; it should be treated as a branch of historical materialism, dealing with the 'question of fact' – the conditions of production of theoretical discourses. At the same time, they would like to retain the distinction between sciences and theoretical ideologies.[20] This position is incoherent. To call a discourse scientific is, in Althusser's terms, to state that it provides access to reality in a manner which an ideology cannot. Such a move presupposes the existence of some general criterion in terms of which discourses may be evaluated as scientific or pseudo-scientific – in Popper's terms, a demarcation criterion. But Althusser, since he abandoned the old definition of dialectical materialism as the theory of theoretical practice, has denied that any such criterion exists. Internalising this criterion within historical materialism, so that the theory of ideology enables us to detect ideological discourses, only shifts the problem, since the scientificity of marxism is assumed. Hindess and Hirst seem far more consistent when they deny both epistemology and the science/ideology distinction.

DISCOURSE AND TRUTH

I now wish to offer a defence of objective knowledge and of epistemology. This defence is made from the standpoint of materialism, in the sense given the term by Lenin in *Materialism and Empirio-Criticism*, where he argues that 'the sole property of matter with whose recognition philosophical materialism is bound up is the property of *being an objective reality*, of existing outside the mind'.[21] Materialism thus understood does not commit us to any particular theory of the structure of matter (e.g. the three 'laws of the dialectic'). It is a purely epistemological doctrine, that sometimes known as 'realism', according to which reality exists independently of discourse. It is closely related to the traditional concept of truth as the correspondence of thought and reality.

I shall not here consider the objections raised against the correspondence theory of truth by some marxists – namely that it treats thought as the passive reflection of an unchanging reality. These objections have been dealt with very well by

David-Hillel Ruben and I have nothing to add to what he has
to say on this subject.[22] There is, however, a deeper difficulty
with this concept, which springs from the denial of immediate
knowledge: what sense is there in calling truth the correspondence of discourse and reality if we have no access to reality
except through discourse?

Let us try to clarify the issue by looking at Alfred Tarski's
semantic definition of truth, regarded by some – notably
Popper – as the rehabilitation of the classical theory of truth.
Take the following sentence – 'the grass is green' (1). On
Tarski's definition, ' "The grass is green" is true if and only if
the grass is green' (2). (2) seems utterly trivial until we realise
that the two sentences are in different languages. (1) belongs
to the 'object language', the language which is under consideration; (2), on the other hand, is a sentence of the 'metalanguage', whose peculiarity lies in the fact that it is particularly
concerned with what Tarski calls the semantics of the object
language, namely, 'the totality of considerations concerning
those concepts which, roughly speaking, express certain
connections between the expressions of a language and the
objects and states of affairs referred to by these expressions'.
The metalanguage, therefore, encompasses both the object
language and the entities to which it refers; it contains
both the expressions of the object language and expressions
(not to be found in the former) designating these expressions and their properties. The necessity for such a distinct language in which we talk about the language in question arises in part from certain paradoxes which arose in
the traditional theory of truth, and need not concern us
here.[23]

The obvious difficulty with this definition of truth is that it
seems to deal with the problem of the relation between
discourse and reality merely by the further proliferation of
discourse – the construction of a metalanguage. It is this sort
of consideration which leads Barry Hindess to write: 'Tarski's
theory tells us nothing about the relation of language to the
world and it certainly cannot legitimise any concept of truth as
correspondence with some extra-linguistic reality'.[24] Hindess
is, I think, wrong. Tarski's definition of truth is part of a
theory of semantics which, as we have seen, is concerned with
the relation between discourses and the entities to which they

refer. It is true that this relation is one that can be dealt with only in discourse, by means of a metalanguage, and we may also accept that the entities to which discourses refer are 'constituted in and by it', as Hindess and Hirst, following Quine, argue. This does not alter the fact that discourses do constantly posit the existence of entities external to them to which they refer. In other words, discourse presupposes a reality outside it. The highly abstract distinctions between object language and metalanguage, ontology and conceptual scheme, reference and sense, real-object and thought-object are examples of the way in which a contrast is drawn between reality and our talk about it. Because we have no direct access to reality this contrast can only be made out in discourse. So, paradoxically, our attempts to close the gap between words and things simply leads to the proliferation of discourse, as is illustrated in Tarski's definition of truth.

This process, through which we are continually led to posit the existence of a reality to which we are denied direct access, is not simply, as Derrida claims, the search for a 'transcendental signified' which will halt the endless 'play' of language. Once immediate knowledge is ruled out as impossible then this play cannot be halted. But one constitutive feature of language is the constant reaching out to a reality outside it. This feature can only be explained by the fact that there *is* such a reality, and that human beings and their discourse are dependent and subordinate aspects of this reality. In other words, the semantic dimension of language can be accounted from only from a materialist standpoint. The denial of this dimension, the reduction of it to a mere search for 'presence' and *parousia* which we find in Derrida and his disciples have led in there case to a new form of theology, one that strips God of his attributes only to transfer them to Language, omnipotent source of meaning.

The great merit of Tarski's definition of truth is that it highlights the *objectivity* of truth. Whether or not a sentence is true depends normally on its relation to a reality outside discourse; it is true or false irrespective of its conditions of utterance or the state of mind of whoever utters it (unless, of course, the sentence is context-bound or refers to its utterer's state of mind). Moreover, the 'correspondence' between discourse and reality which it asserts to hold in the case of a true sentence is not a pictorial one – the sentence and the state of affairs it describes do not somehow share the same structure. Whether or not they 'correspond' depends simply on whether or not the state of affairs designated by the sentence actually exists. However, the classical theory of truth does not tell us how to go about establishing whether or not a given sentence is true. It is, as Tarski's reformulation suggests, a *definition* of truth rather than a criterion. Indeed, truth as such is unattainable. This must be so; if truth is the correspondence of discourse and reality we could only definitively establish the truth of a sentence by comparing the two terms of the relation, which is impossible since we only have access to one term – reality – through the other – discourse. As Xenophanes of Colophon put it in the fifth century BC: 'no man knows, or will ever know, the truth about the gods and about everything I speak of: for even if one chanced to say the complete truth, yet oneself knows it not'.[25]

This consideration does not lead to scepticism, but merely to fallibilism – i.e. to the recognition that our knowledge is always open to correction and revision. The concept of truth becomes no less important once we recognise that it is unattainable. For the specific feature of theoretical discourses is that they purport to convey information, and in particular to add to our knowledge. Therefore, the question of their relation to reality, and the question of the degree to which they succeed in adding to our knowledge of it, are of special interest. The writings of Foucault and of Hindess and Hirst, despite their authors' rejection of concepts such as truth and objective knowledge, are intended to alter the manner in which we conceive of reality and thereby to influence our attitudes to political practice. They therefore involve claims about reality just as much as the most naively realist and empiricist of sociology texts. Once we accept that theoretical discourses are constructed at least in part to convey information, then we are interested in their truth – the limiting point at which discourse and reality correspond. The fact that we can never knowingly attain this point does not alter the fact that the concept of truth may, as Popper puts it, function as a 'regulative principle', so that discourses as evaluated in terms of the degree to which they approximate to the truth.[26] Now this degree cannot be established from the standpoint of truth itself, as if it were a goal which had already been achieved. To do so would be to give epistemology the status of absolute knowledge, looking back across history and evaluating discourses as anticipations of itself. Discourses approximate to the truth in a peculiar sense; their degree of approximation can only be established relative to one another, in contexts, that is, where two or more discourses compete with each other.

Before going on to consider in detail the evaluation of competing discourses, I would like to deal with one possible misunderstanding of my position. It might be argued that since I deny the possibility of direct access to reality and reduce truth to a purely regulative role I am a 'neo-kantian'. Such a claim would be mistaken. Kant held that the conditions of possible experience set limits to the form and content of our knowledge; this implied that there were 'things-in-themselves' which could not be experienced and were therefore unknowable. Some philosophers have invoked Kant in support of the claim that the acceptance or rejection of scientific theories depends on considerations of convenience rather than truth. It should be obvious that I reject the latter claim. Nor do I believe that reality 'in itself' is unknowable, merely that our knowledge of it is fallible. No ultimate resting point can ever be reached at which, in Hegel's terms, truth and certainty are identical. Lenin insisted on the approximate nature of knowledge: 'Man cannot comprehend = reflect = mirror nature *as a whole*, in its completeness, its "immediate totality", he can only *eternally* come closer to this'; and 'cognition is the eternal, endless approximation of thought to the object'.[27] Usually statements of this sort are justified on the grounds of the infinity of reality and the finitude of human thought. One could equally say that discourse itself is infinite. Human language is so constructed that the terms and sentences it contains proliferate endlessly. However, it also constantly reaches out to a reality beyond it. Both these features should be taken into account in philosophical discussion.

A THEORY OF IMMANENT RATIONALITY

An epistemology which evaluates theoretical discourses from

the standpoint of their approximation to the truth must insist on the objectivity of knowledge. The criteria for determining which out of a set of competing discourses approximates most closely to the truth must be objective ones applicable to all discourses. Questions of political or ethical preference must be ruled out of order. Epistemology is normative only in the sense of evaluating discourses in terms of their relation to the truth. Furthermore, discourses must be judged from the standpoint of whether they add to, or at least seek to add to, our knowledge of reality. In this sense, they must be empirical. However, our discussion of the denial of immediate knowledge should have made it clear that there is no layer of neutral 'facts' independent of our discourse, while Hindess and Hirst's critique of epistemology does highlight the dogmatic dangers involved in insisting that all scientific statements conform to some set of principles which have a privileged relation to reality. The way round this problem can only be a theory of *immanent rationality*. In other words, theoretical discourses must be evaluated in terms of their degree of success in resolving the problems which they set themselves. Thus discourses are *not* required to conform to some universal pattern of explanation, such as the three laws of the dialectic. At the same time the definition of success must be one applicable to all discourses. Imre Lakatos' methodology of scientific research programmes offers such a theory of the immanent rationality of theoretical discourses.

The posthumous publication in 1978 of Lakatos' *Philosophical Papers* has underlined the immense importance of his (tragically incomplete) project. Starting with the application of Popper's falsificationist methodology to the history of mathematics (above all in the revolutionary *Proofs and Refutations* and associated writings, which showed that mathematics and logic were themselves fallible, 'quasi-empirical' disciplines),[28] Lakatos went on to challenge Popper's model of science as depending essentially upon the confrontation between an isolated hypothesis and a fact. He did so, first by arguing that this model did not fit the history of the sciences, and secondly by pointing out, as we have seen, that 'hypothesis' and 'fact' are both equally fallible, equally theoretical propositions. So 'why aim at falsification at any price? Why not rather impose certain standards on the theoretical adjustments by which one is allowed to save a theory?' What matters now is the relation between successive versions of a theory – the way in which it is modified in the face of anomalies and inconsistencies. Therefore, 'what we appraise is a *series of theories* rather than isolated theories'.[29]

The basic unit of appraisal, according to Lakatos, is a *research programme*, 'a developing series of theories'.

> Moreover, this series has a structure. It has a tenacious *hard core* . . . and it has a *heuristic*, which includes a set of problem-solving techniques. . . . Finally, a research programme has a vast belt of auxiliary hypotheses on the basis of which we establish initial conditions. I call this belt a *protective belt* because it protects the hard core from refutations: anomalies are not taken as refutations of the hard core but of some hypothesis in the protective belt. Partly under empirical pressure (but partly *planned* according to its heuristic), the protective belt is constantly modified, increased, complicated, while the hard core remains intact.[30]

A research programme is defined by its heuristic, which involves two components, the negative heuristic, which prohibits refutations of the hard core, and the positive heuristic, which 'consists of a partially articulated set of suggestions of hints on how to change, to develop the "refutable variants" of the research programme, how to modify, sophisticate, the "refutable" protective belt'.[31] Methodological appraisal concentrates on the way in which its 'refutable variants' are modified. Say an anomaly is discovered in a research programme – a clash between an observational statement and a prediction derived from the hard core in conjunction with some of its auxiliary hypotheses. It does not matter according to Lakatos whether we drop the hypothesis which was falsified or the observational theory in terms of which the falsifying evidence was interpreted, provided that the new auxiliary hypothesis is not *ad hoc*:

> I distinguish three types of *ad hoc* auxiliary hypotheses: those which have no excess empirical content over their predecessor ('*ad hoc$_1$*'), those which have such excess content but none of it is corroborated ('*ad hoc$_2$*') and finally those

which are not *ad hoc* in these two senses but do not form an integral part of the positive heuristic (*'ad hoc₃'*).[32]

A research programme is theoretically progressive if its latest version predicts novel facts, theoretically degenerating if it does not and empirically progressive if some of its predictions are corroborated, empirically degenerating if they are not.

Obviously much turns on the meaning of 'excess empirical content' or 'novel fact'. Elie Zahar offers this definition: '*A fact ∙ will be considered novel with respect to a given hypothesis if it did not belong to the problem situation which governed the construction of the hypothesis*'. Thus a fact need not be unknown in order to corroborate a hypothesis – Zahar gives the example of the anomalous precession of Mercury's perihelion, which was recorded long before Einstein's general relativity theory explained it. As he acknowledges, Zahar's definition of novel fact implies that the conception of a theory's 'empirical content' depends, not on experience conceived of as independent of discourse, but on the internal constitution of the research programme in question:

> My definition of novelty amounts to the claim that *in order to assess the relation between theories and empirical data within a research programme, one has to take into account the way in which a theory is built and the problems it was designed to solve.*[33]

Furthermore, Lakatos argues, research programmes are born loaded down with anomalies (clashes between auxiliary hypotheses and the 'facts') and inconsistencies. What counts, at least in the initial stages, is less the research programme's success in rapidly eliminating them or even in arriving at predictions of novel facts, than its ability to suggest fertile lines of research which eventually lead to theoretical and empirical progress. The 'verification' or 'falsification' of a research programme is less a matter of a theory and the 'facts' confronting each other than a three-cornered fight between two competing research programmes and their conflicting predictions, and it is usually only long after the event that a particular experiment comes to be regarded as a 'crucial' one adjudicating between a degenerating and a progressive programme. There are no quick kills in epistemology.

The methodology of scientific research programmes enables us to avoid the traps of empiricism and rationalism. Science progresses through the elaboration of auxiliary hypotheses in accordance with a programme's positive heuristic. The criteria of theoretical and empirical progress and degeneration do not invoke an 'empirical basis' of 'facts' constituted outside discourse. Nor do they predetermine what is to count as an explanation, since the form taken by auxiliary hypotheses is specified by the positive heuristic, which is internal to the programme in question. However, both the positive heuristic and the hard core are themselves subject to rational evaluation: if successive versions of a research programme are *ad hoc* then we have rational grounds for abandoning it (should a more successful rival be available). Moreover, progress and degeneration are linked to the growth of knowledge, since they depend upon the prediction of novel facts. We could put it like this: acceptable forms of explanation are laid down by the heuristic of the research programme, but the standards to be met in formulating explanations are applicable to all research programmes and enable us to evaluate them in the light of their contribution to our knowledge of reality.

Lakatos' approach leaves a number of questions unresolved. As he points out himself, Popper's definition of science, which provided the starting point for his own methodology, 'says nothing about the epistemological value of the scientific game'; it merely sets out the rules governing that game, without making any claims as to whether more successful scientific theories bring us closer to the truth; consequently, 'there is nothing in the *Logik der Forschung* [Popper's main work – AC] with which the most radical sceptic may disagree'.[34] Interestingly, in a much earlier paper only published after his death, Lakatos invoked *Anti-Duhring* and *Materialism and Empirio-Criticism* in support of 'metaphysical realism' or 'materialism' – belief in 'a real world independent of our mind and governed by some sort of natural laws', and 'epistemological optimism' – the belief that 'we can somehow explore the laws of nature and form either an exact or at least an approximate idea of them'.[35] These two theses, and the correspondence theory of truth which they involve, provide the epistemological under-pinnings which Lakatos's methodology of scientific research programmes requires, transforming it into a full-blooded epistemology which not only provides objective criteria for the evaluation of discourses but in doing so relates them to the regulative principle of truth. The criteria of theoretical and empirical progress and degeneration must be taken as the means through which their degree of approximation to the truth is established. Without the concept of truth methodology lacks a rationale; without methodology the concept of truth is an empty definition.

Then there is the question of the status of the materialist theses. Although there has been one rather hamfisted attempt to 'prove' them,[36] it seems to me that David-Hillel Ruben is closer to the truth when he writes:

> Ultimately the choice between materialism and idealism is the choice between two competing ideologies. The choice is not an 'epistemological' choice to be made on grounds of stronger evidence or more forceful argument, but is a 'political' choice made on class allegiance.[37]

This position, terminology aside, seems little different from the later Althusser's claim that 'philosophy is the class struggle in theory'. Apart from the immense reductionist dangers involved in statements of this sort – they run the risk of turning the history of philosophy into a sort of prize-fight between progressive materialists and reactionary idealists – they do not account for the fact that philosophers whose 'class allegiance' is very firmly to the bourgeoisie can be materialists – Popper and Lakatos are two examples of this phenomenon. The 'rational kernel' of this position lies in Althusser's insistence since 1967 that philosophy cannot be assimilated to a science. Thus he writes:

> Philosophy states theses. Propositions which give rise neither to demonstration nor to *scientific* proofs in the strict sense, but to *rational justifications* of a particular, distinct type.[38]

In other words, there are no criteria comparable to those of theoretical and empirical progress and degeneration which may be applied to philosophical positions, although Lakatos mistakenly sought to offer one in the shape of a 'methodology of historiographical research programmes'.[39] This does not mean that the decision to adopt a particular philosophical position is an irrational or arbitrary one – we can give 'rational justifications' for a particular theory and attempt to persuade others of its validity. From this point of view it is quite legitimate to invoke political considerations in support of a philosophical position, but there is no reason why these should be given preference over others, as Hillel-Ruben and Althusser seem to claim. In any case, if someone should choose to be, say, an absolute idealist there is no set of criteria itself lacking any philosophical presuppositions which could establish that this position is further from the truth than, say, materialism. There is nothing surprising about this situation, or there should not be, once we realise that there are no indubitable first principles on which our knowledge can rest. Beneath the apparently stable structure of the sciences there is only an endless struggle of ideas.

SCIENCE AND IDEOLOGY

Lakatos claims that 'the methodology of scientific research programmes accounts for the *relative autonomy of theoretical science*'. Research programmes have a mode of existence different from that of either physical objects or mental states; they exist *'in the world of ideas, in Plato's and Popper's "third world"*, in the world of articulated knowledge which is independent of the knowing subject'. Attempts to account for the history of theoretical discourses other than in terms of their intrinsic rationality deal in mere *'mob psychology'*.[40] Lakatos distinguishes between the 'internal' and 'external' history of a science – the former pertains to research programmes, the latter to the social and psychological conditions in which they produced. 'External history', he claims, 'is irrelevant to the understanding of science'.[41] This approach is very similar to those of Bachelard and Althusser, at least in the sense of insisting that theoretical discourses must be analysed exclusively from the point of view of their internal conceptual organisation (their heuristic for Lakatos, their problematic for Althusser).

Barry Hindess attacks this approach. 'Any proposition stated in . . . a discourse' has *'logical or conceptual conditions of existence'*. However, these conditions have no ' "real effectivity" in the generation of discourse'. One way in which Hindess tries to justify this claim is by considering the case where the logical conditions of existence of a discourse are incompatible. He seems to regard this as a sort of *reductio ad absurdum*: 'The process of production of discourse cannot be constrained to conform to the requirements of mutually conflicting presuppositions'.[42] This argument is a good example of what one might call the 'logicist' or 'deductivist' conception of discourse, which rests on the claim that what Hindess calls the 'internal relations between concepts' can only be those of logical consistency or implication. But precisely what is involved in concepts such as heuristic and problematic is the claim that discourses have internal relations which cannot be reduced to those of consistency and implication. Lakatos argues that

> *Some of the most important research programmes in the history of science must be grafted onto older programmes with which they are blatantly inconsistent.* For instance, Copernican astronomy was 'grafted' onto Aristotelian physics, Bohr's programme onto Maxwell's.

This should not be taken to support some sort of 'dialectical' logic or to licence foolish attacks on 'bourgeois' formal logic – Lakatos goes on to argue that *'consistency . . . must remain an important regulative principle'*.[43] But the relations intrinsic to discourses cannot be reduced to those of deductive inference. Theoretical discourses are constituted by *problems*, not derived from axioms.[44] When Hindess dismisses the notion of problematic as 'an extra-discursive totality' he merely assumes the point at issue.[45]

Foucault, like Hindess, denies the internal relations between concepts any real effectivity in the production of discourse. The conditions of possibility of statements depend on the prevailing 'diagram' of 'power-knowledge', which is immanent in statements without being reducible to them. Deleuze writes that 'the diagram is like an intense abstract light which makes the statement visible, and the action sayable (*dicible*) – but for another language, for another mode of action'.[46] This poses the obvious question of the status of this other language and mode of action. If the 'abstract machine' constitutive of a 'diagram' is immanent in the whole social body then it is not clear how there can be a point outside the 'diagram' from which one can grasp its nature. Foucault's problems in accounting for the status of his own discourse are not new. In *The Order of Things* he claims that one *epistemé* cannot be known from the standpoint of another: in which case, as Georges Canguilhem asks, 'how can one explain the appearance, today, . . . of a work such as *The Order of Things*' which is concerned precisely with the transition from one *epistemé* to another?[47]

In any case Foucault does choose rather easy targets when he seeks to show that discursive formations are produced within 'power-knowledge'. However illuminating the analyses of *Discipline and Punish* it would hardly surprise anyone of a left-wing frame of mind to discover that disciplines like criminology and sociology have some connection with power-relations. When he first became interested in the problems of 'knowledge' and 'power' in the 1950s Foucault chose to study the history of psychology rather than that of physics, because of the difficulty of detecting power-relations in the latter:[48] quite so. I await a foucaudian genealogy of general relativity theory with interest. Theoretical physics provides the most important single counter-example to Foucault's approach, for it appears to display a relative autonomy which endows it with a continuity and a history across *epistemés* and 'diagrams' (and even modes of production). As Canguilhem puts it:

> Because one ceases to understand, at the end of the nineteenth century, what physicists who spoke of ether were talking about, one does not therefore cease to understand the mathematical apodicticity of Fresnel's theories and one does not commit an anachronism in seeking in Huygens, certainly not the origin of a melodic history, but the beginning of a progress.[49]

However, theoretical discourses are produced within

definite social relations, and these relations have an effect, not simply on the constitution of discourses, but on the manner in which they are recorded, transmitted and reorganised. The effectivity of social relations upon and within discourses cannot be accounted for in terms of the althusserian concept of ideology, where ideology is assimilated to error and error thereby treated as the index of the intervention of an extra-discursive instance. Althusser does seem here to collapse back in the dogmatic 'justificationist' tradition in which science is identified with proven knowledge and error is a sort of paroxysm arising from the use of defective methods.[50] Fallibilism involves accepting that even the most corroborated research programme may be false and applying common standards to all discourses, rather than, as Barry Hindess puts it, adopting 'different modes of analysis' in the case of the sciences and of the theoretical ideologies.[51]

Rejction of the science/ideology distinction, at least in the sense in which it is used by Althusser, does not involve reducing theoretical discourses to their social conditions. What it does involve is recognising that the difference between science and ideology cuts discourses not *vertically* but *horizontally*. There is no once-and-for-all break through which a theoretical discourse is freed from outside interference. Discourses do not occupy a platonic realm of ideas, Popper's 'third world', Althusser's 'theoretical practice', but are pro-duced and reproduced within social relations. The possibility of a discourse acquiring the sort of 'relative autonomy' analysed by Lakatos depends upon certain extra-discursive conditions. Without the emergence of working-class move-ments and socialist ideologies in the early nineteenth century, the set of problems which give *Capital* its unity – the nature of value, the origins of profit, etc. – would not have seemed relevant to scientific theorising. Similarly, the rejection of Aristotle's conception of the universe as a *cosmos*, a qualitative hierarchy of being, implicit in the adoption by Galileo and other seventeenth-century physicists of the assumption that physical reality is intrinsically mathematical, involved a strug-gle against certain forms of feudal ideology. Foucault's error is to deduce from facts of this sort the claim that science is *nothing but* ideology. Indeed, he seems to go further and to argue that the mere existence of constraints upon the sort of statements which may be produced within a given discourse is an index of the power-relations to which the discourse owes its identity. This position is first cousin to Lacan's claim that it is through language that the subject is placed under the law. To reject this view is to assert that theoretical discourses have (at least) two distinct determinations – their internal structure (heuristic, problematic) and their extra-discursive conditions of existence. It is possible, therefore, by comparing, say, marxism and neo-classical economics, both to determine their theoretical and empirical progress degeneration with respect to one another and to analyse the different social positions they occupy. The two operations are, however, distinct. Theoretical discourses have their own rhythms, which cannot be reduced to those of power.

ABSTRACT AND CONCRETE

Hindess, Hirst and their co-thinkers claim that one implication of their critique of epistemology is that the concept of mode of production cannot be sustained. On the epistemology 'under whose sign' *Capital* is written,

> the significant objects encountered in social knowledge are totalities, definite unities of being, and these finite objects (which in their form transcend the concrete circumstances of their existence) are defined by a single general order of causes.

The capitalist mode of production is an example of such an object. It is a 'concrete generality', that is, 'an entity the effects of which are given in its concept'. In this case, 'the effects of the economy are present in its concept'. Marx's epistemology, therefore, implies the 'auto-effectivity of the economy in providing its own . . . conditions of existence', or 'economism'. The relations between the entities specified in discourse cannot be reduced to the relations between concepts:

> We must therefore distinguish between conditions of existence and the social relations and practices which provide them. The first can be inferred from the concept of

determinate relations of production but the second cannot.

It follows, the authors claim, that 'there is no necessity for the conditions of existence to be secured and no necessary structure of the social formation in which these relations and conditions can be combined'.[52]

It is interesting that Edward Thompson also wishes to free historical materialism from the prison in which the concept of mode of production has enclosed it, thus permitting the concrete analysis of social formations. Of course, in his case, this move is justified by invoking concepts such as 'history', 'experiences', 'culture', 'values', 'process', which seem less solutions than problems, but underlying both his argument and that of the authors of *Marx's 'Capital' and Capitalism Today* is the common idea that the concept of mode of production must be rejected because it sets limits to analysis. They do not explain how in this respect the concept of mode of production differs from any other concept. Precisely what concepts do is set limits, implicitly distinguishing those cases which fall under them from those that do not. As Hegel put it, 'a thing is what it is, only in and by reason of its limit'.[53] Otherwise discourse would be an undifferentiated, chaotic flux rather like the deleuzian body without organs. In order to show that the concept of mode of production is defective arguments are necessary that apply to it alone, rather than all concepts. It is ironic to see 'post-althusserians' and 'anti-althusserian' united in invoking a metaphysics of the concrete which is little more than an incoherent empiricist attack on all conceptual thought.

This rejection of the concept of mode of production is politically motivated. Thompson claims that the concept of mode of production, as a form of secularised hegelianism, requires that '"reformism" must be incorporation within capitalist structures: it cannot *also* be reforms and the modification of those structures to allow a space for incorporation'.[54] The same point is made in *Marx's 'Capital' and Capitalism Today*:

> If the social formation is not conceived as governed by the essential structure of a mode of production and its corresponding forms of state, politics and ideology then the

options facing socialist politics can no longer be reduced to confronting this essential structure or refusing to do so. . . . This means that socialists should be concerned with expanding the areas of socialisation and democratisation in the social formation and that existing struggles to these ends cannot be judged as diversionary merely because they fail to confront the overall structures of the state and the economy.[55]

In part this argument is a confusion. None of the classical marxists (and it is against them that the latter passage is aimed) regarded the struggle for reforms as a *diversion*. What they did oppose was identifying social revolution with this struggle. As Rosa Luxemburg put it,

From the viewpoint of a movement for socialism, the trade-union struggle and parliamentary practice are vastly important in so far as they make socialist the *awareness*, the consciousness, of the proletariat and help to organise it as a class. But once they are considered as instruments of the direct socialisation of capitalist economy, they lose not only their usual effectiveness but cease being means for preparing the working class for the conquest of power.[56]

What both Thompson and the authors of *Marx's 'Capital' and Capitalism Today* object to in the concept of mode of production is that it implies that there are certain limits beyond which change is incompatible with a given set of relations of production; changes which challenge these limits require for their implementation a social revolution which overturns the 'essential structure' of that mode of production. Getting rid of the concept of mode of production enables them to argue that the transition to socialism (which is what is at stake here) can be effected by a series of piecemeal reforms which at no single moment involve a sharp break with the prevailing capitalist order. Epistemological arguments are here closely bound up with a political strategy – gradualism of the traditional social-democratic sort. So the critique of classical marxism need not lead one to the anarchism of Foucault and Deleuze or the liberalism of Glucksmann; it can take one back simply to the reformism of Bernstein and Kautsky. The irony is that the political conclusions drawn by Thompson and by Hindess and Hirst are so similar. One may choose between them on grounds of intellectual style, but not on those of political substance.

To return, however, to the epistemological questions here under consideration, one could put Hindess and Hirst's argument against the thesis of the explanatory primacy of production relations as follows. This thesis inevitably leads to reductionism because it privileges a certain level of discourse, excluding those statements which do not conform to it. The concepts of other social relations are treated as the mere exemplications of those of relations of production. Underlying Hindess and Hirst's argument is what I called above the 'logicist' or 'deductivist' conception of discourse, which reduces relations between concepts to those of consistency and implication. And indeed the model of explanation adopted by orthodox philosophers of science such as Popper and Carl Hempel is precisely of this sort: a phenomenon is held to have been explained if it derived from a conjunction of a universal proposition and a set of initial conditions (certain other requirements are made, but these do not alter the deductive, 'covering-law' type of explanation involved here). Rationality here consists essentially in the subsumption of particulars under universals. Explanation proceeds, as Hegel put it, by 'abstraction, which omits the particular and ascends to higher and highest genus',[57] the premiss of each explanation in turn being explained by its deduction from some more general propositions. The particular counts merely as an exemplification of the universal under which it is subsumed.

The approach which I have sought to outline in this chapter involves a theory of immanent rationality, where, as Hegel put it, 'the proof comes with the proposition' and explanation is not deductive but *heuristic* or *problematic*. What counts in a theoretical discourse (from an epistemological point of view at any rate) is the problems which provide it with its identity, the techniques it specifies to solve these problems and the manner in which it applies these techniques. It follows that there can be no conclusion to a research programme, for it forms, not a closed axiomatic system, but an open process in which the application of certain problem-solving techniques specified in the heuristic may lead to the transformation of that heuristic, just as Galileo's attempt to develop Copernicus's heliocentric research programme led him to abandon aristotelian mechanics.

Applied to marxism this approach displaces the two traditional ways of conceiving the relation between the economy and the social whole – cause/effect (the primacy of the productive forces) and essence/phenomenon (hegelian marxism, capital-logic, etc.). Both are forms of reductionism since non-economic relations are treated as the passive effects of the economy. If, however, we understand the primacy of the relations of production as heuristic, reductionism is no longer such a problem. The concept of relations of production may be taken to constitute the heuristic of the marxist research programme; it specifies the form explanations must take within this programme. However, concepts of particular modes of production and social formations and of non-economic social relations are not merely the exemplifications of the concept of relations of production – they presuppose this concept without being derived from it alone. In this sense we can say that marxism is, like any theoretical discourse, a process of production, of internal transformation, not a deductive system.

This argument is, in a sense, a generalisation of Marx's approach in *Capital*. For the process of 'rising from the abstract to the concrete' involved in the move from 'capital in general' to 'many capitals' is not a deductive one. Concepts such as constant and variable capital, aggregate social capital, price of production etc, are not somehow contained within the concept of the commodity; they had to be *produced* on the basis on that concept, not derived from it. One merit, then, of the philosophical position outlined in this chapter is that it captures Marx's epistemology, as outlined in the Introduction to the *Grundrisse* and actually developed in *Capital*, where, as we saw in Chapter 5, 'science consists precisely in demonstrating *how* the law of value asserts itself'.[58] Moreover, it corresponds quite closely to Lenin's epistemology, at least in the mature form in which it is presented in the *Philosophical Notebooks*:

Knowledge is the reflection of nature by man. But this is not a simple, not an immediate, not a complete reflection, but the process of a series of abstrations, the formation and development of concepts, laws, etc., and these concepts, laws, etc. (thought, science = 'the logical idea') embrace conditionally, approximately, the universal law-governed character of eternally moving and developing nature.[59]

Many of the formulations in this chapter are, however, crude and unsatisfactory and it would take more space than would be appropriate here to develop a fully adequate account of the epistemology I have sought to defend.

More to the point, perhaps, is the following consideration: even if the epistemology set out above is both defensible and indeed that accepted at least implicitly by Marx and Lenin, does marxism itself meet the criteria of theoretical and empirical progress it involves? Lakatos thought not:[60] and we have seen that even Lucio Colletti believed that 'the falling rate of profit has not been empirically verified'. Very often criticisms of *Capital* of this nature are based on a misunderstanding of Marx's arguments. To take the example given by Colletti, Ben Fine and Lawrence Harris argue (in my view correctly) that Marx conceives of the tendency of the rate of profit to fall (TRPF) as an 'abstract tendency' arrived at by ignoring all counter-acting influences, which arise from 'accumulation's effects on distribution and on the value-composition of capital'. As such the TRPF 'yields no general predictions about the actual movements in the rate of profit'; these movements depend upon the 'particular balance' between tendency and counter-acting influences. However,

> an abstract tendency *does* have a connection with observable phenomena even though it does *not* involve simple predictions of trends. The TRPF and tendency for counter-acting influences to operate actually exist in capitalism in a contradictory relationship with each other. The existence of these contradictions gives rise to crises, booms and the associated cycles of production and exchange. This, with their rhythm of unemployment, concentration and centralisation and other phenomena are the observable 'predictions' of Marx's abstract tendency.[61]

Colletti, then, failed to distinguish between the different

levels of abstraction involved in Marx's *Capital*. Many other attributions to Marx of falsified predictions arise from comparable misinterpretations of Marx's method, or of specific propositions he advances.[62] However, it does not seem to me to be an adequate defence of marxism merely to defend its conceptual edifice against distortion and misinterpretation, important though this activity may be. Too much of contemporary marxist theory remains satisfied by an explication of the concepts of historical materialism. A research programme must be judged, however, by the extent to which it gives rise to new theoretical work involving the prediction of novel facts, thereby adding to our knowledge. In the final chapter I shall consider the extent to which marxism meets the standards of theoretical and empirical progress outlined above, and in doing so seek to indicate the relevance of the interpretation of marxism developed in this book for concrete problems of analysis and political practice.

8 Classical Marxism and Contemporary Capitalism

THE CRITIQUE OF POLITICS

The most important theoretical issue confronting Marxism today is that of the state, for it is the point at which practical political considerations converge with those of scientific research. This is evident in the German 'state-derivation' debate, underlying which is the following question: does the west German economic 'miracle' signify that the capitalist state today can overcome the contradictions Marx saw as inherent in capitalist relations of production? More generally, what are the forms and limits of state economic intervention? This question has become even more urgent since it was first formulated in the 1960s. One of the main axes of political debate in the western capitalist countries is the demand that the economic role of the state be both altered and reduced – consider the influence of monetarist economic theories and political currents as diverse as Margaret Thatcher in Britain, Valery Giscard d'Estaing in France and Ronald Reagan in the US.

Among marxists in France also the question of the state appears increasingly to have become the focus of debate. As represented by Nicos Poulantzas in *State, Power, Socialism*, the issues involve both political strategy – can socialism be achieved gradually and by peaceful means, as the eurocommunists claim, or does it require the armed conquest of power by the working class, as the classical marxists insisted? – and the very conception of socialism – does it depend on the self-activity of the masses or can it be achieved on their behalf? These questions, brought into sharp focus by Solzhenitsyn's *The Gulag Archipelago* and the arguments of the *nouveaux philosophes*, have received attention in recent writings by Althusser and his collaborators, which have pointed to the incomplete nature of Marx's 'critique of politics' in comparison with the critique of political economy he developed in *Capital*.[1]

The question of the state is at the centre of those of Marx's early writings, notably his *Critique of Hegel's Doctrine of the State* and *On the Jewish Question*, which represent his transition from radical liberal-democracy to revolutionary communism. For Hegel the state was the highest form of social rationality, reconciling the substantial organic unity characteristic of social bonds sanctioned by custom and the particularistic, self-seeking activities of individuals in civil society, in an 'articulated and genuinely organised' set of institutions. The principle underlying the modern state is that 'the interest of the whole is realised in and through particular ends' – the pursuit of individual self-interest actually contributes, through its unintended consequences, to the whole; thus, with the framework of the state, 'subjectivity . . . must attain its full and living development'. As the reconciliation of substance and subject, universal and particular, custom and individual freedom, 'the state is the divine will, . . . mind present on earth, unfolding itself to be the actual shape and organisation of a world'.[2] Although expressed in terms of his speculative philosophy, Hegel's argument is a summation of the main theme of classical bourgeois political thought from Hobbes and Locke to Rousseau and Smith, that a rational political community requires both scope for the pursuit of individual ends characteristic of civil society (and the institutions of private property and civil liberties that this involves) and their containment within a state which transcends the self-seeking realm of civil society.

It is this entire tradition which Marx sets out to challenge in his *Critique of Hegel's Doctrine of the State*. Following Feuerbach he claims that Hegel's method involves a transposition of subject and predicate such that the properties of nature (and man as a part of nature) are attributed to thought, so that the mental reflection of reality becomes the Absolute Idea, autonomous and omnipotent.[3] Thus, for Hegel 'the concern of philosophy is not the logic of the subject-matter but the subject matter of logic. Logic does not provide a proof of the state but the state provides a proof of logic'. The result is that Hegel fails to explain the separation between state and civil society, merely treating it as part of the process through which Absolute Spirit comes to self-consciousness: 'the fact which serves as a starting point is not seen as such but as a mystical result'. In reality the emergence of the state as an autonomous set of institutions is a product of the process through which civil society became dominated by the egoistic pursuit of private interest. Far from being 'the divine will', 'the *political state is an abstraction from civil society*', a form of alienation reflecting the contradiction at the core of social life, its domination by the pursuit of money.[4] Human emancipation can be completed, Marx argued in *On the Jewish Question*, not through the perfection of the state as an autonomous institution by means of its further democratisation, but by its abolition, and with it the abolition of the distinction between the state and civil society, the resumption of the state into civil society and the substitution of communist for competitive relations between people.

There is no need to trace here the way in which, in subsequent writings, Marx found the source of the abstraction of the state from civil society in the division of labour, and in turn sought to give the latter concept greater definition by means of the concept of the relations of production. The critique of politics led Marx to explore 'the anatomy of civil society' and thereby to the critique of political economy.[5] More to our purpose is to grasp the implication of Marx's critique of Hegel: far from being the highest form of social rationality, the state is the product of contradictions specific to certain forms of society. Further human development requires its abolition. This theme is developed more fully by Marx towards the end of his life, in *The Civil War in France* and *The Critique of the Gotha Programme*, where he insists on the necessity of the destruction of the capitalist state apparatus and its replacement by a transitional form of political rule along the lines of the Paris Commune, in which the distinction between rulers and ruled is abolished and power is exercised directly by the working masses. The most important continuations of Marx's arguments are Engel's *The Origins of the Family, Private Property and the State*, where the state is analysed as the product of irreconcilable class antagonisms, and Lenin's *The State and Revolution*, where the dictatorship of the proletariat is conceived of as a 'Commune-State' based upon soviets or workers' councils preliminary to the abolition of any specialised repressive institutions consequent upon the disappearance of classes and the rule of the associated producers under communism.

Hal Draper has written of 'the two souls of socialism' – revolution from below, through the self-activity of the masses, revolution from above, through the conquest of the state.[6] Marx, Engels and Lenin's writings place them firmly in the tradition of revolution 'from below'. Their difference with the anarchists lies not in any doubt that communism involves the abolition of the state but in their belief that the transition between capitalism and communism must involve a specific form of political rule, the dictatorship of the proletariat, in which the working class collectively exercise power. They emphasise, however, the temporary and unprecedented nature of this state-form – for the first time it is the majority ruling the minority, the proletariat repressing the bourgeoisie on the basis of collective control over the making and implementation of decisions.

By contrast, both stalinism and social-democracy belong to the tradition of revolution 'from above' and conceive of the state as the highest form of social rationality. For example, Kautsky argued that the liberal-democratic state was a product as much of technical necessities inherent in any large-scale industrial society as of capitalist social relations and that it provided the framework in which the working class would take power and collective ownership of the means of production be organised.[7] Hilferding believed that the growing economic role of the state reflected an expansion in social control over the economy and provided the institutional framework for socialism.[8] A similar viewpoint underlies the Communist Parties' claim that the nature of state economic intervention under state monopoly capitalism implies that 'public forms are not only used by the monopolies, they can offer new arms for the revolutionary movement' rendering possible 'a direct, peaceful *transition* to socialism' if only the state is removed from the monopolies' control.[9] The same emphasis on the possibilities offered the socialist movement by the apparatus of economic intervention created by modern capitalism is to be found on the left wing of the Labour Party, notably among those grouped around Tony Benn.[10]

One of the difficulties involved in bringing Marx's theory of the state to bear on contemporary political debates is the extremely undeveloped nature of this theory. Marx tends not to distinguish between the *capitalist* state and the state in general. Engels and Lenin's contributions are concerned mainly with the latter question – the state as the product of class antagonisms, reflecting the need of those owning the means of production to secure also a monopoly of the means of force. The merit of the 'state-derivation' debate in Germany is that it has focussed upon the specific nature of the capitalist state, arguing that it is correlated to the autonomisation of the relations of production resulting from the fact that surplus-labour is appropriated and social labour distributed through the purchase and sale of commodities. However, this argument merely gives us the general *form* of the capitalist state. The chief constraint it imposes upon the activities of the state is their dependence on the extraction and accumulation of surplus-value. Beyond that it could be a free-floating 'relatively autonomous instance' for all that the theoreticians of 'capital-logic' tell us. This weakness reflects, I suspect, the nature of their method – they concern simply to *derive* the capitalist state from the relations of production, rather than going beyond the analyses of *Capital* to produce the new concepts necessary to grasp the role of the state in contemporary capitalism.

One of the most important recent contributions to the discussion of the state is an essay by the Italian communist philosopher Cesare Luporini, who argues that we must distinguish the *state* from the *political*. The latter involves 'the presence of a relation leaders – led and/or governors – governed' and 'arises... when society has need of an organised extra-economic force ... to maintain and reproduce the unequal economic and social relations which are established within it'. The political, that is, is a product of class antagonisms. It is not identical with the state, 'if by state, properly understood, one means an entity institutionally separate from society, and superimposed on it with its apparatus'. Thus in classical Greece the land- and slave-owning dominant class were able to enforce their rule through institutions controlled by the citizenry, property-owning and propertyless alike, which operated as a *force* which act[ed] on individuals and groups, and protect[ed] the reproduction of social relations', a 'quasi-state'. The distinction between public and private, collective and individual, precedes that between state and civil society. The peculiar feature of the latter distinction is that here the 'organised extra-economic force' becomes independent of society as a whole; even the owners of the means of production do not directly control it, and the mass of decision-making falls to a specialised, professional bureaucracy. It is only with the autonomisation of the relations of production specific to capitalism that this separation arises.[11]

Luporini argues that 'law and politics (the class struggle) are organically present in *Capital* . . . but within the domain of politics we don't find the state'. Marx inherited the distinction between state and civil society from Hegel, merely reversing the relationship (the state as product of antagonisms not their reconciliation) without adequately conceptualising it. The relation between the bourgeoisie and the political state 'remains in Marx the mere statement of an empirical fact'. The opposition between state and civil society cannot be assimilated to that between base and superstructure, since the former merely describes a state of affairs characteristic of bourgeois society without explaining it, while the latter asserts the necessity of explaining social formations in terms of the relations of production they involve: 'between these two oppositional couples, there is a logical heterogeneity'.[12]

Marx's failure to analyse the capitalist state does not derive from the fact that he never finished *Capital*,[13] but, according to Luporini, from the following assumption:

> In order to examine the object of our investigation in its integrity, free from all subsidiary circumstances, we must treat the whole world of trade as one nation, and assume that capitalist production is established everywhere, and has taken possession of every branch of industry.[14]

This assumption, that the world economy is one big capitalist nation, ignores the fact that the development of capitalism involves

(1) the constitution of an internal market of determinate dimensions (through which the bourgeoisie becomes do-

minant and ruling class on generally 'national' bases, united into states); within it is established the competition of capitals; . . . (2) the 'global system' (i.e. the creation of the world market) within which competition between different national bourgeoises, protected by their state structures, takes place, and where the *uneven* development of different countries enters the sphere of capitalist development.[15]

Marx's failure to take into account the fact that capitalism involves the organisation of the world economy into a system of nation-states makes sense from the point of view of the argument of *Capital*. For before analysing the different forms of competition between capitals (national and international) it is necessary first, in line with Marx's general approach of 'rising from the abstract to the concrete', to examine the nature of competition as such and the effect of the interaction of 'many capitals' on the 'inner mechanisms' of capitalist production – this is the subject of *Capital* Volume 3. However, Marx's abstraction from the existence of nation-states helps explain the failings of the 'capital-logic' theorists. For, since they seek to derive the nature of the capitalist state directly from capitalist relations of production they, following Marx, 'tend to treat "the state" in the singular', as Colin Barker put it.[16] Yet unless existence of nation-states in the *plural* is grasped as a prerequisite of the existence of capitalist relations of production, then the 'derivation' of the state will be purely formal, offering no insight into the role played by the state in different phases of capitalist development. To quote Luporini again:

> One cannot arrive conceptually at the notion of the political state, *directly*, starting from the class struggle, but one can do it beginning with this configuration and from this articulation [i.e. internal market/world market – AC] of the totality (national and international) of capital.[17]

The 'capital-logic' school's formalism is no doubt tied up with their tendency to collapse the sphere of 'many capitals' into that of 'capital in general'. The authors of *Marx's 'Capital' and Capitalism Today* commit precisely the reverse error. As part of their overall critique of *Capital*'s 'rationalism' and 'essentialism' they claim that because Marx conceives the capitalist mode of production as a 'concrete generality' necessarily securing its conditions of existence 'definite economies are conceived as exemplars of capitalism'. The result is that 'marxism has consistently neglected "national" economies as units of analysis', which is a bad thing because 'definite capitalist economies' provide the framework within which political struggles take place. Curiously, despite the emphasis laid on definite capitalist national economies, their nature goes unanalysed. The two dimensions specified by Luporini – the internal market and the world economy – receive no serious attention. The world economy is treated as a mere aggregate of national economies, while it is assumed, without discussion or analysis, that nation-states pursue economic policies. 'Capital in general' has been collapsed into 'many capitals', with the result that the constraints upon and determinants of the activities of 'definite capitalist economies' are not considered to be a problem worthy of analysis. This approach leads to rather questionable results – for example, the claim that socialist planning necessitates 'non-racist' immigration controls.[18]

THE THEORY OF STATE CAPITALISM

Marx's 'Capital' and Capitalism Today offers us a caricature of classical marxism, which it depicts as hypnotised by the prospect of the imminent and inevitable collapse of capitalism, prevented by its 'rationalism' and 'essentialism' from analysing concrete social formations. In fact, Lenin's and Luxemburg's first major works were studies of the development of capitalism in Russia and Poland respectively. Both Kautsky's *The Agrarian Question* and Lenin's writings on the same subject were attempts to the problems posed for socialist strategy in social formations where peasants and agricultural labourers form a large proportion of the working population, while Trotsky's *Results and Prospects* and *1905* centre on a brilliant analysis of class relations in the Russian social formation. More generally, the tendency by many contemporary marxists to dismiss the theoretical productions of the Second and Third Internationals as unvarnished 'economism' reflects the idealism and formalism rampant on the academic left today as well as a lack of acquaintance with the classical texts. It is closer to the truth to suggest that classical marxism is a complex discursive formation containing warring tendencies towards both evolutionism and a radically non-teleological mode of analysis, as I suggested at the end of Chapter 5. This is one reason why we cannot merely live off the classics, but at least let us not make our task more difficult by dismissing these classics as the product of a 'rationalism' which effaces the concrete.

My concern here is with the writings of the marxists of the Second and Third Internationals who sought to provide a middle term between *Capital* and the study of specific social formations, i.e. with the theory of the capitalist world economy. Luxemburg's *The Accumulation of Capital* and Hilferding's *Finance Capital* were major contributions to this theory. Their defects – Hilferding is perhaps most successful in the rather technical task of extending Marx's value-analysis to the intricacies of the stock market and monopoly pricing, while Luxemburg's misinterpretation of *Capital*, volume 2 leads her to predict the inevitable economic collapse of capitalism – should not be allowed to obscure their importance as pioneering studies of imperialism.[19] Trotsky made an important methodological contribution when he developed the concept of uneven and combined development. Trotsky argued that the development of the capitalist world economy had drawn together social formations with widely differing class relations and productive forces into a single integrated system. The effect was to create within each social formation, whether 'developed' or 'peripheral', a specific combination of 'advanced' and 'backward' features, and to leave the bourgeoisie in what is now the Third World, heavily dependent on its counterparts in the imperialist countries. This analysis implied that in the epoch of imperialism bourgeois-democratic and proletarian revolutions did not represent separate and distinct stages but aspects of a single process tending towards the seizure of power by the working class. Trotsky thereby challenged the evolutionist conception of history accepted by both Stalin and Kautsky, according to which modes of production succeeded one another inevitably.[20]

The most important attempt to arrive at an overview of the nature of imperialism is to be found in the writings of Nikolai Bukharin. First in *Imperialism and World Economy* (1917) and then in a more abstract form in *The Economics of the Transformation Period* (1920), Bukharin argued that the tendencies analysed by Hilferding – the formation of monopolies, the dominance of money-capital, the world struggle for markets – were part of a broader process of transformation in which the state and monopoly capital became ever more closely linked and in which competition between capitals had ceased to be merely commercial and was increasingly assuming a military form. The nation-state was, therefore, supplanting the individual firm as the organising centre of capitalist production and accumulation. In 1916 Bukharin wrote that under imperialism

> *The state power thus sucks in almost all branches of production; it not only maintains the general conditions of the exploitative process, the state more and more becomes a direct exploiter, organising and directing production as a collective capitalist.*[21]

This organisation of the *national* economy by the state in no way implied the abolition of capitalism. For individual nation-states formed part of a world economy within which competition between capitals continued to take place, although competition now tended to take the form of military as well as economic struggles between 'state capitalist trusts'. Competition, albeit transformed, still reflected the absence of any collective organisation of the units of production: 'The system of world economy is just as blindly irrational and "subjectless" as the earlier system of *national* economy'.[22]

Bukharin's writings represent the most important single contribution to marxist economic theory this century. Marx had stated that 'competition on the world market' is 'the basis and vital element of capitalist production',[23] but it was only Bukharin who conceptualised the world market as an integrated system of which individual nation-states were component parts. Similarly, while Marx and Engels had entertained the possibility of the formation of a single 'state capitalist trust' dominating the entire national economy, they conceived this as a hypothetical limiting case unlikely to be realised in practice. Bukharin showed that 'competition on the world market' gave rise to a tendency towards state capitalism within individual national economies. His analysis is not without its defects – many of his formulations in *The Economics of the Transformation Period* reflect the influence of A. A. Bogdanov's 'empirio-monist' philosophy of 'organisation' (much to Lenin's annoyance, as his marginal notes to the book show), while he tended, in line with his highly deductive method of analysis, to treat the *tendency* towards state capitalism as if it were an already realised result.[24] However, his approach was an immensely fruitful one. I shall try to indicate some of its applications.

One such application has been to the analysis of social relations in the USSR. As we have seen, one of the most thorny questions with which contemporary marxist theorists have sought to grapple is that of stalinism. Althusser has ended by confessing that marxism in its present state is unable to deal with this question. Others have sought to account for the class nature of the Soviet Union in terms of Trotsky's concept of degenerated workers' state. This concept was intended to suggest that, while the relations of production in the USSR were post-capitalist, the relations of distribution and politico-ideological superstructure, reflecting the pressure of material scarcity on the isolated and backward Russian economy, involved the domination of a bureaucratic stratum alienated from the working class and its interests. There are obvious difficulties with this analysis – Marx had argued, as we saw, that the distribution of income depended on the distribution of the means of production; furthermore, he distinguished between legal property forms and the relations of production themselves, which Trotsky appeared to conflate in identifying the transcendence of capitalism with state ownership of the means of production. In any case, Trotsky had regarded a degenerated workers' state as an intrinsically unstable state of affairs, likely to give way rapidly either to the restoration of the political power of the working class or to the reimposition of capitalism by imperialism. Neither of these alternatives eventuated; far from the Second World War leading to the fall of the soviet bureaucracy, as Trotsky predicted, it emerged from the conflict greatly strengthened and reproduced itself from the Elbe to the Pacific between

1944 and 1949. Rather than place in question Trotsky's assumptions, his epigones extended his analysis from the USSR to China and eastern Europe, even though this made his definition of a workers' state entirely formal, since none of the 'socialist' regimes to have emerged since the war can trace their origins to the seizure of power by the working class. From being in Trotsky's words 'social excrescences' arising from 'an "accidental" (i.e. temporary and extraordinary) enmeshing of historical circumstances' – the isolation of the bolshevik revolution – the 'bureaucratised workers' states' have become a phase of the transition to socialism.[25] Orthodox trotskyism became a degenerating research programme, lagging behind the facts rather than predicting them.

One of Trotsky's followers, Tony Cliff, was however, led by his researches to reject this analysis of the 'socialist countries'. In a study written in 1947 (and originally planned as a defence of Trotsky's theory!) Cliff challenged the identification (by both stalinists and orthodox trotskyists) of socialism with the expansion of the productive forces:

> From a socialist standpoint . . . the decisive criterion is not the growth of production *per se*, but the social relations acompanying this tremendous development of the productive forces. Is it or is it not accompanied by an improvement in the economic position of the workers, by an increase in their political power, by a strengthening of democracy, a reduction of economic and social inequality, and a decline of state coercion? Is the industrial development planned, and if so, planned by whom, and in whose interests? These are the basic socialist criteria for economic advance.[26]

Applying these criteria to the USSR led Cliff to the conclusion that the working class was separated from the means of production, that the latter were in the effective possession of the party-state bureaucracy, a social group with the essential attributes of a ruling class, and that production of means of consumption was subordinated to that of the means of production. This situation was drastically at variance with the characteristics of the dictatorship of the proletariat outlined by the marxist classics, which made the collective control of the means of production by the working class, and therefore the widest possible workers' democracy, the decisive feature of the transition to communism. Yet if the USSR was a class society could it be described as capitalist, since relations between enterprises were governed, not by the exchange of their products, but by state planning, however irrational?

However, those who claimed that the USSR represented a new mode of production, sometimes called 'bureaucratic collectivism', were unable to distinguish it from certain forms of capitalism, since the most extreme features of stalinism (forced labour, state control of the labour market) were shared by Nazi Germany, and failed to produce an adequate or coherent definition of the new form of class society they claimed to have discovered.[27]

To solve this problem, Cliff turned to the theory of state capitalism. He started from the same premiss as Trotsky, namely that the degeneration of the Russian revolution originated in its failure to spread to western Europe after 1917. We have already seen that, according to Marx, 'the influence of individual capitals on one another has the effect precisely that they must conduct themselves as *capital*'.[28] Conceived in isolation from the rest of the world, the USSR could not be regarded as capitalist. But, seen as one aspect of a global system governed by both the struggle for markets and military competition, the Soviet social formation took on quite another aspect. The priorities reflected in the elimination after 1928 of most of the remaining gains the working class had won in the revolution and in subsequent Soviet decision-making were determined not by the autonomous will of the bureaucracy but by pressures arising from its relations with the western imperialist powers. The fact that these relations took the form primarily of military competition altered the case not at all. It was their subordination to a world system of competing nation-states which forced the Soviet rulers to concentrate resources on the military; the equalisation of private labours analysed by Marx in *Capital* still took place, albeit in the form of comparisons of the share of national income devoted to, and the productivity of labour in, arms and related industries in the USSR. The development of monopoly arising from the tendencies towards the centralisation and concentration of capital inherent in the capitalist mode of production had modified but not overthrown the law of value. The further tendency towards a world economy consisting of state capitals competing militarily now introduced only a new inflection to the analysis of *Capital*. The application of the theory of state capitalism to the USSR, reinforced Marx's identification of capitalist relations of production based on two fundamental antagonisms – that between labour and capital and that between capitals.[29]

It is impossible to trace here the detail of Cliff's analysis of the Soviet Union. Its merit was to develop an explanation of stalinism which was developed directly from the marxist classics. Thus his discussion of the role of arms production and of the form taken by capitalist crises in the USSR is a dialogue with, and a development upon, the writings of theorists as diverse as Luxemburg, Bukharin, Hilferding and Tugan-Baranovsky. As an analysis of the Soviet social formation it has stood the test of time. In particular, its prediction that once the Russian economy had passed through its phase of 'primitive accumulation' it would be liable to stagnate was a remarkable anticipation of more recent developments.[30] The theory proved to be easily extendible to the other 'socialist' regimes.[31] Far then from being an aporia of marxism, as Foucault, Glucksmann and company claim, stalinism proved readily amenable to explanation on the basis of *Capital*.

'*A given fact is explained scientifically only if a new fact is explained with it*'.[32] Thus wrote Imre Lakatos. From this point of view, the theory of state capitalism, in the form developed by Tony Cliff, represented what Lakatos would call a 'theoretically and empirically progressive problem-shift'. Constructed to account for stalinism, the theory anticipated a variety of other developments. Cliff identified the predominant form of competition between capitals on a world scale as military competition. He also pointed out that arms production can serve as a stabilising factor, offsetting capitalism's inherent liability to crises. The commodities produced in the arms sector are means neither of production nor of consumption. They are sold neither to firms nor to workers but supplied directly to the state. The realisation of their value in the market implies an increase neither in the rate of wages (and a fall in the rate of surplus-value) nor in the rate of accumulation (and a fall in the rate of profit). Value created in arms production does not add to the supply of goods thrown on the market, but merely increases the demand for means of production and of consumption produced in other sector. Furthermore, since the rate of profit on arms contracts is normally fixed in advance by negotiation between the firm concerned and the state, capital in the arms sector does not participate in the formation of a general rate of profit on the basis of competition and therefore the existence of a higher than average organic composition of capital in this sector need not cause the average rate of profit to fall. It was these factors which led Cliff and his collaborators, notably Michael Kidron, to attribute the unprecedented expansion of post-war capitalism – world gross national product rose 3½ times between 1948 and 1973 – to the emergence of a 'permanent arms economy' in both western and eastern blocs.[33]

This theory avoided the two errors fallen into by many marxists or former marxists after the Second World War – to detect at every turn, in defiance of all empirical evidence, signs of the final, catastrophic collapse of capitalism (many varieties of orthodox trotskyism), or to assert that capitalism had, thanks to Keynes, overcome its contradictions (John Strachey, Corlineus Castoriadis). The system's new stability rested on foundations of sand – the accumulation by rival super-powers of means of destruction capable of wiping out humanity many times over. Moreover, the decline in the arms economy (measured both in terms of the percentage of national income devoted to arms production and the portion of the investible surplus diverted from the accumulation of productive capital to this sector) evident in the 1960s and 1970s, and arising from American capital's need to recover the competitive position lost to Japanese and German capital, could only mean a return to the classical pattern of boom and slump.

Finally, the theory of state capitalism provides a framework within which to analyse the new period of crises which the world economy entered somewhere between 1968 and 1973. As we saw at the beginning of this chapter one feature of this period has been a renewed ideological offensive against economic intervention by the state. In itself this is no novelty: Milton Friedman and his cohorts are simply parroting, with greater technical sophistication, the demands for cuts in social expenditure, exclusive reliance on the mechanisms of the market, etc. made by F. A. Hayek, Lionel Robbins and others in the 1930s. The difference lies in the nature of the crises. During the great depression output, employment and price levels fell catastrophically. Today a less acute crisis of over-production has not prevented prices from continuing to rise.

The theory of state capitalism may help to explain this situation. One of the defects of the 'capital-logic' approach, as Colin Barker points out, is that it treats 'the state as a necessarily unproductive sphere of activity, as being outside the concept of "capital" itself, as non-capital though necessary for capital'. But 'it seems to me to fly in the face of current actual developments in the world economy to deny that the state can be a *productive* capitalist, that is, a capitalist under whose direct dominion surplus-value is produced'.[34] In other words, not the state *and* capital, but the state *as* capital. The merit of the approach initiated by Bukharin and further developed by Cliff and his collaborators is that it highlights the tendencies towards state capitalism within the western economies. These tendencies take the form of the state acting as productive capital (e.g. nationalised industries) and assuming overall responsibility for the direction of the national economy (planning, monetary and fiscal policy, etc.) That these tendencies exist is undeniable – it can be seen in the role of states in rescuing unprofitable firms whose collapse would have harmful implications for the national economy on the world market (e.g. British Leyland, and Chrysler) and the activities of highly profitable and competitive state-owned firms (e.g. Renault and BP). Their effect is to make the nation-state – even in western capitalism – the most important unit through which the extraction and accumulation of surplus-value is organised. However, the result is not a system of co-equal, autonomous national capitals colliding like billiard balls. The different relative strengths of national capitals, and the activities of their international extensions, the multinational companies, means that individual economies are as much disarticulated as articulated by competition on a global scale. For concurrent with the tendency towards state capitalism is the increasing organisation of production on an international basis. The activities of multinational corporations and in particular their ability to operate across national borders seriously compromises the power of weaker states to plan their own economies. One must therefore distinguish between bureaucratic state capitalism as it exists in the 'socialist' countries, where, in principle at least, one centre controls the entire national economy, and state monopoly capitalism in the west, where state capital, private national capital and foreign multinationals uneasily co-exist within the same economy.[35]

Crises can no longer take their classical form in this new situation. For, as we saw in Chapter 5, crises served to provide conditions for renewed accumulation through bankrupting the weaker capitals and forcing workers, under the whip of unemployment, to accept lower wages and worse conditions. A situation in which the state assumes direct responsibility for the overall management of the national economy and in particular intervenes to prop up lame ducks which, if left to themselves, market forces would drive into liquidation, prevents this mechanism from being fully operative. The necessity of the most effective possible (international) reorganisation of capital clashes with the priorities of national capital. A good example is provided by the European steel, textiles and shipbuilding industries which by the standards set by world levels of productivity are uncompetitive. The social and economic consequences of total closure are such that European governments prefer protectionism, cartellisation and phased reductions in output and employment. It follows that inflation can no longer be simply flushed out of the system by drastic falls in production (or rather, national capitals are unwilling and unable to countenance sufficiently drastic falls). The inevitable result is stagflation, and a state-induced restructuring of capital which proceeds by attrition.

One consequence of this analysis is that there is no national solution to the crisis. The programmes for the state direction of investment, further nationalisations and 'reindustrialisation' advocated by the left wing of the Labour Party and by the western European Communist Parties could at best improve the competitive position of individual national capitals and would in all likelihood involve further reductions in working-class living standards. But since the crisis is produced by a global system of competition and exploitation it is amenable only to international solutions. Even less than in the 1920s and 1930s is 'socialism in one country' possible.

REVOLUTION, CLASS STRUGGLE AND THE STATE

The merit of the modified version of classical marxism developed by Tony Cliff and his collaborators is that it starts from Marx's analysis of capitalist relations of production while recognising that this analysis conceives of capitalism as a system whose very structure – the contradictions of 'capital in general' and 'many capitals' – engenders a continual process of transformation. Capitalism today is very different from the capitalism of Marx's time. It is multinational, closely interwoven if not identified with the state, and heavily armed. Too often marxists try to analyse it formally, by showing that one or other of Marx's propositions holds true today. Absent from such an approach is any sense of the inner dynamic of the system.[36] The authors of *Marx's 'Capital' and Capitalism Today* tell us that the search for the laws of motion of capitalism rests upon a 'rationalist' misconception and invite us to bow down before the infinite openness of discourse and the infinite complexity of social life. The theory of state capitalism, by contrast, insists that the very characteristics of the modern world economy which differ from those of Marx's day can only be understood of the basis of *Capital*. It refuses, therefore, to ignore the changes in the nature of capitalism over the last century but does not infer either that these changes refute *Capital* or that we should give up the attempt to understand capitalism (or indeed anything else) as a bad job. It is a powerful vindication of the continued scientific validity of *Capital*.

It does not follow that all is well with marxism. There is no satisfactory theory of ideology – neither Marx's discussion of fetishism, nor Gramsci's adoption of Machiavelli's distinction between law and force, nor Althusser's borrowings from Lacan's theory of the imaginary provides the basis of such an account. Furthermore, we have yet to arrive at an adequate analysis of the relationship between class-relations and sexual oppression. I have no answer to the questions posed by these gaping holes in historical materialism, beyond a (hardly original) hunch that the work of Foucault and Deleuze, Lacan and Derrida is of relevance, both because they accord the discourses within which ideologies are reproduced and transmitted a specificity denied them by traditional marxist discussions, and because they concern themselves with the relationship between political oppression and human sexuality. Classical marxism would, in my opinion, benefit from a confrontation with French 'structuralist' and 'post-structuralist' thought – a confrontation, however, that went beyond the latter's uncritical assimilation or wholesale rejection.

Meanwhile, I would like to conclude by considering some of the political implications of the version of marxism I have sought to explicate and defend in this book. My starting point is provided by Nicos Poulantzas' arguments in *State, Power, Socialism*. In many ways this is a remarkable book, representing considerable progress over earlier works by the same author. Poulantzas abandons the old talk of relatively autonomous instances: 'the *relative* separation of the state and the economic sphere (accumulation of capital and production of surplus-value)' is 'specific to capitalism' and '*is nothing other than the capitalist form of the presence of the political in the constitution and reproduction of the relations of production*'. The state is no longer 'the factor of cohesion between the different levels of a social formation', rather it is 'the *specific material condensation* of a relationship of forces among classes and class fractions'. It follows that the class struggle is not external to the state – 'class contradictions are the very stuff of the state: they are present in its material framework and pattern its organisation; while the state's policy is the result of their functioning within the state'. In particular, the state's structure and internal organisation – what Poulantzas calls its 'institutional materiality' – depend upon and are shaped by the relations of production and the class struggles to which they give rise.[37]

This approach seems to me to be a useful one. In particular, it serves as a corrective to the tendency (from which the theory of state capitalism has not always been free) to read off the nature and mode of operation of the capitalist state from its economic functions. The state is not, as Poulantzas rightly emphasises, a thing, a neutral instrument which may be used by different classes for different purposes; it is a social relation whose nature depends upon the relations of production but which does not simply passively reflect these relations, playing a critical role in crystallising the prevalent system of class domination. Marx had written of the 'concentration of bourgeois society in the form of the state' and of the state as 'the concentrated and organised force of society',[38] and Lenin followed him in declaring that 'politics is the most concentrated expression of economics'.[39] These formulations deny to politics any autonomy of class struggle and the relations of production; at the same time politics is not a passive medium of class contradictions, it *concentrates* them, bringing them together in an articulated and organised form in which is inscribed the domination of a particular class. The concept of the state as 'the *specific materialised condensation*' of the balance of class forces captures exactly these different aspects: the state not as 'factor of cohesion' where contradictions are overcome – rather, here they are concentrated, but in a specific organised form, a set of structures, an 'institutional materiality' through which one class secures its domination. Political class struggle is thereby accorded a specificity it is often denied by the 'capital-logic' school, for whom politics merely registers subterranean economic changes; at the same time its dependence on the relations of production is firmly asserted.

Poulantzas here offers a framework by means of which to restate the classical marxists' insistence on the centrality of political struggles, and of the conquest of state power, for the transition to socialism. This framework depends upon the proposition that it is the state's monopoly of legitimate violence which underpins any system of class domination. Poulantzas challenges the eurocommunist claim that the western bourgeoisie has come to rely less on 'force' than on 'consent':

Physical violence and consent do not exist side by side like two calculable homogeneous magnitudes, related in such a way that more consent corresponds to less violence. Violence-terror always occupies a determining place – and not merely because it remains in reserve, coming into the open only in critical situations. *State-monopolised physical violence permanently underlies the techniques of power and mechanisms of consent: it is inscribed in the web of disciplinary and ideological devices; and even when not directly exercised, it shapes the materiality of the social body upon which class domination is brought to bear.*[40]

This argument would seem to provide powerful support to Lenin's claim in *The State and Revolution* that the transition to socialism cannot be effected peacefully and necessitates the destruction of the capitalist state machine. However, Poulantzas explicitly rejects such a strategy, arguing that a revolution which replaced parliament with soviets would be constantly liable to the danger of stalinism. The only tenable strategy for socialists in the west is, he argues, the gradual transformation of capitalism within the framework of a political regime which progresssively 'articulates' the institutions of parliamentary democracy at the centre with those of direct democracy at the base. One can only speculate about the reasons for this apparent contradiction. We saw in Chapter 6 that Poulantzas goes a long way towards accepting the foucauldian thesis that power-relations are anterior to and subsume relations of production. Even his discussion of the 'institutional materiality' of the state involves an analysis of the 'social division of labour', which he had already come close to assimilating to relations of domination/subordination in *Classes in Contemporary Capitalism*. This enables him to take over many of Foucault's formulations concerning 'power-knowledge' in *State, Power, Socialism* without grasping that, as Stuart Hall points out, Foucault 'is developing a different problematic – one, moreover, which is, at several key points, inconsistent with Poulantzas's framework of "classical marxism"'.[41] The result is a pessimistic political framework: since class-relations do not exclusively determine power-relations there is always the danger that the old totalitarian Adam will spring up again even under socialism and it is therefore necessary to eschew armed insurrection and preserve the institutions of parliamentary democracy as a safeguard against dictatorship. It is a melancholy sight: the most influential marxist political theorist of the last decade collapsing into liberal platitudes.

It does not follow that those who wish to defend the continued relevance of Lenin's political strategy do not have a case to answer. Does not leninism involve a 'voluntarist' and 'instrumentalist' approach to the state, its seizure by a force external to it, the revolutionary party, which then turns it to its own purposes; does not this approach lead in practice to a sterile and purist approach to politics, a refusal to engage in everyday struggles and thereby to transform the state gradually for the sake of an insurrection that will never come? Obviously, no fully satisfactory answer to these questions can be provided here. However, a number of points can be made.

The classical marxist theory of revolution rests upon the proposition that it is the socialisation of the labour-process brought about by capitalist relations of production that makes proletarian revolution and socialist democracy possible. Marx writes that the centralisation and concentration of capital engender

> the growth of the co-operative form of the labour-process, the conscious technical application of science, the planned exploitation of the soil, the transformation of the means of labour into forms in which they can only be used in common, the economising of all means of production by their use as the means of production of combined, socialised labour, the entanglement of all peoples in the net of the world market and, with this, the growth of the international character of the capitalist regime.

The capitalist accumulation process, in other words, socialises labour, not only within the factory, but on a national and international scale. Capitalism creates the 'collective worker'. But, since this process takes place on the basis of exploitative relations of production,

> along with the constant decrease in the number of capitalist magnates, who usurp and monopolise all the advantages of this process of transformation, the mass of misery, oppression, slavery, degradation and exploitation grows; but with this there also grows the revolt of the working class, a class constantly increasing in numbers, and trained, united and organised by the very mechanism of the capitalist process of production.[42]

Because their exploitation necessitates the socialisation of the labour-process workers, in order to fight for the most limited improvements in their position within the process of production, must organise and act collectively. The basic weapons of the economic class struggle – the strike, the picket, blacking – are not the inventions of socialists; they arose spontaneously from workers' battles against exploitation at the point of production. Moreover, the creation of the 'collective worker' and the 'transformation of the means of labour into forms in which they can only be used in common' mean that the proletariat can only appropriate the means of production *collectively*. It makes no sense to talk about dividing up a factory among individual workers the way a landed estate may be shared out among peasants. It is for this reason that Marx and Engels write: 'we call communism the *real* movement which abolishes the present state of things'.[43] Communism, the rule of the associated producers, is not, primarily, a prescription derived from a moral critique of capitalism; the collective appropriation of the means of production which it involves is made possible by the socialisation of the labour-process effected by capitalism.[44]

The marxists of the Second and Third Internationals were in agreement that, in the sense outlined above, capitalism created the conditions of communism. They differed, however, on two crucial issues. First, what form would the transition to communism take? Kautsky in particular vehemently rejected the notion of a 'Commune-State' that would supplant the existing state machine. The transfer of power to the working class would take place within the framework of the existing parliamentary-democratic state; the sole means of political representation for workers would be provided by the social-democratic parties.[45] Ironically, like the stalinists after them, the social-democrats conflated party and class; socialist revolution was identified by both with the capture of the state machine by the party, with no role allowed for the self-activity of the mass of workers.[46]

By contrast, Lenin, Trotsky and Gramsci all argued that the spontaneous struggles of workers would throw up forms of organisation wider than the party which would provide the basis for the new, radically democratic form of state which the proletarian revolution would establish – soviets, or councils of workers' delegates. The significance of these institutions was, first, that they were class-wide organisations in a sense that neither parties nor trade unions were, embracing organised and unorganised workers, revolutionaries, reformists and the previously apathetic. Second, they were organs of struggle, usually formed spontaneously in pursuit of ends initially falling far short of the seizure of power – for example, the first soviet was formed in St Petersburg in 1905 to co-ordinate a print-workers' strike called to win payment for setting punctuation marks as well as letters. Third, however, the soviets were potentially a new form of state, providing the workers with the means to co-ordinate and act nationally, yet on the basis of their power to paralyse and assume control of the process of production. Implicit, then, in the formation of soviets was a situation of dual power, in which the working class could challenge the bourgeoisie's ability to rule.[47]

Let us note that this is in no sense a 'voluntarist' or 'insurrectionist' concept of the transition to socialism. It conceives of proletarian revolution as a *process* whose roots lie in the elementary forms of working-class struggle. Working-class power and the new form of state it involves exists in embryo in the day-to-day struggles and organisations of the proletariat. Gramsci wrote that 'the socialist state already exists potentially in the institutions of social life characteristic of the exploited working class'[48] and saw the internal commissions (the Italian shop-stewards' committees) as the institutions which could form the basis of a proletarian dictatorship, organising rank-and-file workers within the factories to assume control of production. However, to describe revolution as a process is not to assert that it involves no ruptures. Lenin, Trotsky, Luxemburg and Gramsci argued that socialist revolution was impossible without the armed seizure of power by the working class. They did so because bourgeois class rule was underpinned by the state's monopoly of legitimate violence. The expropriation of the capitalist class would be impossible without the dissolution of what Engels called the 'special bodies of armed men' – the army and police – on which this monopoly depended and the arming of the working masses. This is no mere theorem. Historical experience since their time has confirmed the classical marxists' claims; to cite merely the most recent events – Chile 1970–3, Portugal 1974–5, Iran 1978–9, – no revolution which leaves the repressive state apparatus intact can hope to succeed.

The second issue over which Lenin, Trotsky and Gramsci differed sharply with the marxists of the Second International was the question of class consciousness. Kautsky and

Plekhanov, here following Marx and Engels, believed that revolutionary consciousness among the masses would be the product of a process of 'natural development'. In *What is to be Done?* Lenin denied that 'the working class *spontaneously* gravitates towards socialism'.[49] Although formulated in terms borrowed from Kautsky, Lenin's argument represented a radical challenge to evolutionist marxism, since it laid great emphasis on the active intervention of socialist political organisation in the class struggle. To be fully satisfactory, it required the formulation of a theory of the obstacles to the formation of revolutionary class consciousness, a task for which, ironically, Lenin was ill fitted, since many of these obstacles – notably the separation of economic and political struggles, the existence of mass trade unions and working-class parties pledged to respect the framework of capitalism, the evolution of the trade union bureaucracy as a social layer whose *raison d'etre* is to negotiate social peace – were present either to a very limited extent or not at all in tsarist Russia; it was in western Europe and north America that the problem of a legal workers' movement integrated within the capitalist system and concerned to achieve its piecemeal reform not its overthrow was – and is – of central importance.[50]

Lenin's theory of the revolutionary party represented, however, an immense breakthrough. It stressed that the party's task was not to substitute itself for the working class, but to make their struggles conscious and directed towards the seizure of power. Lenin wrote in 1907 that the bolsheviks' success

> was due to the fact that the working class . . . for objective economic reasons possesses a greater capacity for organisation than any other class of capitalist society. Without this condition an organisation of professional revolutionaries would be nothing more than a plaything, an adventure, a mere signboard. *What is to be Done?* repeatedly emphasises this, pointing out that the organisation it advocates has no meaning apart from its connection with the 'genuinely revolutionary class that is spontaneously rising to struggle'.[51]

The revolutionary party, on Lenin's conception, is that section of the working class consciously and actively committed to the revolutionary transformation of society. It seeks to achieve this aim by winning the support of the majority of the working population. 'To win,' Lenin said,

> we must have the sympathy of the masses. An absolute majority is not always essential; but what is essential to win and retain power is not only the majority of the working class . . . but also the majority of the working and exploited population.[52]

Revolution, then, is not a blanquist coup. It depends on the active support and participation of the working masses, who, organised into soviets, directly take power. Lenin argued that the only way to achieve such a majority was by the involvement of revolutionaries in the everyday struggles of workers; only by activity within the trade unions around partial demands stopping well short of the seizure of power, by participation in united fronts with reformist workers, could the revolutionary party conquer the masses. It is, as Gramsci put it, 'the result of a dialectical process, in which the spontaneous movement of the revolutionary masses and the organising and directing will of the centre converge'.[53]

The conception of the revolutionary process espoused by Lenin, Trotsky and Gramsci was a profoundly democratic one. The revolutionary party was conceived, not as a substitute for the working class, but as the most conscious and active section of that class. Revolution itself could only be the act of the working class; in Marx and Engels' words, 'the emancipation of the working class must be the work of the working class itself'.[54] The identification of socialism with the self-emancipation of the working-class is, for some – E. P. Thompson, for example – an essentially moral decision, involving a commitment to humanistic and libertarian ideals. For Marx, however, and for the tradition which developed this insight, working-class power arises from the tendencies inherent in capitalist relations of production which drive workers collectively to organise themselves in defence of their interests.[55] This conception of socialism was lost with the degeneration of the Russian revolution in the 1920s. Even Trotsky and his followers, by identifying socialism with the legal form of state ownership, assented to the denial of the self-activity of the working class. Socialism and working-class power came to be both logically, and in actuality, distinct. The application of the theory of state capitalism to 'really existing socialism' restored the identity of the two concepts. It explained stalinism as the effect of the pressure of world capitalism on a regime isolated by the failure of the revolution to spread beyond Russia after 1917 and the virtual destruction of the working class by civil war, famine and blockage.[56] Far from being the inevitable outcome of marxism, stalinism was the product of the revolution's defeat. The immense expansion of 'socialism' after 1945 signified in reality the growth of a specific form of capitalism. Workers' democracy was not merely the icing on the socialist cake but the constitutive element of the revolutionary process; socialism was inseparable from the action of the working class.[57]

From this point of view, the classical marxist preoccupation with the conquest of political power is entirely justified. It reflects, not the will to power which Foucault, Deleuze and the *nouveaux philosophes* detect secreted within marxism, but the realisation that the state is the 'specific materialised condensation' of the contradictions constitutive of capitalist society. No serious socialist strategy can ignore the question of the state. Two errors reinforce each other – on the one hand, the failure to grasp that it is the social distribution of the means of production and the corresponding mode of appropriation of surplus-labour on which the nature of every social formation depends; on the other hand, the refusal to confront the fact that the reproduction of these relations of production depends on the 'concentrated and organised force of society' – the state. These errors are involved in the dissolution of economics and politics into relations of power which is characteristic not only of Foucault's work, but also of the writings of many who believe they are thereby rescuing marxism from 'economism'. They tend either to the adoption of a strategy of piecemeal reform, the return of Kautsky and Bernstein from the grave, or to a great renunciation, the refusal to sully one's hands with power, which can take a variety of forms, from the aimless terrorism of some of the *autonomisti* to the cosy 'prefigurative' socialism of sections of the British left. The retreat from the central insights of classical marxism as outlined in this book leads to the pursuit of utopia, whether it be the peaceful transformation of capitalism or the 'resistance' of power in the name of an unattainable natural man. The strategy defended by Lenin, Luxemburg, Trotsky and Gramsci sought instead to supplant the 'imperialist robber state' with a form of political power based on the forms of organisation created by workers out of their daily struggles with capital as a stage towards the abolition of all relations of exploitation and their 'condensation' in the state.

The continued relevance of classical marxism seems to me unarguable. Neither of the two main forms of orthodox economic analysis – monetarism and keynesianism – offers a satisfactory account of the economic crisis; indeed, both close off the most important questions. The theory of state capitalism, by contrast, offers an explanation of this phenomenon which grounds it in the internal structure of capitalism, and in particular in the manner in which competition on a world scale has come to be dominated by multinational firms closely integrated in the national state. Furthermore, the expansion of capitalism, albeit in a peculiar form, in many parts of the Third World, has meant that the patterns of working-class struggle studied and sometimes led by the classical marxists in Manchester and St Petersburg are being reproduced in the industrial estates of São Paolo and Durban and in the oilfields of Khozestan. The articulation of capital accumulation, the socialisation of the labour-process and 'the revolt of the working class, a class constantly increasing in numbers and trained, united and organised by the very mechanism of the capitalist process of production' now exists on a world scale.[58] In particular political conjunctures this articulation has led to the emergence of organs of working-class power to challenge the state's monopoly of violence – Russia 1905 and 1917, Italy 1918–20, Germany 1918–23, China 1925–7, Spain 1936–7, Hungary 1956, Portugal 1975. The red thread of soviet power runs through the history of the twentieth century. There is no reason to believe that its tale has yet been told.

None of this guarantees the triumph of socialism. In the west at least the mass reformist unions and parties provide a framework within which workers may improve their position but which binds them to the *status quo*. It was with this problem that Gramsci grappled in his *Prison Notebooks*, not wholly successfully – namely, the ideological and political conditions of bourgeois rule.[59] Both Lenin and Trotsky were careful to emphasise that socialism would depend on the outcome of the class struggle, not the iron laws of capitalism. When Bukharin declared that 'a restoration of the *old* capitalism is impossible', Lenin commented: 'this depends upon whether the pro-letariat "on the basis of class struggle" . . . would be able to bring about the total downfall'.[60] And Trotsky warned the Third Congress of the Comintern in 1921 against 'faith in automatic evolution' which, he said, was 'the most important and the most characteristic trait of opportunism'. He went on to say:

> If we grant – and let us grant it for the moment – that the working class fails to rise in revolutionary struggle, but allows the bourgeoisie the opportunity to rule the world's destiny for a long number of years, say, two or three decades, then assuredly some new sort of equilibrium will be established.

Therefore, 'speaking theoretically and abstractly, the restora-tion of capitalist equilibrium is possible. But it does not take place in a vacuum – it can only take place through the classes'.[61] Marxism, in Lenin and Trotsky's hands, became not a secularised theology but a means for analysing the objective conditions of the class struggle without claiming to predeter-mine that.struggle's outcome. Trotsky's prediction proved to be correct: the failure of proletarian revolution in the 1920s and 1930s permitted a new capitalist equilibrium to be established. We are now witnessing the breakdown of that equilibrium. The defeat of the last revolutionary wave helped ensure the triumph of vulgar evolutionism within marxism, even in Trotsky's last writings,[62] so that when marxist theory revived in the 1960s it did so in distorted often idealist forms, as we have seen in Althusser's case. We cannot simply 'return' to classical marxism; its silences and lacunae are too evident and filling them may involve transforming marxism. But this theoretical labour takes place in conditions more favourable to socialist revolution than any since the end of the First World

War. Classical marxism is, as I have sought to indicate, uniquely fitted to analyse these conditions. We can only hope to develop marxism starting from the classics, resting on the shoulders of giants, as Newton put it. Moreover, the situation of crisis within which we live today offers an opportunity to close the gap between marxist theory and working-class struggle which opened up, with such harmful results, in the 1920s. In Britain at least a considerable socialist intelligentsia exists side by side with an economically militant working class like two closed vessels which do not communicate. This situation can only be remedied within the framework of a party which insists that theory relate to the problems of the class struggle and which engages in day-to-day battles as part of an overall revolutionary strategy. Without Gramsci's Modern Prince – the revolutionary party – marxist theory cannot escape the seminar room.

Notes and References

DEFINITIONS

1. N. Poulantzas, *Classes in Contemporary Capitalism* (London: New Left Books, 1975) p. 200.

CHAPTER 1

1. *Power and Opposition in Post-Revolutionary Societies* (London: Ink Links, 1979) pp. 9, 10.
2. Ibid., p. 226.
3. Ibid., p. 231.
4. E. Altvater and O. Kallscheuer, 'Socialist politics and the crisis of marxism', in R. Miliband and J. Saville (eds), *The Socialist Register 1979* (London: Merlin, 1979) p. 116.
5. This tension was noted by Trotsky as early as 1938 – see L. Trotsky, 'A Fresh Lesson', in *Writings 1938–39* (New York: Pathfinder Press, 1974) pp. 68–72.
6. On the evolution of the Communist Parties, see I. Birchall, *Workers Against the Monolith* (London: Pluto, 1973); F. Claudin, *The Communist Movement* (Harmondsworth: Penguin, 1975).
7. See C. Harman, 'Eurocommunism, the state and revolution', *International Socialism* (old series), no. 101, September 1977; E. Mandel, *From Stalinism to Eurcommunism* (London: New Left Books, 1978).
8. L. Althusser, 'Unfinished history', introduction to D. Lecourt, *Proletarian Science?* (London: New Left Books, 1977) p. 13.
9. *Power and Opposition in Post-Revolutionary Societies*, p. 227.
10. R. Debray, 'Springtime weepers', originally published in *Le Nouvel Observateur*, 13 June 1977, English translation in *Telos*, Fall 1977.
11. K. Marx, *Capital*, vol. 3 (Moscow: Progress, 1971) p. 791.
12. See R. Debray, 'A modest contribution to the rites and ceremonies of the tenth anniversary', *New Left Review*, no. 105, May–June 1979.
13. P. Sweezy, 'A crisis in marxian theory', *Monthly Review*, vol. 31, no. 2, June 1979, p. 23.
14. L. Colletti, 'A political and philosophical interview', *New Left Review*, no. 86, July–August 1974, p. 24.
15. D. Widgery, 'Ten years for Pandora', *Socialist Review*, no. 2, May 1978.
16. C. Harman, 'The crisis of the European revolutionary left', *International Socialism* (new series), no. 4, Spring 1979.

17. See the critical discussion of their own history by two leading members of the French section of the Fourth International – A. Artous and D. Bensaid, '*Que faire* (1903) et la création de la Ligue Communiste (1969)', *Critique Communiste*, no. 6, April/May 1976.
18. C. Harman, 'Everything seemed possible...', *Socialist Review*, no. 2, May 1978.
19. See, for example, A. Callinicos and P. Goodwin, 'On the perspectives of the Fourth International', *International Socialism* (new series), no. 6, Autumn 1979.
20. See E. Balibar, *On the Dictatorship of the Proletariat* (London: New Left Books, 1977) and L. Althusser, 'What must change in the party', originally a series of articles in *Le Monde*, 25–8 April 1978, English translation in *New Left Review*, no. 109, May–June 1978.
21. See the special issue of *Critique Communiste* on 'Militantisme et vie quotidienne', no. 11/12, December 1976/January 1977.
22. See M. Holborow, 'The women's movement in Italy', *Socialist Review* no. 13, July/August 1979.
23. See R. Challinor, *The Origins of British Bolshevism* (London: Croom Helm, 1978); J. Hinton, *The First Shop Stewards' Movement* (London: George Allen and Unwin, 1973); D. Widgery, *The Left in Britain 1956–68* (Harmondsworth: Penguin, 1976); S. Macintyre, *A Proletarian Science* (Cambridge University Press, 1980).
24. See T. Cliff, 'The balance of class forces in recent years', *International Socialism* (new series), no. 6, Autumn 1979; D. Beecham, 'The employers' offensive', *Socialist Review*, no. 15, October 1979.
25. See S. Jefferys, 'Out at 60?', *Socialist Review*, no. 13, July/August 1979 and no. 14, September 1979.
26. A. Cutler, B. Hindess, P. Hirst and A. Hussain, *Marx's 'Capital' and Capitalism Today*, vol. 1 (London: Routledge and Kegan Paul, 1977) pp. 2, 10, 179, 222, 242.
27. P. Anderson, *Considerations on Western Marxism* (London: New Left Books, 1976) p. 29.
28. F. Parkin, *Marxism and Class Theory* (London: Tavistock, 1979) p. ix.
29. See R. Blackburn in the *Times Higher Education Supplement*, 5 December 1979.
30. E. P. Thompson, *The Poverty of Theory and Other Essays* (London: Merlin, 1978) p. 383.
31. V. Descombes, *La Même et l'Autre* (Paris: Minuit, 1979), p. 152.
32. *Le Monde*, 21–22 January 1979.
33. N. Poulantzas, *State, Power, Socialism* (London: New Left Books, 1978) p. 265.

CHAPTER 2

1. E. Jolas, 'The revolution of language and James Joyce', in S. Beckett and others, *Our Exagmination Round his Factification for Incamination of Work in Progress* (London: Faber and Faber, 1972) p. 77.
2. M. Foucault, 'Politics and the study of discourse', *Ideology and Consciousness*, no. 3, Spring 1978 pp. 17–18.

3. See the discussion of the role assumed by the concept of representation in the seventeenth century in M. Foucault, *The Order of Things* (London: Tavistock, 1970), Chapter 3.
4. F. de Saussure, *Course in General Linguistics* (New York: McGraw-Hill, 1966) pp. 65, 66, 113.
5. R. Jakobson, *Essais de Linguistique Générale* (Paris: Minuit, 1963) p. 162.
6. Saussure, *Course in General Linguistics*, p. 115.
7. Ibid., pp. 117, 117–18.
8. Ibid., pp. 116, 118, 120.
9. Ibid., p. 77.
10. F. Jameson, *The Prison-house of Language* (Princeton: Princeton University Press, 1974) p. 32.
11. G. Deleuze, 'A quoi reconnait-on le structuralisme?' in F. Chatelet (ed.) *Histoire de la Philosophie* t. 8 (Paris: Hachette, 1973) p. 306.
12. See 'Note sur la philosophie de la différence de Heidegger' in G. Deleuze, *Différence et Répetition* (Paris: Presses Universitaires de France, 1968) pp. 89–91.
13. V. Descombes, *La Même et l'Autre* (Paris: Minuit, 1979) p. 13.
14. Ibid, chapter 1.
15. Ibid., p. 40.
16. See, for example, J. Hyppolite, *Logique et Existence* (Paris: Presses Universitaires de France, 1953) pp. 50, 91–2.
17. M. Poster, *Existential Marxism in Postwar France* (Princeton University Press, 1975) p. 19.
18. Quoted in W. Kaufmann, *Hegel* (London: Weidenfeld and Nicholson, 1965) p. 176.
19. See especially G. W. F. Hegel, *The Science of Logic* (London: George Allen and Unwin, 1929) vol. 1, pp. 53–75, and p. 81.
20. See G. Stedman Jones, 'The marxism of the early Lukács', *New Left Review*, no. 70 November–December 1971.
21. M. Foucault, 'Nietzsche, Freud, Marx', in *Cahiers de Royaumont: Philosophie* no. VI, *Nietzsche* (Paris: Minuit, 1967) pp. 183–5.
22. Ibid., pp. 187, 189, 190, 188.
23. C. Levi-Strauss, 'Introduction à l'oeuvre de Marcel Mauss', in M. Mauss (ed.), *Sociologie et Anthropologie* (Paris: Presses Universitaires de France, 1950) XLIX, XLVII–XLVIII.
24. Ibid., XLIX, XLIV, XLIX.
25. Ibid., XXXII.
26. J. Lacan, *Ecrits: A Selection* (London: Tavistock, 1977) p. 147.
27. Lacan wrote in the Rome report that 'the undertaking of the psychoanalyst acts in our time as a mediator between the man of care and the subject of absolute knowledge' – i.e., between existentialism and the dialectic (ibid., p. 105). Kojeve's influence is evident here.
28. Ibid., p. 64.
29. J. Lacan, *The Four Fundamental Concepts of Psychoanalysis* (London: The Hogarth Press and the Institute of Psychoanalysis, 1977) pp. 154, 177.
30. Hegel, *The Science of Logic*, vol. 2, p. 413.
31. A. Lemaire, *Lacan* (London: Routledge and Kegan Paul, 1977) p. 162.
32. J. Lacan, *Ecrits*, pp. 264, 286, 287.

33. G. W. F. Hegel, *The Phenomenology of Mind* (London: George Allen and Unwin, 1966) p. 229. Lacan refers to the dialectic of master and slave on a number of occasions – for example, Lacan, *Ecrits*, pp. 26, 80.
34. Lacan, *Ecrits*, p. 264.
35. Ibid., pp. 166, 264, 284, 234.
36. Ibid., p. 126.
37. Jakobson, *Essais*, p. 63. See generally ibid., chapter 2.
38. See J. Lacan, 'The agency of the letter in the unconscious or reason since Freud', in Lacan, *Ecrits*. The identification may seem a little arbitrary. Indeed, Jakobson also applies the metaphor/metonymy distinction to Freud, but with different results (see Jakobson, *Essais*, pp. 65–6).
39. Lacan, *Four Fundamental Concepts*, pp. 150, 149, 153, 155, 154.
40. Ibid., p. 172.
41. Foucault, *The Order of Things*, pp. 386, 387.
42. D. C. Woods, 'An introduction to Derrida', *Radical Philosophy*, no. 21, Spring 1979, provides an excellent presentation of Derrida's approach.
43. M. Heidegger, *Being and Time* (Oxford: Blackwell, 1967) p. 47. Derrida acknowledges his debt to Heidegger in *Positions* (Paris: Minuit, 1972) pp. 18–19. George Steiner's description of Derrida as a disciple of Lacan in *Heidegger* (London: Fontana/Collins, 1978) p. 144 is superficial and inaccurate: compare Derrida's critical discussion of Lacan in *Positions*, pp. 112–19, n. 33.
44. J. Derrida, *Writing and Difference* (London and Henley: Routledge and Kegan Paul, 1978) p. 291.
45. See J. Derrida, *Of Grammatology* (Baltimore: Johns Hopkins Press, 1976) p. 98.
46. Ibid., p. 69.
47. Ibid., p. 52. And see the discussion of Saussure in J. Derrida, *Positions*, pp. 27–50.
48. Descombes, *La même*, p. 173–4.
49. Derrida, *Writing and Difference*, p. 292.
50. Derrida, *Positions*, pp. 29–30.
51. Derrida, *Of Grammatology*, pp. 158–9, 3, 10, 87, 337 n. 8.
52. Ibid., pp. 47, 143.
53. Cf. M. Heidegger: 'Our western languages are languages of metaphysical thinking', *Identity and Difference* (New York: Harper and Rowe, 1974) p. 73.
54. Derrida, *Writing and Difference*, p. 288.
55. Woods, 'Derrida', p. 18.
56. Jameson, *The Prison-house*, p. 176.
57. B. Russell, 'Knowledge by acquaintance and knowledge by description', in *Mysticism and Logic and Other Essays* (London: George Allen and Unwin, 1963) pp. 152, 167.
58. V. I. Lenin, *Materialism and Empirio-Criticism* (Moscow: Progress, 1947) p. 250. For Marx's views, see K. Marx, *Grundrisse* (Harmondsworth: Penguin, 1973) pp. 100–8.
59. B. Spinoza, *Ethics* part II (London: J. M. Dent and Sons, 1959), prop. XLIV and note.

CHAPTER 3

1. M. Poster, *Existential Marxism in Postwar France* (Princeton University Press, 1975) pp. 341–2.
2. D. Caute, *Communism and the French Intellectuals 1914–60* (London: Andre Deutsch, 1964) p. 29.
3. On the Lysenko affair, see D. Lecourt, *Proletarian Science?* (London: New Left Books, 1977).
4. Caute, *French Intellectuals 1914–60* pp. 55, 220, 332, 187.
5. L. Althusser, 'Unfinished history', introduction to Lecourt, *Proletarian Science?* pp. 14, 15. For a detailed discussion of dialectical materialism, see L. Colletti, *Marxism and Hegel* (London: New Left Books, 1973).
6. Lefebvre looked back on the 1940s shortly before his expulsion from the Communist Party – see H. Lefebvre, 'Le marxisme et la pensée francaise', *Les Temps Modernes*, nos. 137–138, July–August 1957.
7. L. Althusser, *For Marx* (London: Allen Lane, 1969) p. 21.
8. On hegelian marxism, see L. Althusser, 'The object of *Capital*', in L. Althusser and E. Balibar, *Reading Capital* (London: New Left Books, 1970) chapter 5 and A. Callinicos, *Althusser's Marxism* (London: Pluto, 1976) chapter 1.
9. J. Rancière, *La Leçon d'Althusser* (Paris: Gallimard, 1974) p. 95.
10. P. Anderson, *Considerations on Western Marxism* (London: New Left Books, 1976) pp. 43–4.
11. L. Althusser, 'Is it easy to be a marxist in philosophy?', in *Essays in Self-criticism* (London: New Left Books, 1976) p. 169.
12. Rancière, *La Leçon*, p. 73.
13. G. W. F. Hegel, *Encyclopaedia of the Philosophical Sciences*, part I, *Logic* (Oxford: Clarendon Press, 1975) p. 296.
14. Althusser, *For Marx*, pp. 101, 113.
15. Ibid., pp. 115–16.
16. L. Althusser, 'From *Capital* to Marx's philosophy', in Althusser and Balibar, *Reading Capital*, pp. 15–16 (Marx, Freud, Nietzsche), 53 (Heidegger), 62–3 (Husserl's *Origins of Geometry*). The references to Hegel are too frequent to be worth listing.
17. Derrida has stated his agreement with Althusser's conception of history – J. Derrida, *Positions* (Paris: Minuit, 1972) pp. 79, 86, 87. The only reference to Derrida by Althusser that I have been able to track down is quite friendly – L. Althusser, *Politics and History* (London: New Left Books, 1972) p. 184.
18. See L. Althusser, 'Freud and Lacan', in *Lenin and Philosophy and Others* (London: New Left Books, 1971) p. 185. Althusser also acknowledges his debt to Lacan in the opening pages of *Reading Capital* – 'From *Capital* to Marx's philosophy', p. 16 n. 1.
19. Anderson, *Considerations*, p. 64. Anderson's discussion of Althusser's 'spinozism' is something of an oddity. He rather undermines his case by writing that 'nearly all the novel concepts and accents of Althusser's marxism, *apart from those imported from contemporary disciplines*, were in fact directly drawn from Spinoza' (p. 64, emphasis added) – hardly a very rigorous or informative statement without any discussion of these

importations. Anderson adds a footnote in which he claims that in 'Elements of Self-criticism' (1974) 'Althusser has for the first time acknowledged his debt to Spinoza' (p. 65 n. 38). Consultation of the indexes to *For Marx* and *Reading Capital* reveals no less than thirteen references to Spinoza, the earliest dating from 1961, one of which Anderson had cited on the previous page! For a recent althusserian interpretation of Spinoza see P. Macherey, *Hegel ou Spinoza* (Paris: Maspero, 1979).

20. Althusser, *For Marx*, pp. 198–9.
21. See K. Marx, *Capital*, vol. 1 (Harmondsworth: Penguin, 1976) pp. 283–92.
22. Althusser, *For Marx*, pp. 166, 167.
23. G. W. F. Hegel, *The Phenomenology of Mind* (London: George Allen and Unwin, 1966) p. 800.
24. Althusser, 'The object of *Capital*', in Althusser and Balibar, *Reading Capital*, pp. 99, 100.
25. Derrida, *Positions*, p. 79.
26. Althusser, 'From *Capital* to Marx's philosophy', in Althusser and Balibar, *Reading Capital*, pp. 35, 16, 38; and see generally pp. 34–40.
27. Ibid., p. 52.
28. Althusser, *For Marx*, pp. 233–4.
29. L. Althusser, 'Ideology and the ideological state apparatuses', in *Lenin and Philosophy and Other Essays*, pp. 160, 170.
30. Althusser, *For Marx*, p. 232.
31. Althusser, 'From *Capital* to Marx's philosophy', in Althusser and Balibar, *Reading Capital*, p. 17.
32. Ibid., p. 16.
33. B. Spinoza, *Ethics* (London: J. M. Dent and Sons, 1959) part II prop. 40 note II and prop. 51.
34. See especially G. Bachelard, *La Formation de l' Esprit Scientifique* (Paris: Vrin, 1970).
35. See D. Lecourt, *Marxism and Epistemology* (London: New Left Books, 1976) part 1 and D. Lecourt, *Bachelard: Ou, le Jour et la Nuit* (Paris: Grasset, 1974).
36. A. Badiou, 'Le (re)commencement du materialisme dialectique', *Critique*, no. 240, May 1967, p. 449.
37. Althusser, 'Is it simple to be a marxist in philosophy?', in *Essays*, p. 170.
38. A. Badiou, 'Le (re)commencement du materialisme dialectique', *Critique*, no. 240, May 1967, p. 442 n. 8.
39. Althusser, 'The object of *Capital*', in Althusser and Balibar, *Reading Capital*, p. 180.
40. See G. Stedman Jones, 'The marxism of the early Lukács', *New Left Review*, no. 70, November–December 1971.
41. See Callinicos, *Althusser's Marxism*, pp. 57–60, 72–7.
42. Althusser, 'From *Capital* to Marx's philosophy', in Althusser and Balibar, *Reading Capital*, pp. 60, 56.
43. Althusser distinguishes this question from that of the conditions of production of theoretical discourses – the problem of the history of the sciences. Paul Patton, 'Althusser's epistemology', *Radical Philosophy*, no.

19, Spring 1978, rightly criticises the conflation of these questions by a number of commentators, including myself. I should add that I also failed adequately to distinguish the question of the 'knowledge-effect' from that of the difference between science and ideology.

44. A. Badiou, 'Le (re)commencement du materialisme dialectique', *Critique*, no. 240, May 1967, p. 449.
45. Althusser, *For Marx*, p. 169.
46. See A. Glucksmann, 'A ventriloquist structuralism', *New Left Review*, no. 72, March–April 1972 (first published in 1967).
47. See the texts by Lecourt cited in n. 35 above, and E. Balibar, 'From Bachelard to Althusser: the concept of epistemological break', *Economy and Society*, vol. 7, no. 3, August 1978.
48. See J. Derrida, 'Structure, sign and play in the discourse of the human sciences', in *Writing and difference* (London and Henley: Routledge and Kegan Paul, 1978); G. Besse, 'Deux questions sur un article de Louis Althusser', R. Garaudy, 'Les manuscrits de 1844', both in *La Pensée*, February 1963, and G. Mury, 'Materialisme et hyper-empirisme', *La Pensée*, April 1963.
49. Althusser, 'The object of *Capital*', in Althusser and Balibar, *Reading Capital*, pp. 188, 189.
50. Althusser, 'Elements of self-criticism', in *Essays in Self-Criticism*, p. 127 n. 20.
51. Balibar, 'The basic concepts of historical materialism', in Althusser and Balibar, *Reading Capital*, pp. 207, 215, 216.
52. See A. Glucksmann, 'A ventriloquist structuralism', *New Left Review*, no. 72, March–April 1972.
53. N. Poulantzas, *Political Power and Social Classes* (London: New Left Books and Sheed and Ward, 1973) p. 44. This is all the odder, since in 'Vers une théorie marxiste', *Les Temps Modernes*, no. 240, May 1966, Poulantzas made some perceptive criticisms of Althusser's functionalist tendencies.
54. See J. Rancière, 'On the theory of ideology', *Radical Philosophy*, no. 7, Spring 1974; P. Q. Hirst, 'Althusser and the theory of ideology', *Economy and Society*, vol. 5, no. 4, November 1976.
55. Althusser, 'The object of *Capital*', in Althusser and Balibar, *Reading Capital*, p. 174.
56. P. Q. Hirst, 'Althusser and the theory of ideology', *Economy and Society*, vol. 5, no. 4, November 1976, p. 390.
57. N. Poulantzas, *Classes in Contemporary Capitalism* (London: New Left Books, 1975) pp. 207, 242. See P. Q. Hirst, 'Economic classes and politics' in A. Hunt (ed.), *Class and Class Structure* (London: Lawrence and Wishart, 1977) for a systematic critique of 'Poulantzas' conflation of the relations of production with their political/ideological conditions of existence' (p. 138).
58. Bettelheim acknowledges his debt to the 'break made by L. Althusser and his associates with the "economistic" interpretation of Marx's *Capital*', C. Bettelheim, *Class Struggles in the USSR*, vol. 1 (Hassocks: Harvester, 1977) p. 48 n. 2. Althusser gives this book a favourable mention as one of the two exceptions (the other being Fernando

Claudin's *The Communist Movement*) to the 'derisory' analysis of the USSR in terms of the 'cult of personality' – L. Althusser, 'Unfinished history', p. 8 n. 2.

59. A. Callinicos, 'Maoism, stalinism and the Soviet Union', *International Socialism* (new series), no. 5, Summer 1979.

60. See also Callinicos, *Althusser's Marxism*, p. 105.

61. Althusser advocates what he calls 'a very special kind of destruction' of the state, 'not at all an annihilation, but the reorganisation, restructuring and revolutionisation of an existing apparatus' – L. Althusser, 'On the twenty-second congress of the French Communist Party', *New Left Review*, no. 104, July–August 1977, p. 17.

62. T. Bottomore and P. Goode (eds.), *Austro-Marxism* (Oxford University Press 1976) p. 78. It is, by the way, quite wrong to assert, as Perry Anderson does, that Max Adler and the other austro-marxists were 'attracted to Kant's ethics' rather than his epistemology (Anderson, *Considerations* p. 63 n. 28). See Otto Bauer's obituary of Adler (Bottomore and Goode, *Austro-Marxism*, p. 52).

63. See, for example, R. Rosdolsky, 'La situation révolutionnaire en Austriche en 1918 et la politique des sociaux-démocrates', *Critique Communiste*, nos. 8/9, September/October 1976.

64. V. Descombes, *La Même et l'Autre* (Paris: Minuit, 1979) pp. 158–9.

65. A. Cutler, B. Hindess, P. Hirst and A. Hussein, *Marx's 'Capital' and Capitalism Today* (London: Routledge and Kegan Paul, 1977 and 1978).

CHAPTER 4

1. G. W. F. Hegel, *The Phenomenology of Mind* (London: George Allen and Unwin, 1966) p. 105.

2. G. W. F. Hegel, *Encyclopaedia of the Philosophical Sciences*, Part 1, *Logic* (Oxford: Clarendon Press, 1975) p. 174.

3. Hegel, *Phenomenology*, p. 81.

4. F. Nietzsche, *The Birth of Tragedy and The Case of Wagner* (New York: Vintage Books, 1967) p. 170.

5. W. Kaufman, *Nietzsche* (Cleveland: World Publishing Company, 1966) pp. 62, 70–1.

6. F. Nietzsche, *Thus Spake Zarathustra* (Harmondsworth: Penguin, 1969) p. 160.

7. Kaufman, *Nietzsche*, p. 108.

8. F. Nietzsche, *The Will to Power* (New York: Vintage Books, 1968) pp. 339, 335, 340.

9. Ibid., p. 270.

10. Ibid., p. 543.

11. G. Deleuze, *Nietzsche et la Philosophie* (Paris: Presses Universitaires de France, 1962) p. 10.

12. G. Deleuze, *Différence et Répétition* (Paris: Presses Universitaires de France, 1968) p. 79.

13. Ibid., pp. 53, 54.

14. G. Deleuze, *Logique du Sens* (Paris: Minuit, 1969) p. 15. Deleuze here dismisses the three main schools that have dominated Anglo-Saxon philosophy of language; that of Russell and the early Wittgenstein, for whom the sense of a sentence depends on the objects to which it refers; that of the theorists of 'communication-intention' (Austin, Strawson, Grice, Searle) who derive meaning from the speaker's intentions; that of Frege and the theorists of formal semantics (Davidson and his followers), for whom the sense of a sentence is determined by its truth-conditions. One difficulty, however, in comparing Deleuze's philosophy of language with these theories is that, although the analysis of statements is an important aspect of Foucault's work, neither he nor Deleuze (nor indeed Lacan or Derrida) distinguish between sentences and the words of which they are composed. In my exposition I have followed them, although I am aware that this introduces a certain looseness into the discussion.

15. Deleuze, *Différence et répétition*, p. 155.

16. L. Carroll, *The Annotated Snark* (Harmondsworth: Penguin, 1973) p. 42.

17. Deleuze, *Logique*, pp. 201–2.

18. Deleuze, *Différence et répétition*, p. 157.

19. See Deleuze, *Logique*, pp. 75–6, for a discussion of 'ideal games'.

20. Ibid., p. 66.

21. M. Foucault, *L'Ordre du Discours* (Paris: Gallimard, 1971) pp. 56–8.

22. Deleuze, *Logique*, p. 67.

23. See the discussions of Plato in Deleuze, *Différence et Répétition*, pp. 82–9, 165–8.

24. Ibid., pp. 95, 167, 95.

25. Quoted in Deleuze, *Logique*, p. 20.

26. Ibid., p. 101.

27. Ibid., pp. 106–7.

28. Ibid., pp. 109, 107.

29. G. Deleuze and F. Guattari, *L'Anti-Oedipe* (Paris: Minuit, 1972) pp. 7, 11.

30. Ibid. p. 14.

31. J. Derrida, *Writing and Difference* (London and Henley: Routledge and Kegan Paul, 1978) p. 194.

32. See, for example, Deleuze, *Différence et répétition*, pp. 154–5.

33. P. Veyne, 'Foucault révolutionne l'histoire', appendix to *Comment on Ecrit l'Histoire* (Paris: Seuil, 1979) pp. 229, n. 6, 230.

34. Deleuze, *Logique*, pp. 148–9, 151.

35. Ibid., p. 155.

36. Deleuze and Guattari, *L'anti-Oedipe*, p. 26.

37. Ibid., pp. 17, 52, 390.

38. Ibid., pp. 8, 16.

38. Ibid., pp. 8, 16.

39. M. Foucault, 'Nietzsche, Genealogy, History', in *Language, Counter-Memory, Practice* (Oxford: Basil Blackwell, 1977) p. 148.

40. See notably two articles by Colin Gordon – 'Birth of the subject', *Radical Philosophy*, no. 17 Summer 1977; 'Other inquisitions', *I & C*, no. 6, Autumn 1979. The best discussions of Foucault are probably G. Deleuze, 'Ecrivain non: un nouveau cartographe', *Critique*, t. XXXII,

no. 343, December 1975 and Pierre Veyne's beautiful essay, 'Foucault révolutionne l'histoire'.

41. M. Foucault, *The Order of Things* (London: Tavistock, 1970) xxi–xxii.
42. M. Foucault, 'Verité et pouvoir', *L'Arc* no. 70, 1977, pp. 18, 16.
43. See G. Deleuze, 'Un nouvel archiviste', *Critique*, t. xxvi, no. 274, March 1970.
44. M. Foucault, *The Archaeology of Knowledge* (London: Tavistock, 1972) pp. 49, 55.
45. M. Foucault, 'What is an author?', in *Language, Counter-Memory, Practice*, p. 138.
46. See, for example, Foucault, *L'Ordre du Discours*, pp. 54–5.
47. Foucault, *Archaeology*, pp. 122, 121–2.
48. Ibid., pp. 117, 162–5.
49. K. Williams, 'Unproblematic archaeology', *Economy and Society*, vol. 3, no. 1, February 1974, p. 57.
50. It is, therefore, slightly misleading for Peter Dews in an otherwise admirable article ('The *nouvelle philosophie* and Foucault', *Economy and Society*, vol. 8, no. 2, May 1979, pp. 146–7) to suggest that there is a break between *The Archaeology of Knowledge* and Foucault's later writings. The thesis of the *Archaeology* that statements are necessarily rare does not contradict the isolation in *L'Ordre du Discours* of principles determining the 'rarefaction of discourses' which derive from extra-discursive practices. The result – the subsumption of discourses under relations of power – may seem paradoxical, but its avoidance would seem to necessitate rejection of the initial premiss – the rarity of statements, at least in the form in which it is defended by Foucault.
51. M. Foucault, 'History of systems of thought' (summary of a course given at the College de France in 1970–1), in *Language, Counter-Memory, Practice*, p. 199.
52. G. Deleuze, 'Ecrivain non: un nouveau cartographe', *Critique*, t. xxxi, no. 343, December 1975, p. 1215.
53. M. Foucault, *Discipline and Punish* (London: Allen Lane, The Penguin Press, 1977) pp. 27–8.
54. V. Descombes, *Le Même et l'Autre* (Paris: Minuit, 1979) p. 152.
55. M. Foucault, 'Verité et pouvoir', *L'Arc*, no. 70, 1977, p. 17. See also Deleuze, 'Ecrivain non', p. 1208.
56. Foucault, 'Nietzsche, Genealogy, History', in *Language* pp. 142, 148.
57. See Deleuze, 'Ecrivain non', pp. 1208–12.
58. M. Foucault, *Le Volonté de Savoir* (Paris: Gallimard, 1976) pp. 123–8.
59. Foucault, *Discipline and Punish*, pp. 137–8.
60. F. Ewald, 'Anatomie et corps politiques', *Critique*, t. xxxi no. 343, December 1975, p. 1259.
61. Foucault, *Discipline and Punish*, pp. 170, 228, 250, 255.
62. F. Ewald, 'anatomie et corps politiques', *Critique*, t. xxxi, no. 343, December 1975, pp. 1263, 1264.
63. See Foucault, *Discipline and Punish*, p. 226 for some rather trite remarks on the power-relations that made the natural sciences possible.
64. Deleuze, *Logique*, p. 203.

236236   *Is There a Future for Marxism?*

65. G. Deleuze, 'Ecrivain non: un nouveau cartographe', *Critique* t. xxxi, no. 343, December 1975, p. 1223.
66. On programmes, technologies, strategies see G. Gordon, 'Other inquisitions', *I & C*, no. 6, Autumn 1979, pp. 33–42; J. Donzelot, 'Misère de la culture politique', *Critique*, t. xxxiv, nos. 373–4, June–July 1978, p. 577.
67. Foucault, *Le Volonté de Savoir*, pp. 132–3.
68. F. Ewald, 'Anatomie et corps politiques', *Critique*, t. xxxi, no. 343, December 1975, pp. 1232.
69. M. Foucault, 'La grande colère des faits', *Le Nouvel Observateur*, 9 May 1977, p. 84.
70. See also G. Deleuze, 'Ecrivain non: un nouvean cartographe', *Critique*, t. xxxi, no. 343, December 1975, pp. 1208–12 – although Deleuze has at least kept his distance from the *nouveaux philosophes*. See P. Dews, 'The *nouvelle philosophie* and Foucault', *Economy and Society*, vol. 8, no. 2, May 1979 pp. 146–7, for an excellent discussion of Foucault's relationship with Glucksmann and *tutti quanti*. It is incredible in the light of both explicit statements such as that cited in the text to n. 69 (this volume) and the logic of Foucault's arguments that Frank Carlen and Pat Burton can bracket him with Althusser as working 'within marxism' (*Official Discourse* (London: Macmillan, 1979) p. 15).
71. F. Nietzsche, *Beyond Good and Evil* (Harmondsworth: Penguin, 1973) p. p. 49.
72. Foucault, *Le Volonté de Savoir*.
73. Deleuze and Guattari, *L'Anti-Oedipe*, pp. 11, 408. It should be noted that the authors distinguish between two poles of psychosis – the 'schizo-revolutionary' and the 'paranoid-fascist'. See ibid., pp. 329 ff.
74. Foucault and Deleuze, 'Intellectuals and power', in *Language Counter-Memory, Practice*, p. 212.
75. G. Deleuze and F. Guattari, *Rhizome* (Paris: Minuit, 1976) pp. 70–1.
76. See J. Donzelot, *La Police des Familles* (Paris: Minuit, 1977) – one of the best examples of a work inspired by Foucault's genealogy, and one that illustrates very clearly the objective convergence of Deleuze and Foucault's writings.
77. Nietzsche, *Beyond Good and Evil*, p. 175. Vincent Descombes insists on the nietzschean inspiration of *L'Anti-Oedipe* – see Descombes, *Le Même et l'autre*, pp. 201–9.
78. At several points Deleuze explicitly refers to Stirner; see, for example, *Nietzsche et la Philosophie*, pp. 183–6, and *Logique*, p. 130. Dominique Lecourt argues that the *nouveaux philosophes* are a throw-back to Stirner – see D. Lecourt, *Dissidence ou Révolution?* (Paris: Maspero, 1978) chapter 3.

CHAPTER 5

1. M. Foucault, *L'Ordre du Discours* (Paris: Gallimard, 1971) p. 74.
2. G. Deleuze, *Différence et Répétition* (Paris: Presses Universitaire de France, 1978) p. 236.

3. Matters are a little more complicated in the case of Lacan, whose debt to Hegel read through Kojeve is great. However, in *The Four Fundamental Concepts of Psychoanalysis* (London: The Hogarth Press and the Institute of Psychoanalysis, 1977) he adopts the slogan 'Lacan *against* Hegel' (p. 215). Derrida seems to doubt the possibility of ever 'escaping Hegel'. For example, he attacks 'an indicative anti-hegelianism' (Deleuze?) which by reintroducing 'a purity into the concept of differ- ence . . . returns it to nondifference and to full presence', *Writing and Difference* (London and Henley: Routledge and Kegan Paul, 1978) p. 332 n. 20.
4. See p. Anderson, *Considerations on Western Marxism* (London: 1976) pp. 70–3.
5. L. Colletti, 'Marxism and the dialectic', *New Left Review*, no. 93 September–October 1975 pp. 4–9.
6. G. W. F. Hegel, *The Science of Logic* (London: George Allen and Unwin, 1929) vol. II pp. 66, 70.
7. G. Della Volpe, *Logic as a Positive Science* (London: New Left Books, 1980) pp. 151, 178, and see pp. 163–73 (on Galileo's method), and 183–99 (on Marx's).
8. K. R. Popper, *Conjectures and Refutations* (London: Routledge and Kegan Paul, 1969) chapter 15. There are close similarities between Popper's epistemological approach and that of Della Volpe and Colletti.
9. Hegel, *Science*, vol. I, p. 60.
10. G. W. F. Hegel, *The Phenomenology of Mind* (London: George Allen and Unwin, 1966) p. 115.
11. Charles Taylor, *Hegel* (Cambridge University Press, 1975) is, despite its superiority to other treatments of Hegel in English, an example of this sort of reading.
12. Quoted in Della Volpe, *Logic*, p. 53.
13. Hegel, *Phenomenology*, pp. 79, 129.
14. G. W. F. Hegel, *Science*, vol. I p. 243.
15. G. W. F. Hegel, *Lectures on the History of Philosophy* (London: Routledge and Kegan Paul, 1963) vol. II pp. 368–9.
16. Hegel, *Science*, vol. II pp. 477–8.
17. Hegel, *Phenomenology*, p. 80.
18. One could argue that the way was prepared for this transformation by Berkeley's critique of the concept of material substance and by Hume and Kant's refusal to treat the subject as a substance but rather as respectively, a bundle of impressions, and a transcendental unity, whose existence can be inferred but whose nature cannot be known, underlying these impressions. On Kant's 'cracked I' see Deleuze, *Différence et Répétition*, pp. 82, 116–18.
19. Hegel, *Phenomenology*, p. 123.
20. Hegel, *Science*, p. 484.
21. Colletti, 'Marxism and the dialectic', *New Left Review*, no. 93, pp. 23, 23–7, 20–1, 27, 21–2, 27–8.
22. Here are just a few examples, apart from those cited in the text: J. Rancière, 'Le conception de critique et de critique de l'économie politique des *Manuscrits de 1844* au *Capital*', in L. Althusser, E. Balibar, J.

Rancièrs, R. Establet and P. Macherey, *Lire le Capital* (Paris: Maspéro, 1973); G. Lukács, *History and Class Consciousness* (London: Merlin, 1971); N. Geras, 'Essence and appearance: aspects of fetishism in Marx's *Capital*', *New Left Review*, no. 65, January–February 1971; J. Mepham, 'The theory of ideology in *Capital*', *Radical Philosophy*, no. 2, Summer 1972; D. Sayer, *Marx's Method* (Hassocks: Harvester, 1979).

23. K. Marx, *Capital*, vol. I (Harmondsworth: Penguin, 1978) p. 164. See also ibid., pp. 163–77, 433, 675–82; K. Marx, *Capital*, vol. 3 (Moscow: Progress, 1971) pp. 26, 48, 822, 828, 830, 832–51; J. Marx, *Theories of Surplus-Value*, part III (Moscow: Progress, 1972) pp. 453ff.

24. L. Althusser, 'From *Capital* to Marx's philosophy', in L. Althusser and E. Balibar, *Reading Capital* (London: New Left Books, 1970) p. 17.

25. Marx, *Capital*, vol. 1, pp. 165–6.

26. Marx, *Capital*, vol. 3, p. 828.

27. L. Althusser, 'The object of *Capital*', in Althusser and Balibar, *Reading Capital*, pp. 188, 193. It is interesting to note that Deleuze and Guattari attack Althusser for his 'identification of production with a structural and theatrical representation (*Darstellung*)', *L'Anti-Oedipe* (Paris: Minuit, 1972) p. 365.

28. See B. Brewster, 'Fetishism in *Capital* and *Reading Capital*', *Economy and Society*, vol. 5, no. 3, August 1976; N. Rose, 'Fetishism and ideology', *Ideology and Consciousness*, no. 2 Autumn 1977 (although this article contains a serious and elementary misinterpretation of Marx's theory of profits); P. Hirst, *On Law and Ideology* (London: Macmillan, 1979) chapter 4 and an unpublished paper by Mike Rosen.

29. See J. Mepham, 'The *Grundrisse*: method or metaphysics?', *Economy and Society*, vol. 7, no. 4, November 1978, for an excellent critical discussion of Rosdolsky.

30. See Marx's letter to Kugelmann of 11 July 1868, K. Marx and F. Engels, *Selected Correspondence* (Moscow: Progress, 1955) pp. 209–10.

31. See Marx and Engels, *Correspondence*, pp. 192, 199.

32. For claims to the contrary, see F. Engels, 'Supplement to *Capital*, Volume 3', appendix to Marx, *Capital*, vol. 3, pp. 895, 899–900; B. Croce, *Historical Materialism and the Economics of Karl Marx* (London: Howard Latimer, 1914) pp. 134, 135; A. Cutler, B. Hindess, P. Hirst and A. Hussain, *Marx's 'Capital' and Capitalism Today* vol. 1 (London: Routledge and Kegan Paul, 1977) p. 36. Marx, *Theories of Surplus-Value*, part III, pp. 72–4 must count as definitive refutation of this interpretation.

33. The *loci classici* of the 'fundamentalist' and neo-ricardian interpretations of *Capital* are, respectively, D. Yaffe, 'Value and price in Marx's *Capital*', *Revolutionary Communist*, no. 1, January 1975; I. Steedman, *Marx after Sraffa* (London: New Left Books, 1977). For a critique of both positions and much else besides see B. Fine and L. Harris, *Rereading Capital* part 1 (London: Macmillan, 1979). See also P. Armstrong, A. Glyn and J. Harrison, 'In defence of value', *Capital and Class*, no. 5, Summer 1978; S. Himmelweit and S. Mohun, 'The anomalies of *Capital*', *Capital and Class*, no. 6, Autumn 1978.

34. Cutler *et al.*, *Capitalism Today*, vol. 1, p. 116; vol. 2 p. 234.

35. K. Marx, *Grundrisse* (Harmondsworth: Penguin, 1973) p. 449.
36. Ibid., p. 421 n.
37. On the 'transformation problem' see, apart from Marx, *Capital*, vol. 3, part II and the texts cited in n. 33 above, L. Von Bortkiewicz, 'Value and price in the marxian system', *International Economic Papers*, no. 2, 1952; I. I. Rubin, *Essays in Marx's Theory of Value* (Detroit: Black and Red, 1972); F. Seton, 'The "transformation problem" ', *Review of Economic Studies*, vol. XXIV, 1956–7; P. Salama, *Sur la Valeur* (Paris: Maspero, 1975), I. Gerstein, 'Production, circulation and value', *Economy and Society*, vol. 5, no. 3, August 1976; P. Green, 'The necessity of value – and a return to Marx', *International Socialism* (new series), no. 3, Winter 1978–9 and no. 4, Spring 1979.
38. Marx, *Grundrisse*, p. 651.
39. Ibid., p. 657.
40. See Marx, *Capital*, vol. 1, pp. 433–6; vol. 3, pp. 264–5.
41. See J. Hyppolite, *Studies in Marx and Hegel* (London: Heinemann, 1969) chapter 7.
42. See Marx, *Capital*, vol. 3, pp. 196–7, 198; J. Strachey, *The Nature of Capitalist Crisis* (London: Gollancz, 1935) pp. 218–19.
43. Such an analysis of the tendency of the rate of profit to fall is developed in much greater detail in Fine and Harris, *Rereading Capital*, pp. 58–89.
44. E. Balibar, 'The basic concepts of historical materialism', in Althusser and Balibar, *Reading Capital*, pp. 288, 290.
45. See P. Macherey, *Hegel ou Spinoza* (Paris: Maspero, 1979), especially pp. 223–4, 225.
46. See G. Deleuze, *Spinoza et le problème d'expression* (Paris: Minuit, 1969).
47. Marx, *Capital*, vol. 3, pp. 239, 249. See also, ibid., pp. 251–4 (on the devalorisation of capital), and Fine and Harris, *Rereading Capital*, pp. 58–89.
48. L. Trotsky, *The First Five Years of the Communist International* vol. I, (New York: Monad, 1972) p. 200. Compare the following statement by Cornelius Castoriadis, founder of the libertarian marxist *Socialisme ou Barbarie* group and a figure widely respected by French and American left-wing intellectuals: '*economic crises are a relatively superficial phenomenon, which only belonged to a particular phase of capitalism*', P. Cardan (*né* C. Castoriadis), *Modern Capitalism and Revolution* (London: Solidarity, n.d.), p. 29. Which thinker seems more relevant today?
49. L. Althusser, 'Reply to John Lewis', in *Essays in Self-Criticism* (London: New Left Books, 1976), pp. 49–50 n. 12. On the distinction between structures and practices see N. Poulantzas, *Political Power and Social Classes* (London: New Left Books and Sheed and Ward, 1973) pp. 57–8. See B. Hindess and P. Hirst, *Precapitalist Modes of Production* (London:Routledge and Kegan Paul 1975) pp. 272–8 for an account of how the concept of structural causality seems to render the transition from one mode of production to another impossible.
50. K. Marx, *Theories of Surplus-Value*, part II p. 174.
51. Marx, *Grundrisse*, pp. 413–14.
52. Ibid., p. 101.
53. Ibid., pp. 88–98 and see Fine and Harris, *Rereading Capital*, chapter 1.

54. Marx and Engels, *Correspondence*, pp. 209–10.
55. Hegel, *Science*, vol. II, p. 483.
56. E. P. Thompson, *The Poverty of Theory and Other Essays* (London: Merlin, 1978) p. 253.
57. This is the weakness of Scott Meikle's neo-aristotelian interpretation of Marx, 'Dialectical contradiction and necessity', in J. Mepham and D. H. Ruben (eds), *Issues in Marxist Philosophy*, vol. 1 (Hassocks: Harvester, 1979).
58. Marx, *Capital*, vol. 1, p. 928.
59. W. Benjamin, *Illuminations*, H. Arendt (ed.) (London: Jonathan Cape, 1970) p. 255.
60. See (on the party), H. Weber, *Marxisme et Conscience de Classe* (Paris: Union Generale des Editions, 1975) pp. 43–80; J. Molyneux, *Marxism and the Party* (London: Pluto, 1978) chapter 1; (on the national question), G. Haupt, M. Lowy and C. Weill, *Les Marxistes et la Question Nationale 1848–1914* (Paris: Maspero, 1974); (on women), R. Delmar, 'Looking again at Engels's *Origins of the Family, Private Property and the State*', in J. Mitchell and A. Oakley (eds), *The Rights and Wrongs of Women* (Harmondsworth: Penguin, 1976).
61. See L. Althusser, 'Marx's relation to Hegel', in *Politics and History* (London: New Left Books, 1972).

CHAPTER 6

1. G. A. Cohen, *Karl Marx's Theory of History: A Defence* (Oxford: Clarendon Press, 1978) ix, x.
2. K. Marx, *Capital*, vol. 3 (Moscow: Progress, 1971) p. 791.
3. K. Marx, *Capital*, vol. 1 (Harmondsworth: Penguin, 1976) pp. 290, 284.
4. L. Althusser, 'On the materialist dialectic', in *For Marx* (London: Allen Lane, The Penguin Press, 1969); 'The object of *Capital*', in L. Althusser and E. Balibar, *Reading Capital* (London: New Left Books, 1970) chapter 8.
5. Cohen, *Theory of History*, p. 134.
6. Ibid., p. 61.
7. Marx, *Capital*, vol. 1, p. 275.
8. Cohen, *Theory of History*, pp. 158, 162.
9. See, for example, K. Marx and F. Engels, *The German Ideology, Collected Works*, vol. 5 (London: Lawrence and Wishart, 1976) p. 43; ibid., p. 66 where Marx equates capital with the means of production.
10. B. Hindess and P. Hirst, *Pre-capitalist Modes of Production* (London: Routledge and Kegan Paul, 1975) p. 12.
11. See Marx, *Capital*, vol. 1, part IV.
12. See A. Callinicos, 'Maoism, stalinism and the Soviet Union', *International Socialism* (new series) no. 5, Summer 1979.
13. K. Marx, *Grundrisse* (Harmondsworth: Penguin, 1973) p. 96.
14. For a detailed discussion of one such 'functionalist interpretation of the labour theory of value, see A. Callinicos, *'Marx's "Capital" and capitalism*

today – a critique', *International Socialism* (new series) no. 2, Autumn 1978, pp. 87–91.

15. F. Parkin, *Marxism and Class Theory* (London: Tavistock, 1979) p. 27.
16. Cohen, *Theory of History*, p. 75; see. ibid., pp. 73–7. One of the best discussions of the problems posed for the definition of classes by Marx's theory of productive labour is Ernest Mandel's introduction to *Capital*, vol. 2 (Harmondsworth: Penguin, 1978). Harry Braverman's analysis of the labour-process and class-relations, *Labour and Monopoly Capital* (New York and London: Monthly Review, 1974), is a modern classic.
17. See Hindess and Hirst, *Modes of Production*, especially chapter 5. On capitalist control of the labour-process see Marx, *Capital*, vol. 1, chapter 13.
18. Marx, *Capital*, vol. 3, pp. 790–1.
19. P. Anderson, *Lineages of the Absolutist State* (London: New Left Books, 1974) p. 403.
20. Hindess and Hirst, *Modes of Production*, pp. 232, 240–1. For a remarkably similar argument see Cohen, *Theory of History*, p. 103.
21. J. Holloway and S. Picciotto, 'Capital, crisis and the state', *Capital and Class*, no. 2, Summer 1977, pp. 77–8.
22. J. Holloway and S. Picciotto, Editors' introduction to *State and Capital* (London: Edward Arnold, 1978) pp. 14, 29.
23. See the texts by R. Panzieri and M. Tronti, in Conference of Socialist Economists, *The Labour-process and Class Strategies* (London: Stage 1, 1976).
24. See the self-critical remarks in N. Poulantzas, 'The capitalist state: a reply to Miliband and Laclau', *New Left Review*, no. 95, January–February 1976, pp. 77–83.
25. N. Poulantzas, *State, Power, Socialism* (London: New Left Books, 1978) pp. 43, 45.
26. E. P. Thompson, *The Poverty of Theory and Other Essays* (London: Merlin, 1978) pp. 254, 257, 374. A very similar viewpoint is developed in P. Cardan (né C. Castoriadis), *Modern Capitalism and Revolution* (London: Solidarity, n.d.).
27. A. Glucksmann, *Les Maîtres Penseurs* (Paris: Grasset, 1977) pp. 239, 240, 250.
28. F. Ewald, 'Anatomie et corps politiques', *Critique*, t. XXXI, December 1975, pp. 1232, 1241, 1246–7.
29. For example: 'The growth of a capitalist economy gave rise to the specific modality of disciplinary power', M. Foucault, *Discipline and Punish* (London: Allen Lane, The Penguin Press, 1977) p. 221. Ewald's statements cited in the text are, however, more consistent with the general tenor of Foucault's writings.
30. Marx, *Capital*, vol. 1, pp. 477, 450.
31. Ibid., pp. 716, 723–4.
32. Marx, *Grundrisse*, p. 657.
33. Marx, *Capital*, vol. 3, p. 880.
34. J. Holloway and S. Picciotto, 'Capital, crisis and the state', *Capital and Class*, no. 2, summer 1977, pp. 91–2.
35. Poulantzas, *State, Power, Socialism*, p. 174.

36. Versions of this argument are to be found in A. Glyn and B. Sutcliffe, *British Capitalism, Workers and the Profits Squeeze* (Harmondsworth: Penguin, 1972), E. Mandel, *Late Capitalism* (London: New Left Books, 1975) chapter 5; J. Harrison, *Marxian Economics for Socialists* (London: Pluto, 1978).

37. See two articles by Chris Harman, 'Mandel's *Late capitalism*', *International Socialism* (new series), no. 1, July 1978; 'Do wages cause inflation?', *Socialist Review*, no. 10, March 1979.

38. Marx, *Capital*, vol. 3, p. 240; see also ibid., pp. 264–5.

39. See especially S. Himmelweit, 'The continuing saga of the rate of profit', *Conference of Socialist Economists Bulletin*, no. 9, Autumn 1974; A. Shaikh, 'Political economy and capitalism', *Cambridge Journal of Economics*, vol. 2, no. 2, June 1978; B. Fine and L. Harris, *Rereading Capital* (London: Macmillan, 1979) pp. 58–75.

40. Marx, *Capital*, vol. 1, pp. 770, 790; see generally ibid., chapter 25.

41. R. Rosdolsky, *The Making of Marx's 'Capital'* (London: Pluto, 1977) p. 284.

42. K. Marx and F. Engels, *Manifesto of the Communist Party, Collected Works*, vol. 6 (London: Lawrence and Wishart, 1976) p. 483.

43. L. Althusser, 'Reply to John Lewis', in *Essays in Self-Criticism* (London: New Left Books, 1976) p. 47.

44. Ibid., p. 50.

45. For a generalisation of this argument to other modes of production see P. Anderson, *Passages from Antiquity to Feudalism* (London: New Left Books, 1974) p. 198, n. 3, and *Arguments within English Marxism* (London: New Left Books, 1980) p. 55. It is interesting to note that precisely the same issues are raised by marxist discussions of the crisis of feudalism. See the debate provoked by Robert Brenner's article, 'Agrarian class structure and economic development in pre-industrial Europe', *Past and Present*, no. 70, February 1976. Brenner invokes 'the structure of class relations, of class power' to explain why capitalism developed in some countries and not in others. According to Guy Bois, this 'amounts to a voluntarist vision of history in which the class struggle is divorced from all other objective contingencies and, in the first instance, from such laws of development as may be peculiar to a specific mode of production', G. Bois, 'Against the neo-malthusian orthodoxy', *Past and Present*, no. 79, May 1978, p. 67. Bois himself is the author of *Crise du Feudalisme* (Paris: Presses de la fondation nationale des sciences politiques, 1976), an impressive empirical study of late medieval Normandy which integrates both the trends in output, productivity, population and prices studied by bourgeois 'neo-malthusian' historians such as M. M. Postan and Emmanuel Le Roy Ladurie and the struggles between lord and peasant rescued from oblivion by Rodney Hilton, E. A. Kosminsky and others into a global analysis of the feudal mode of production and its laws of motion.

46. F. Ewald, 'Anatomie et corps politiques', *Critique*, t. xxxi, December 1975, p. 1253. See also Pierre Veyne: 'The primacy of relation [in Foucault's philosophy – AC] implies an ontology of the will to power',

'Foucault révolutionne l'histoire', appendix to *Comment on Ecrit l'Histoire*' (Paris: Seuil, 1978) p. 240. Veyne, a colleague of Foucault's at the College de France, showed this essay to him before publishing – see ibid., p. 229.

47. See especially F. Nietzsche, *The Will to Power* (New York: Vintage Books, 1968) pp. 332–41, 544–50.
48. This approach – genealogy as method rather than ontology – is stressed by Foucault in 'Nietzsche, Genealogy, History', in *Language, Counter-Memory, Practice* (Oxford: Basil Blackwell, 1978) and in *La Volonté de Savoir* (Paris: Gallimard, 1976) pp. 123–35.
49. G. Deleuze, 'Ecrivain non: un nouveau cartographe', *Critique*, t. XXXI, no. 343, December 1975, pp. 1218–19, 1221–2.
50. The kantian resonances of Deleuze's writings are considerable. See his *La Philosophie de Kant* (Paris: Presses Universitaires de France, 1963). For a quasi-kantian reading of Foucault, see C. Gordon, 'Other inquisitions', *I & C*, no. 6, Autumn 1979.
51. Foucault, *Discipline and Punish*, p. 216.
52. P. Dews, 'The *nouvelle philosophie* and Foucault', *Economy and Society*, vol. 8, no. 2, May 1979, p. 166.
53. Foucault, *La Volonté de Savoir*, p. 208.
54. See G. Deleuze and F. Guattari, *L'Anti-Oedipe* (Paris: Minuit, 1972) p. 456.
55. See P. Dews, 'The *nouvelle philosophie* and Foucault', *Economy and Society*, vol. 8, no. 2, May 1979, pp. 163–4.
56. Poulantzas, *State, Power, Socialism*, p. 149.
57. Marx, *Capital*, vol. 1, pp. 553, 412–13.
58. M. Foucault, 'My body, this paper, this fire', *Oxford Literary Review*, vol. 4, no. 1, Autumn 1979, p. 27.
59. See, for example, J. Hirsch, 'The state apparatus and social reproduction', in J. Holloway and S. Picciotto (eds), *The State and Capital*, pp. 61–2.
60. E. Laclau, *Politics and Ideology in Marxist Theory* (London: New Left Books, 1977) p. 77. See also ibid., pp. 74–6.
61. See Hindess and Hirst, *Modes of Production*, Introduction; B. Hindess and P. Hirst, *Mode of Production and Social Formation* (London: Macmillan, 1977).
62. S. Clarke, 'Marxism, sociology and Poulantzas' theory of the state', *Capital and Class*, no. 2, Summer 1977, p. 10.
63. See M. Dobb, *Studies in the Development of Capitalism* (London: Routledge, 1946) pp. 199–200 on the inability of the mercantilist economists to conceive of the extraction of surplus-labour taking place other than on the basis of state intervention. Consequently, 'so long as surplus-value was conceived as reliant on conscious regulation to produce it, the notion of *economic objectivity* – of an economy operating according to laws of its own, independent of man's conscious will – which was the essence of classical political economy could scarcely develop' (p. 200).
64. Poulantzas, *State, Power, Socialism*, p. 17.
65. M. Godelier, 'Infrastructures, societies and history', *New Left Review*, no. 112, November–December 1978, pp. 87, 88.

CHAPTER 7

1. I. Hacking, *Why Does Language Matter to Philosophy?* (Cambridge University Press, 1976) pp. 158, 159.
2. Ibid., especially p. 185.
3. See L. Wittgenstein, *Philosophical Investigations* (Oxford: Basil Blackwell, 1968); A. J. P. Kenny, 'Cartesian privacy', in G. Pitcher (ed.), *Wittgenstein* (London: Macmillan, 1970).
4. See, for example, L. Colletti, 'A political and philosophical interview', *New Left Review*, no. 86, July–August 1974, pp. 9–12.
5. See K. Popper, *The Logic of Scientific Discovery* (London: Routledge and Kegan Paul, 1968) chapter 1.
6. D. H. Ruben, *Marxism and Materialism* (Hassocks: Harvester, 1977) pp. 15–17, 86.
7. I. Lakatos, 'Falsification and the methodology of scientific research programmes', in *The Methodology of Scientific Research Programmes* (Cambridge University Press, 1978) p. 16.
8. Ibid., pp. 44, 45.
9. See T. S. Kuhn, *The Structure of Scientific Revolution* (Chicago University Press, 1970), P. K. Feyerabend, *Against Method* (London: New Left Books, 1975) and *Science in a Free Society* (London: New Left Books, 1978).
10. I. Kant, *Critique of Pure Reason* (London: Macmillan, 1970) A84, B117.
11. B. Hindess, *Philosophy and Methodology in the Social Sciences* (Hassocks: Harvester, 1977) p. 208.
12. B. Hindess and P. Hirst, *Mode of Production and Social Formation* (London: Macmillan, 1977) pp. 19–20.
13. Quine is explicitly invoked in S. Graukroger, 'Bachelard and the problem of epistemological analysis', *Studies in the History and Philosophy of Science*, vol. 7, no. 3 (1976), a text at least loosely related to those of Hindess, Hirst and their collaborators.
14. W. V. O. Quine, *From a Logical Point of View* (New York: Harper and Row, 1963) p. 13.
15. A. Cutler, B. Hindess, P. Hirst and A. Hussain, *Marx's 'Capital' and Capitalism Today*, vol. 1, (London: Routledge and Kegan Paul, 1977) p. 315.
16. B. Hindess and P. Hirst, *Pre-capitalist Modes of Production* (London: Routledge and Kegan Paul, 1975) p. 18.
17. The paradox in this case is that Mach's epistemologically motivated of the concepts of absolute space and time in *The Science of Mechanics* had influenced Einstein in the development of the special theory of relativity. See E. Zahar, 'Einstein, Mach and the rise of modern science, *British Journal of the Philosophy of Science*, vol. 28 (1977) pp. 195–213.
18. D. Lecourt, *Proletarian Science?* (London: New Left Books, 1977) pp. 111–12.
19. L. Colletti, 'A political and philosophical interview', *New Left Review*, no. 86, July–August 1974, p. 16.
20. See, for example, L. Althusser, 'The conditions of Marx's scientific discovery', in *Essays in Self-Criticism* (London: New Left Books, 1976); A.

Callinicos, *Althusser's Marxism* (London: Pluto, 1976) pp. 77–88. A paper by Andrew Collier, 'In defence of epistemology', now published in J. Mepham and D. H. Ruben (eds), *Issues in Marxist Philosophy*, vol. 2 (Hassocks: Harvester, 1979), convinced me that the position set out in the latter essay was untenable.

21. V. I. Lenin, *Materialism and Empirio-Criticism* (Moscow: Progress, 1947) p. 248.
22. Ruben, *Marxism and Materialism*, pp. 63–92 and 193–7.
23. A. Tarski, 'The establishment of scientific semantics', in *Logic, Semantics, Metamathematics* (Oxford: Clarendon Press, 1969) p. 401. See also 'The concept of truth in formalised languages' in the same volume.
24. Hindess, *Philosophy and Methodology*, p. 178.
25. Fragment 189 in S. Kirk and J. E. Raven, *The Presocratic Philosophers* (Cambridge University Press, 1976) p. 179.
26. See K. Popper, 'Truth, rationality and the growth of knowledge', in *Conjectures and Refutations* (London: Routledge and Kegan Paul, 1969). This essay greatly influenced the arguments in this chapter; note, however, that Popper's concept of 'verisimilitude', the measure of a theory's degree of approximation to the truth, has been challenged on logical grounds.
27. As Barry Hindess points out, see Hindess, *Philosophy and Methodology*, p. 178.
28. See I. Lakatos, *Proofs and Refutations* (Cambridge University Press, 1976) and the papers collected together in I. Lakatos (ed.) *Mathematics, Science and Epistemology* (Cambridge University Press, 1978).
29. Lakatos, 'Falsification and the methodology of scientific research programmes', in *Scientific Research Programmes*, pp. 32, 33.
30. I. Lakatos and E. Zahar, 'Why did Copernicus's research programme supersede Ptolemy's?', in *Scientific Research Programmes*, p. 179.
31. Lakatos, 'Falsification', p. 50.
32. Lakatos, 'History of science and its rational reconstructions', in *Scientific Research Programmes*, p. 112 n. 2.
33. E. Zahar, 'Why did Einstein's programme supersede Lorentz's?', *British Journal of the Philosophy of Science*, vol. 24 (1973) p. 103.
34. Lakatos, 'Popper on demarcation and induction', in *Scientific Research Programmes*, p. 156.
35. I. Lakatos, 'Necessity, Kneale, Popper', in I. Lakatos, *Mathematics, Science and Epistemology*, pp. 125, 123–4, 124.
36. See R. Bhaskar, *A Realist Theory of Science* (Hassocks: Harvester, 1975). This much over-rated book rests on a 'transcendental' argument which is not transcendental in any sense which Kant might have recognised but which does seem to me (and to others – see Ruben, *Marxism and Materialism*, p. 101) to be circular. Its 'rational kernel' – the doctrine of natural kinds – is much better stated elsewhere, for example in R. Harre and E. Madden, *Causal Powers* (Oxford: Basil Blackwell, 1975), and in any case provides no criteria on which to choose between different theories.
37. Ruben, *Marxism and Materialism*, p. 109.

38. L. Althusser,*Philosophie et Philosophie Spontanée des Savants (1967)* (Paris: Maspèro, 1974) p. 15.
39. See I. Lakatos, 'History of science and its rational reconstructions' in *Scientific Research Programmes*.
40. Lakatos, 'Falsification and the methodology of scientific research programmes', in Lakatos *Scientific Research Programmes*, pp. 52, 92, 91. The concept of the 'third world' is developed in K. Popper, *Objective Knowledge* (Oxford: Clarendon Press, 1973).
41. Lakatos, 'History of science and its rational reconstructions', in *Scientific Research Programmes*, p. 102.
42. Hindess, *Philosophy and Methodology*, pp. 215, 219.
43. Lakatos, 'Falsification and the methodology of scientific research programmes', in *Scientific Research Programmes*, pp. 43, 44.
44. For arguments in favour of the priority of a logic of problems and questions over that of propositions, see R. G. Collingwood, *Autobiography* (Oxford: Clarendon Press, 1979), *An essay on metaphysics* (Oxford University Press, 1940). G. Deleuze,*Différence et répétition* (Paris: Presses Universitaires de France, 1968) pp. 203–13, 228–36.
45. See Hindess, *Philosophy and Methodology*, p. 214.
46. G. Deleuze, 'Ecrivain non: un nouveau cartographe', *Critique*, t. xxxi, no. 343, December 1975, p. 1226.
47. G. Canguilhem, 'Mort de l'homme ou épuisement du cogito?', *Critique*, t. xxiii, July 1967, p. 606.
48. See M. Foucault, 'Verité et pouvoir', *L'Arc*, no. 70. (1977).
49. Canguilhem, 'Mort de l'homme on épuisement du cogito?', *Critique*, t. xxiii, July 1967, p. 613.
50. On 'justificationism' see the essays in I. Lakatos (ed.), *Mathematics, Science, Epistemology*.
51. See Hindess, *Philosophy and Methodology*, pp. 206–9.
52. Cutler *et al.*, *Capitalism Today*, vol. 1, pp. 113, 116, 118, 121, 219, 222.
53. G. W. F. Hegel, *Encyclopaedia of the Philosophical Sciences*, part 1, *Logic* (Oxford: Clarendon Press, 1975) p. 136.
54. E. P. Thompson, *The Poverty of Theory and Other Essays* (London Merlin, 1978) p. 305.
55. Cutler *et al.*, *Capitalism Today*, p. 317.
56. R. Luxemburg, 'Reform or Revolution?', in M. A. Waters (ed.), *Rosa Luxemburg Speaks* (New York: Pathfinder, 1970) p. 58.
57. G. W. F. Hegel, *The Science of Logic* vol. ii (London: George Allen and Unwin, 1929), p. 253.
58. Some have claimed to discover in Marx an empirical, inductive moment of his method prior to the 'rising from the abstract to the concrete' – see, for example, G. Della Volpe, *Logic as a Positive Science* (London: New Left Books, 1980) pp. 183–99; E. Mandel, Introduction to K. Marx, *Capital*, vol. 1 (Harmondsworth: Penguin, 1976) pp. 17–25; D. Sayer, *Marx's Method* (Hassocks: Harvester, 1979). Three comments are in order. First, if these commentators are right then so much the worse for Marx: Hume and Popper showed convincingly that induction is logically impossible since a universal proposition (such as a scientific law) cannot be derived from a set of particular propositions,

however many members that set may have. But, secondly they are wrong: Marx, no more than Newton (a self-proclaimed inductivist) or any other great scientist, went around collecting facts and then devised a theory to fit them. The starting point for Marx's investigations was provided by the concepts he inherited from the classical economists, on which he set to work his own concepts (notably that of relations of production) in the process transforming the latter and producing many new ones (labour-power, constant and variable capital, etc.). Thirdly, this mistaken interpretation derives in part from a failure to distinguish between Marx's writings of the 1840s (including the so-called 'Works of the Break' – e.g. *The German Ideology*), where he was still deeply influenced by Feuerbach's empiricism and vulgar materialism, and *Capital* and related works, where Hegel, as we have seen, looms large.

59. V. I. Lenin, *Philosophical Notebooks, Collected Works*, vol. 38 (Moscow: Progress, 1963) p. 182.
60. I. Lakatos, 'Science and pseudo-science', in *Scientific Research Programmes.*
61. B. Fine and L. Harris, *Rereading Capital* (London: Macmillan, 1979) pp. 63–4, 71.
62. See, for example, the discussion of misinterpretations of Marx's theory of wages in R. Rosdolsky, *The Making of Marx's 'Capital'* (London: Pluto, 1977) pp. 282–313.

CHAPTER 8

1. See, for example, E. Balibar, C. Luporini and A. Tosel (eds), *Marx et sa Critique de Politique* (Paris: Maspero, 1979).
2. G. W. F. Hegel, *The Philosophy of Right* (New York: Oxford University Press, 1971) pp. 280, 283, 280, 166.
3. See K. Marx and F. Engels, *The Holy Family, Collected Works*, vol. 4 (London: Lawrence and Wishart, 1975) pp. 57–61 on 'the mystery of speculative construction'.
4. K. Marx, 'Critique of Hegel's doctrine of the state', in *Early Writings* (Harmondsworth: Penguin, pp. 73, 63–4, 145.
5. See Marx's own account in the preface to *A Contribution to the Critique of Political Economy* (London: Lawrence and Wishart, 1971).
6. H. Draper, 'The two souls of socialism', *International Socialism* (old series), no. 12.
7. See M. Salvadori, *Karl Kautsky and the Socialist Revolution 1880–1938* (London: New Left Books, 1979).
8. See Yvon Bourdet's Introduction to R. Hilferding, *Le Capitalisme Financier* (Paris: Minuit, 1970).
9. P. Boccara, *Etudes sur Capitalisme Monopoliste d'Etat, sa Crise et son Issue* (Paris: Editions Sociales, 1973) pp. 30, 32.
10. See especially S. Holland, *The Socialist Challenge* (London: Quartet, 1975).
11. C. Luporini, 'Le politique et l'étatique: une ou deux critiques?', in

248   *Is There a Future for Marxism?*

Balibar, Luporini and Tosel, *Critique de Politique*, pp. 83–4, 85, 86, 87–9.

12. Ibid, pp. 92–3, 96–7.
13. Roman Rosdolsky shows that Marx had abandoned, by the time he came to write *Capital*, the project of a multi-volumed work starting with capital and ending with the state, see *The Making of Marx's 'Capital'* (London: Pluto, 1977) pp. 10–62.
14. K. Marx, *Capital*, vol. 1 (Harmondsworth: Penguin, 1976) p. 727 n. 2.
15. Luporini, 'Le politique et l'étatique: une ou deux critiques?', in Balibar, Luporini and Tosel, *Critique de Politique*, p. 104.
16. C. Barker, 'The state as capital', *International Socialism* (new series), no. 1, July 1978, p. 24.
17. Luporini, 'Le politique et l'étatique: une ou deux critiques?', in Balibar, Luporini and Tosel, *Critique de Politique*, p. 104, See also C. von Braumuhl, 'On the analysis of the bourgeois nation-state within the world market context', in J. Holloway and S. Picciotto (eds), *State and Capital* (London: Edward Arnold, 1978).
18. A. Cutler, B. Hindess, P. Hirst and A. Hussain, *Marx's 'Capital' and Capitalism Today* vol. 2. (London: Routledge and Kegan Paul, 1978) pp. 235, 244, 251–2.
19. On Hilferding see Athar Hussain's stimulating 'Hilferding's *Finance Capital*', *Bulletin of the Conference of Socialist Ecnomists*, vol. iv (13) March 1976. However, Hussain's failure to distinguish between money as universal equivalent and as measure of value both lays the foundations of and undermines the discussion of money in Cutler *et al.*, *Capitalism Today*; Bukharin's essay in R. Luxemburg and N. Bukharin, *Imperialism and the Accumulation of Capital* (London: Allen Lane, The Penguin Press, 1972), provides the definitive critique of Luxemburg's theory of realisation, but see the comprehensive discussion of Marx's reproduction schemes in Rosdolsky, *The Making of Marx's 'Capital'*, pp. 445–505.
20. L. Trotsky, *The Third International After Lenin* (New York: Pathfinder, 1970).
21. N. Bukharin, 'Towards a theory of the imperialist state', quoted in S. F. Cohen, *Bukharin and the Bolshevik Revolution* (London: Wildwood House, 1974) p. 29.
22. N. Bukharin, *The Economics of the Transformation Period* (New York: Bergmann, 1971) p. 19.
23. K. Marx, *Capital*, vol. 3 (Moscow: Progress, 1971) p. 110.
24. The best overall discussion of Bukharin is M. Haynes, 'The resurrection of Nikolai Bukharin', *International Socialism* (new series), no. 2, Winter 1978. On Bogdanov see the appendix to D. Lecourt, *Proletarian science?* (London: New Left Books, 1977).
25. L. Trotsky, *In Defence of Marxism* (New York: Pathfinder Press, 1970) p. 6. Ernest Mandel offers a profoundly evolutionist version of Trotsky's theory of 'degenerated' or 'deformed' workers' states in *Revolutionary Marxism Today* (London: New Left Books, 1979). For a critique of the theory, see P. Binns and D. Hallas, 'The Soviet Union – state capitalist or socialist?', *International Socialism* (old series), no. 91, September 1976.
26. T. Cliff, *State Capitalism in Russia* (London: Pluto, 1974). This work first

appeared in June 1948 as an internal document in the British section of the Fourth International. It was published in 1955 and republished, in an expanded form, in 1964.

27. See T. Cliff, 'The theory of bureaucratic collectivism – a critique', in *Origins of the International Socialists* (London: Pluto, 1971). For a critical discussion of more recent versions of this theory see P. Binns and M. Haynes, 'New theories of eastern European class societies', *International Socialism* (new series), no. 7, Winter 1980.

28. K. Marx, *Grundrisse* (Harmondsworth: Penguin, 1973) p. 657.

29. See Cliff, *State Capitalism in Russia*, chapter 7; P. Binns, 'The theory of state capitalism', *International Socialism* (old series), no. 74, January 1975. This approach differs fundamentally from Charles Bettelheim's *Class Struggles in the USSR* (Hassocks: Harvester, 1977 and 1978), where the restoration of capitalism after the October revolution is attributed almost solely to the power of bourgeois ideology. It is also quite different from that of social-democratic theorists such as Kautsky, for whom the USSR was state capitalist from October 1917 (rather than, as Cliff argues, 1928–9) when the bolsheviks sought to establish the dictatorship of the proletariat rather than parliamentary-democratic regime.

30. Cliff, *State Capitalism in Russia*, chapter 7. This point is also made very strongly by Peter Binns in an unpublished paper, 'The arms economy and the rise of state capitalism'.

31. See Y. Gluckstein, *Stalin's Satellites in Europe* (London: George Allen and Unwin, 1952); *Mao's China* (London: George Allen and Unwin, 1957); C. Harman, *Bureaucracy and Revolution in Eastern Europe* (London: Pluto, 1974); 'Poland and the crisis of state capitalism', *International Socialism* (old series), no. 93, November–December 1976 and no. 94, January 1977; N. Harris, *The Mandate of Heaven* (London: Quartet, 1978).

32. I. Lakatos, 'Falsification and the methodology of scientific research programmes', in *The Methodology of Scientific Research Programmes* (Cambridge University Press, 1978) p. 34.

33. The connection between the theories of state capitalism and the permanent arms economy is made forcefully, in P. Binns, 'The theory of state capitalism', *International Socialism* (old series), no. 74, January 1975. For formulations of the latter theory, see M. Kidron, 'Rejoinder to left reformism II', *International Socialism* (old series), no. 7, Winter 1961; *Western Capitalism Since the War* (Harmondsworth: Penguin, 1970); *Capitalism and Theory* (London: Pluto, 1974).

34. C. Barker, 'The state as capital', *International Socialism* (new series), no. 1, July 1978, pp. 24, 25.

35. See M. Kidron, 'Two insights don't make a theory', and C. Harman, 'Better a valid insight than a wrong theory', *International Socialism* (old series), no. 100, July 1977.

36. See C. Harman, 'Mandel's *Late Capitalism*', *International Socialism* (new series), no. 1, July 1978.

37. N. Poulantzas, *State, Power, Socialism* (London: New Left Books, 1978) pp. 18–19, 129, 132.

38. K. Marx, *Grundrisse* (Harmondsworth: Penguin, 1973) p. 108; *Capital*, vol. 1, p. 915.
39. V. I. Lenin, 'The trade unions, the present situation and Trotsky's mistakes', in *Collected Works*, vol. 32 (Moscow: Progress, 1965) p. 32.
40. Poulantzas, *State, Power, Socialism*, p. 81.
41. Stuart Hall, review of Poulantzas, *State, Power, Socialism*, *New Left Review*, no. 119, January–February 1980, p. 66.
42. Marx, *Capital*, vol. 1, p. 929.
43. On the relation between the 'real subsumption' of the worker under capital involved in the extraction of surplus-value and the creation of the 'collective worker' see Marx, 'Results of the immediate process of production', Appendix to *Capital*, vol. 1, pp. 1039–40.
44. K. Marx and F. Engels, *The German Ideology, Collected Works*, vol. 5 (London: Lawrence and Wishart, 1976) p. 49.
45. On Kautsky see Salvadori, *Socialist Revolution 1880–1938*, pp. 273–7.
46. See C. Harman, 'Party and Class', *International Socialism* (old series), no. 32, Winter 1968–9.
47. See A. Callinicos, 'Soviet power', *International Socialism* (old series), no. 103, November 1977.
48. A. Gramsci, *Selections from the Political Writings 1910–1920* (London: Lawrence and Wishart, 1977).
49. V. I. Lenin, *What is to be done?*, *Collected Works*, vol. 5 (Moscow: Progess, 1961) p. 386 n.
50. H. Weber, *Marxisme et Conscience de Classe* (Paris: Union Generale des Editions, 1975) pp. 207–324.
51. V. I. Lenin, 'Preface to the collection *Twelve Years*', *Collected Works*, vol. 13 (Moscow: Progress, 1962) pp. 103–4.
52. V. I. Lenin, 'Speech in defence of the tactics of the Comintern', Third Congress of the Comintern, *Collected Works*, vol. 32 (Moscow: Progress, 1965) p. 476.
53. A. Gramsci, *Selections from the Political Writings 1921–1926* (London: Lawrence and Wishart, 1978) p. 198. For more on the revolutionary party see J. Molyneux, *Marxism and the Party* (London: Pluto, 1978); T. Cliff, *Lenin*, vol. 1 (London: Pluto, 1974).
54. K. Marx and F. Engels, 'Circular letter to Bebel, Liebknecht, Bracke, et al.' in K. Marx, *The First International and After* (Harmondsworth: Penguin, 1974) p. 375.
55. For two critical discussions of Thompson's 'astrategic' conception of socialism, see A. Callinicos, 'The ingredient of humanity', *Socialist Review*, no. 9, February 1979; P. Hirst, 'The necessity of theory', *Economy and Society*, vol. 8, no. 4, November 1979. The most substantive critique of *The Poverty of Theory* is P. Anderson, *Arguments within English Marxism* (London: New Left Books, 1980), but see my review of the latter, *New Statesman*, 27 June 1980.
56. See C. Harman, *How the revolution was lost* (London: n.d.).
57. The issue of socialist democracy is discussed in Mandel, *Revolutionary Marxism Today*; H. Weber, 'Goulag, Glucksmann, et democratie socialiste', *Critique Communiste*, no. 18/19, October/November 1977; 'Eurocommunism, socialism and democracy', *New Left Review*, no. 110,

July–August 1978. Both Mandel and Weber tend to overestimate the efficacy of institutional safeguards of democratic rights and to blur the issue of whether soviet power is compatible with parliamentary institutions. See also C. Barker, 'A "new" reformism' *International Socialism* (new series) no. 4, Spring 1979; P. Spencer, ' "Left-Wing" eurocommunism' *International Socialism* (new series), no. 5, Summer 1979.

58. See especially N. Harris, 'The world crisis and system', *International Socialism* (old series), no. 100, July 1977.

59. See P. Anderson, 'The antinomies of Antonio Gramsci', *New Left Review*, no. 100, November 1976–January 1977.

60. Bukharin, *Transformation Period*, pp. 58, 214 (L 37). See also p. 214 (L 33) – comment on passage on p. 54.

61. L. Trotsky, *The First Five Years of the Communist International*, vol. 1 (New York: Monad, 1972) pp. 211, 212.

62. See D. Hallas, *Trotsky's Marxism* (London: Pluto, 1979).

Name Index

Subject Index